Western Frontiersmen Series
XXIV

Adventurers and Prophets

American Autobiographers
in Mexican California
1828-1847

by
Charles B. Churchill

THE ARTHUR H. CLARK COMPANY
Spokane, Washington
1995

LIBRARY OF CONGRESS CARD CATALOG NUMBER 94-47236
ISBN 0-87062-228-5

Library of Congress Cataloging-in-Publication Data
Churchill, Charles B.
    Adventurers and prophets : American autobiographers in Mexican
California, 1828-1847 / by Charles B. Churchill.
        p.   cm. -- (Western frontiersmen series ; 24)
    Includes bibliographical references and index.
    ISBN 0-87062-228-5
    1. California --History --To 1846 --Biography. 2. California-
-History --1846-1850 --Biography. 3. Autobiographies --California-
-History and criticism. I. Title. II. Series.
F864.C53   1994
979.4'03'0922 --dc20   94-47236
                                                 CIP

Contents

Illustrations

Acknowledgements

I am indebted to many people who have given me help and encouragement over the course of my research and writing and it is a pleasure to acknowledge them here.

This book began as a doctoral dissertation, and I owe the greatest appreciation to Professor Harold Kirker for guiding it through to completion. As a teacher and scholar he has been an inspiration; his timely encouragement and overall kindness to me will never be forgotten. I want to thank Professors Albert Lindemann and Richard Oglesby for showing an interest in my work, and for taking time from the demands of their own teaching and research to read my manuscript. Their comments and criticisms have been invaluable. Dr. Jerry Jackman also aided me with good advice. It goes without saying, of course, that any blunders belong to me.

The staffs of the Huntington and Bancroft Libraries have been unfailingly kind and consistently helpful. I would like in particular to mention Walter Brem, an old friend from Santa Barbara whose personal attentions made my stay at the Bancroft especially enjoyable.

I have been singularly blessed with friends and relatives who have believed in me and supported me (in more ways than one) for years. I would like to thank my parents, Margaret and Ray Johnson, Vernon and Paula Churchill, for their faith and encouragement. My brothers, Bill and David Churchill, have never ceased to buoy my spirits. My children, Joe, Sophie and Dori, are constant loving presences. My close friends John Mraz, Eli Bartra, Stefan Dasho, Nancy Edwards, Jack and Cathy Estill, Reid and Madeline Parker, continue to give me the greatest intellectual and emotional satisfaction, without which my life and work would be poorer.

Finally, I want to express, however inadequately, my deep love and appreciation for my wife, Lisa. She has been unfailingly optimistic and supportive. She has made the writing of this book, and my life, easier and more rewarding. More than any other person she deserves credit for anything that is good in my work. It is to her that I dedicate this book.

CHARLES B. CHURCHILL

Introduction

In the late eighteenth century American sailing ships began to arrive off the Pacific Northwest and California. They were China Traders from Boston in search of valuable sea-otter pelts.[1] Spanish prohibitions against trade with foreigners did not entirely prevent these enterprising people from landing, requesting water and supplies, and illicitly exchanging goods for otter skins. The first Americans to spend time in California were undoubtedly sailors from these vessels who had either deserted or been put ashore by unscrupulous sea captains who wanted to avoid paying them.[2]

By the 1820s Mexico had gained independence from Spain, and California was opened to trade. Between that time and the Mexican War, a significant number of Americans began to visit Mexican California in pursuit of commercial profits, furs, and land. They came on the merchant ships and they came overland across the continent. Some returned to the United States to tell glowing stories of the wealth and potential of California. Many remained to take up residence, and a few even became citizens of Mexico, taking wives from among the Spanish-Mexican Californians. Several of these Americans have left autobiographical accounts of their lives and experiences in Mexican California, and it is these works that are the subject of this study.

Autobiography combines the personal and historical in revealing ways. Perceptions, attitudes, ideals and self-images are placed in a dialectical relationship with historical experiences. Autobiographies can provide "windows" on these interactions. They can reveal the factors which might contribute to or detract from a clearer and deeper self-understanding, and a sense of the general historical tendencies of the times. Autobiographies can show people assessing their lives, their struggles, their surroundings and options, and the lessons of their personal experiences. Even their exaggerations, pride and bombast, or their omissions, can prove revealing and useful.

---

[1]See Samuel Eliot Morison, *The Maritime History of Massachusetts*, 59. Morison, citing H. H. Bancroft, states that the first American ship to anchor in California waters was the ship *Otter*, Ebenezer Dorr, Jr., master, which stopped at Monterey for provisions in 1796.

[2]Adele Ogden, *The California Sea Otter Trade, 1784-1848*, 45-52.

Many of the personal narratives written by Americans in California during the Mexican period take for granted the superiority of Anglo-Americans and their institutions. These writings also display certain general traits created by a frontier existence; they reveal an ever-present desire for land and wealth in the West, and they show the respect for efficiency, ingenuity and enterprise just then being instilled by the beginnings of industrialism. The United States of the Jacksonian era was a dynamic, diverse, optimistic and self-confident society, increasingly holding out the lure of material success to more and more of its citizens.

In contrast to this, Americans found in California a remote and neglected outpost of a Mexican nation which had just completed a long and bloody struggle for independence from Spain, a struggle that had little direct impact on California, but left Mexico with only a feeble grip on its outlying provinces.[3] The potential for effective government in remote California suffered from the chaos and anarchy that characterized Mexican society after independence. Mexican liberals had tried to restructure the economic, social and political life of their country along lines suggested by the United States' history and institutions. But they lacked experience at self-government, while unresolved social and economic tensions continued with great explosive potential. Threats of intervention by Spain and interference in internal political and economic affairs by England and the United States further contributed to Mexico's instability. With its economy in ruins, and the traditional ruling classes (clergy, landowners, mine owners) hostile to changes that would threaten their interests, Mexico was hardly governed at all.[4]

California could not help but be affected by Mexico's travails. Californians needed both the flexibility to deal with their own particular problems, and the financial, military and bureaucratic support of the central government. They were to receive neither. Many of the "revolutions" that observers from the United States commented on during this period were due to the problems created by California's isolation and Mexico's inablility to establish viable political institutions there, or to permit the Californians to establish their own. The Mexican Constitution of 1824, which was in operation until 1835 and permitted a measure of autonomy to the territories, still did not provide a set of specific regulations for their inter-

---

[3] See John Lynch, *The Spanish American Revolutions, 1808-1826*, 326-328.
[4] David J. Weber, *The Mexican Frontier, 1821-1846: The American Southwest Under Mexico*, 31-32.

nal government. Local institutions such as the town councils *(ayun-tamientos)* lacked sufficient authority to function effectively; the territorial congress *(diputación)* drew up its own laws but never received confirmation or approval of these from the central government in Mexico City, nor was it ever made clear which regulations left over from Spanish rule remained in force. After 1835, the central government in Mexico City attempted to tighten control over the territories, but with much vacillation and little success. The civilian and military spheres of governance were never clearly separated, and the result was friction between Mexican military officers sent to govern California and the local California elites who viewed military rule as despotism. Several of the revolutions were in fact efforts to expel Mexican Governors who were seen by prominent Californians like Juan Bautista Alvarado as a threat to the right of Californians to have a civil government separate from the military power.[5]

Americans in California during this period came into contact with an emerging ranchero class which was not the product of an old established economy and culture. This class of people was a new phenomenon in California and owed its existence to frontier developments dominated by the secularization of the missions and the hide and tallow trade. Thoughtful and ambitious Californians looked upon the missions, which tied up enormous amounts of land, as obstacles to California's development. But prior to the establishment of a more extensive trade and the creation of major markets for hides and tallow, the missions were almost the sole providers of food, labor and revenues for the territorial government. Secularization made available to certain prominent and well-placed Californians the opportunity to assume positions as administrators of mission properties and to petition for grants of former mission lands. The secularization plans of Governor José Figueroa in 1833 benefited an elite group of Californians by blocking the acquisition of mission lands by the few immigrants from Mexico, foreigners, or lower class Californians. After Figueroa's death, all the missions were secularized and became sources of revenue for acquisitive California politicians. Mission administrators sold off cattle and grain, and acquired lands which were confirmed as grants by California's governors. Those foreigners who became Mexican citizens, of course, were then eligible for land grants.[6]

[5]Ibid., 27-29.
[6]Ibid., 60-67, 205-206.

The American autobiographers who witnessed this process were therefore seeing a society in flux. The last of the old order in the form of the missions was being dismantled, and a new political class was just coming to prominence, all in the span of ten to fifteen years. Not all of the rancheros acquired great wealth, but quite a few enriched themselves in a relatively brief period of time solely through the singular market for the products of their cattle. They had little need or incentive to diversify, any more than did the American plantation owners of the South who grew cotton exclusively. Like the Southern plantation owner, they relied on a servile labor force — the former mission Indians who were rapidly converted into peons on the ranchos everywhere in California. Such a fluid situation, with immense tracts of fertile land becoming available, and a tiny population to compete for them, was obviously attractive to those Americans, ever growing in numbers, who were making their way to California.[7]

As these Americans began arriving they found not the raw wilderness of earlier American frontiers, but a pastoral country that had been "softened up" by seventy years of Spanish-Mexican occupation. The missions, pueblos and ranchos were a kind of civilization, though different from what most had known (if indeed some of the mountain men had known much of any civilization at all!). A revealing confrontation between several cultures—American, Spanish-Mexican Californian, and the remains of an indigenous native tribal culture—then emerges from the autobiographies of this period to illuminate American attitudes and expose some of the contradictions to be found in holding to a set of beliefs while having to deal with the practical realities of surviving and prospering in a new and complex setting.

Like the Spanish and French on the North American continent, Americans had developed ideas and practices that stood them in good stead as they pushed westward to conquer a wilderness. By the 1820s and 1830s, when the first of them began arriving in California, the English-speaking people of North America had experienced several hundred years of conflict with native American cultures. They were also beginning to press south and west into the Spanish-Mexican border regions, and in their dealings with these different cultures, American technological superiority was clearly evident to all parties. Perhaps this

[7] Ibid., 211.

contributed to a certain inclination for some of these Americans to look down on the people they would eventually displace. Success tends to reinforce structures of belief, and American cultural and ethnocentrism can also be understood as an ideological reflection of the successful struggle for predominance and control over lands to which the Indians—and the Spanish-Mexicans—asserted their own claims. Its roots go back to the earliest meetings between Europeans and native Americans.

From these contacts there emerged two sharply divergent images of the Indians. They were either seen as hostile and savage men, cannnibalistic, bestial, and dominated entirely by their ungovernable passions; or they were viewed as a generous and hospitable people, childlike perhaps in their innocence, but definitely men who were, in the words of an English sailor left on shore along the northern coast of the Gulf of Mexico in 1568, "Naturally very courteous, if you do not abuse them."[8] Both of these images were grounded in actual experiences with the Indians, some resulting in hostilities and some in friendships. Those culture contacts which were based primarily on trade, and thus on mutual benefits to be derived by both peoples, tended to favor the development of the second, more positive image. But where the Europeans competed for possession of the land—a process that went on throughout most of the history of European immigration—the former harsh characterization of the Indians came to predominate, and in the English case at least, it was reinforced by a puritanical division of people into the saved and the damned. As we shall see, similar conflicting images of the Spanish-Mexican Californians were also expressed by Americans in California during the first half of the nineteenth century.[9]

There was a "racial" component to the Anglo-American sense of superiority as well. Its origins were in English history and culture, but it became firmly rooted in the course of struggle against the Indians, and in the use of African slave labor.[10] It called upon a puritanical concept of

---

[8]Quoted in Gary B. Nash, *Race, Class, and Politics: Essays on American Colonial and Revolutionary Society*, 36-37. The Indians also considered themselves superior to the first Europeans with whom they had extensive relations. See James Axtell, *The Invasion Within: The Contest of Cultures in Colonial North America*, 80.

[9]Ibid., 40-50.

[10]See Winthrop D. Jordan, *White Over Black*, for an extended discussion of the formation of American attitudes toward blacks and Indians.

predestination that singled out Americans as a people uniquely chosen to conquer and settle a wilderness. This gave them a kind of built-in cultural self-confidence, not to say arrogance, as they pushed their way westward. They also deployed against the Spanish-Mexican people of the southwest, elements of the so-called "Black Legend," a legacy from the 16th century contest between Spain and England in which the Spanish were characterized as authoritarian, corrupt, decadent, bigoted, cruel, fanatical, treacherous and lazy.[11] All of these elements were crystalized in the concept of Manifest Destiny, which mandated that Americans believe in their inevitable right to expand across the continent. So when they confronted the Spanish-speaking people of California and the southwest, people who were often of mixed Spanish, Indian and even African blood, Americans frequently responded in a prejudicial manner to individuals they assumed were both racially and culturally inferior.[12]

It is this process of interaction between peoples of different historical, cultural and ethnic backgrounds that Americans in Mexican California illustrated in their autobiographies. In spite of a legacy of ethnocentric attitudes and beliefs, several individuals were able to fairly evaluate and appreciate the different cultures they encountered. Those with the longest contact, who had developed the greatest intimacy with the local people, were almost always the most insightful and the least overcome by their biases. Yet all of them reveal attitudes, expectations, ideals and identities that shed important light on trans-ethnic and trans-cultural interactions, and on the contradictions and complexities of what it can mean to be an American.

---

[11]See Phillip Wayne Powell, *Tree of Hate: Propaganda and Prejudices Affecting United States Relations with the Hispanic World,* 7, 10-11, 117-118.

[12]See David J. Weber, ed., *Foreigners in Their Native Land: Historical Roots of the Mexican Americans,* 59-60.

PART I
Merchants and Traders

CHAPTER I

Alfred Robinson

Merchants and traders from the United States were among the first Americans to establish themselves on the coast of Mexican California. Most of them came from New England and formed economic and friendship ties first with the missions and then with the powerful ranchero families who succeeded to most of the mission land. They often married into these families, becoming Catholics and accepted members of California's upper class. Alfred Robinson's *Life in California* is an important reflection of such an experience. First published in 1846, it was never to achieve the fame of Richard Henry Dana's *Two Years Before the Mast,* which appeared six years earlier. Dana's autobiographical account of his voyage to Mexican California and his experiences there in the mid-1830s has become a classic of American literature. Yet as a source of insight into the people and institutions of early California it is arguably inferior to Robinson's *Life in California.* Robinson's attitudes and mentality were those of a representative American type whose pioneering commercial activities constituted the entering wedge of American power on the Pacific. Dana was on the coast for just a little over a year; Alfred Robinson spent much of his adult life in California.

Robinson, Dana, and a lesser-known sea captain, William Dane Phelps, wrote about their experiences in California while all were in the employ of the New England mercantile house of Bryant, Sturgis and Company. This firm was the first American company to trade in the hides and tallow that were the products of the California missions and ranchos of this period. The era of regularized, legal trade was begun, after the Mexican revolution against Spanish rule, by the British firm of McCulloch, Hartnell and Company. During the first full year of Mexican rule in California, there were twenty ships trading on the coast, and fourteen of them were there exclusively for California products. A shortage of hides and tallow on the world market, the lifting of the Spanish trade embargo, rumors and reports of windfall profits to be made in California, all contributed to stiff competition for the California trade. But the Boston ships had an advantage. Their hold capacities were much greater than those of their rivals. These ships weighed three to four hundred tons, whereas rival ships averaged only one to two hundred tons. The Yankee traders, therefore, soon held prominent place in the California trade, with Bryant, Sturgis and Company in the lead.[1]

Bryant and Sturgis were instrumental in beginning the process of binding California to the United States through trade and economic ties, well before the Mexican War brought the territory into American hands. Taking advantage of a recently independent Mexican government preoccupied with its own internal problems of underdevelopment and economic prostration, Yankee traders ignored or circumvented Mexican restrictions, often with the connivance of the Californians who desired the many luxuries and necessities brought round the Horn in Boston ships. The hide and tallow trade first offered the missions a market for their produce in cattle, and then after secularization, became the means of enrichment for the new ranchero class. The firm of Bryant and Sturgis dominated this trade from 1829 to 1840.[2]

Robinson began his career in California as a clerk for Bryant and Sturgis, arriving on the *Brookline* in 1829. His mentor was the experienced trader William Gale. It was Gale who came up with the idea to branch out from the fur trade traffic between the Pacific Northwest and China, and tap the potential for profits by exchanging the manufactured goods of New England for the raw materials of California. Gale was known in California as "cuatro ojos"—four-eyes—because of his thick glasses, and Alfred Robinson always spoke of him with affection.[3]

Robinson was only twenty three in 1829, but soon advanced from clerk to "supercargo." He was responsible for lining up customers for American trade goods and arranging for the purchase of hides, horns and tallow all along the California coast. In *Life in California* he described a typical trading scene aboard ship:

---

[1]Sherman F. Dallas, "The Hide and Tallow Trade in Alta California, 1822-1846" (Ph.D. dissertation, Indiana University, 1955), 86-87, 136, 160-162.

[2]Adele Ogden, "Boston Hide Droghers Along California Shores," 289-305.

[3]Alfred Robinson, *Life in California,* 19.

As we anticipated, our friends came in the morning, flocking on board from all quarters; and soon a busy scene commenced, afloat and ashore. Boats were plying to and fro—launches laden with a variety of our cargo passing to the beach, and men, women and children crowding upon our decks, partaking in the general excitement. On shore all was confusion. Cattle and carts laden with hides and tallow, 'gente de razón' and Indians, busily employed in the delivery of their produce, and receiving in return its value in goods; groups of individuals seated around little bonfires upon the ground, and horsemen racing over the plain to the town, appeared a living panorama.[4]

As Bryant and Sturgis' commercial agent, Robinson was required to travel extensively in California, and this gave him the opportunity to know the mission padres and the leading land-owning families. He eventually married into one of these families, the de la Guerras of Santa Barbara, where he too would make his home. Robinson was a keen observer of California life, as well as an adopted son and a participant in the culture and customs of the native Californians. He would become, as a biographer explained it, a kind of business and cultural middleman between the natives and the Americans who were beginning to arrive in California by land and sea.[5] He was a man with a foot in both worlds, though his New England origins and Yankee outlook are readily apparent in the judgements about California and the Californians that emerge from the pages of his autobiographical *Life in California*. This work offers an important starting point for comparing the experiences of Robinson's contemporaries and later visitors to (and settlers in) California. Indeed, this is what makes it an excellent place to begin examining the interactions between cultural attitudes, personality and historical setting. Alfred Robinson was one of the first Americans to become a part of the life of Mexican California, and to write about what he saw and felt.

His local connections notwithstanding, Robinson had a low opinion of the Mexican government in California. He scorned its weakness and disagreed with its policies. Its apparent powerlessness was highlighted for him shortly after his arrival, by an incident involving the Boston ship *Franklin*. The ship's captain had been caught smuggling by the Mexican port authorities in San Diego and faced the confiscation of his cargo. But instead of submitting to this, the captain (John Bradshaw) sailed out of

---

[4]Ibid., 26-27.
[5]Adele Ogden, "Alfred Robinson, New England Merchant in Mexan California," 193-218.

San Diego harbor underneath the guns of the fort there, firing his own cannons, according to Robinson, "as if in derision of a government of such weakness and pusillanimity." Throughout his narrative, Robinson would criticize what he saw as "the want of sagacity and energy of the government."[6]

Mexico's hold on California was indeed so loose that it had very inconsistent success in regulating the Californians' trade with the United States. Even in the days of Spanish rule when trade was virtually prohibited, Robinson noted that "the old friars sometimes secretly purchased goods of the American trading ships." The Californians were almost exclusively an agricultural and stock-raising people. Not only the old friars, but everyone else in California relied on trade for their luxuries and manufactured goods. Robinson pointed out that this commerce was "confined principally to American ships, direct from the United States; for they have but two or three small vessels of their own, and not more than twenty or thirty on the whole extent of the Mexican coast!" The United States would first dominate California's trade before finally moving to incorporate the territory, and U.S. commercial interests would be in the vanguard of those seeking United States control.[7]

Mexico's tenuous grip on "Alta California" was also evidenced by the "revolutions" and factional strife among the leading California families. These struggles often pitted northern against southern centers of power. By the 1840s in-fighting among the Californians was starting to draw in the Americans who had begun to increase the province's small and scattered population. Robinson pointed out that during this time, if a California leader could gather about him as many as one hundred men, he was considered to have a powerful force at his command.[8] The Mexican authorities in California—or would-be authorities—hoped to use, yet feared, the tough, hardened mountain men who had begun to wander into the territory as the beaver were trapped out in the Rocky Mountains. These men found the climate congenial and the opportunities abundant, and many of them stayed. While visiting a friend in Santa Barbara, Robinson watched a party of these American hunters taking target practice. He was impressed by one of them: "A tall, gigantic Kentuckian,

[6]Robinson, op. cit., 5, 11.
[7]Ibid., 59, 154.
[8]Ibid., 48-49.

named Galbraith, was retiring from the scene as I entered, with extravagant boastings of his superior skill." Robinson was invited to try his hand at shooting, and luckily hit the bullseye. This aroused Galbraith's jealousy, and he challenged Robinson to try again. The latter declined, however, saying "this was enough for me; a chance shot had gained my victory, and I had no idea of losing my credit by a second attempt, particularly with a person who amused himself daily by shooting off the heads of little 'chenates' (blackbirds) at the distance of twenty paces." Robinson's "chance shot" had placed him on a par with men whose legendary stature was even then beginning to take shape.[9]

In Santa Barbara in the 1830s there was some anti-foreign agitation. But this did not worry Alfred Robinson, perhaps because he knew he could call on Americans like Galbraith and others who were "well-armed and ready to unite on the first alarm." At his Santa Barbara residence, Robinson himself kept several muskets, pistols and an old sword within easy reach. He thought just the sight of these "appalling instruments was ample security against the rogues, who were generally lounging about the door, leading from the corridor to the street." But the ill-will against foreigners at that time apparently originated with some soldiers from Mazatlán and not the native Californians; these latter had their own grievances against the governors sent from Mexico and their convict troops (Robinson's "rogues"). Therefore Robinson could feel reasonably secure that the Americans would not be threatened, nor would he himself have to take sides.[10]

Foreigners were usually treated well in Mexican California; their skills were often valued, and there was little discrimination against them. In 1840, however, a native Californian, Governor Juan Bautista Alvarado, ordered the arrest and expulsion of a number of foreigners, many of whom had not bothered to obtain passports and were therefore in the country illegally. Quite a few of these people were American sailors who had "jumped ship" and American fur trappers from across the mountains. In this instance Robinson could not remain noncommittal, but clearly took sides. He described one of the mountain men arrest-

---

[9]Ibid., 60-61. I could find no other sources to corroborate Robinson's story of this contest, though Robinson does not appear in general to have been the boastful sort, unlike some of his mountain man contemporaries. Isaac Galbraith had stayed behind when Jedediah Smith led the first group of American trappers into California in 1826. See Dale L. Morgan, *Jedediah Smith and the Opening of the West*, 243.

[10]Ibid., 61-69

ed, an individual of dubious character, as "a bold Tennessean, whose name was Graham." He claimed that Alvarado had used his considerable talent in learning enough English to gain "access to their [the Americans] amusements and convivialities, and prepared for him that support which he subsequently received." Alvarado had employed Isaac Graham and his fellow Americans to help him defeat and expel the Mexican commander Nicolás Gutierrez, promising the Americans that California would be declared independent of Mexico. To be governor, however, Alvarado had first to reconcile the southern Californians to his rule. In the process, allegiance to Mexico was continued, though Robinson implied that the north/south disagreement was mainly over how to divide the proceeds from secularizing the missions; he said that under Alvarado the Presidios were allowed to fall into ruin, and he chided Alvarado for caring "little for the safety of any other place but the one where he was located." Ignoring the passport issue, Robinson scored the new governor for treating the Americans unjustly. He made light of Alvarado's charges that the men were plotting to detach California from Mexico, claiming instead that an agreement setting the terms for a horse race between animals belonging to Graham and some Californians had been construed by Alvarado as a plan to overthrow the government. The only mitigating circumstance in the governor's favor was his statement to Robinson that Graham had repeatedly insulted and badgered him. As a highly respected and well-connected foreigner, Robinson himself was not targeted for arrest. But his sympathies were with "our countrymen" and he called those who made the arrests "villains." It was yet another instance of the California authorities' bad judgement . If they had been, in Robinson's words, "wise enough to have examined into the charges, and chastised where chastisement was due, the affair would have ended where it commenced; but, erring, as they always did, when meddling with foreign interest, they were sure to be on the wrong side." It seems likely that the California government could have done very little to please Alfred Robinson; still, his reactions to the arrests were by no means the most censorious. In fact another American, Thomas Jefferson Farnham, was visiting California just at that time and would also write about this "Graham Affair." Farnham's point of view was ethnocentric and expansionist in the extreme, and his entirely negative and racist portrayal of the Californians as villains would receive widespread coverage in the American press.[11]

Alfred Robinson was hardly immune to the expansionist sentiments sweeping over the United States at that time. By 1847 such sentiments had helped to make California a province of the United States. The westward flow of United States power became a flood with the gold rush of 1849-50, and men like Alfred Robinson were in the van of this movement. Robinson could see that California was ripe for the taking, by *some* power capable of governing. California's distance from Mexico, and the new country's preoccupation with her own problems, left the Californians in a state of neglect that was often considerably less than benign. The Californians' remoteness spared them the high casualties and widespread destruction visited upon Mexico during the revolution against Spain, yet they were no less divided in their loyalties. There was factional strife between the mission padres and Spanish loyalists on one hand, and a military group of republicans on the other. The latter was agitating for secularization of the missions, and division of the mission lands. This process was beginning when Alfred Robinson arrived, and he was a witness to the disruption of what at the time was the principal economic unit in California. The missions were at first almost the sole trading partners for Bryant and Sturgis, so it is not surprising that Robinson criticized secularization. Yet most of the leading Californians favored secularization, wished for more autonomy, and opposed the sporadic attempts of the Mexican government to impose on them centralizing governors and policies, especially when these threatened their own ambitions for control of mission lands. Alfred Robinson could see that the Californians had, as he put it, "an inveterate dislike towards the Mexicans, which has given rise to sundry revolutions in their government." Nevertheless he would sometimes express support for a governor

---

[11]Ibid., 121-127. There seem to have been grievances and provocations on both sides in this affair. Graham and his followers felt that their services to Alvarado had been insufficiently rewarded. Alvarado, for his part, came to regret having employed Graham, and feared that the latter was plotting a Texas-style revolution. Robinson had nothing to say about any such plot, and clearly felt that Alvarado was out of line in his treatment of the foreigners. From an American's point of view, rumors of plots were hardly sufficient to warrant or justify such highhanded treatment. See John Walton Caughey, *California: A Remarkable State's Life History*, 141-142, 157; Walton E. Bean, *California: An Interpretive History*, 68,85. See below Chapter 10 for a discussion of Thomas Jefferson Farnham and the Graham Affair.

sent from Mexico, if that person was opposed to secularization.[12]

Industrializing and empire-building nations of the early nineteenth century generated in their peoples a certainty of the righteousness and superiority of their civilizations. The United States was expanding geographically and industrially, and New England was at the center of this ferment. Alfred Robinson's New England background no doubt contributed significantly to the formation of his attitudes toward the people and institutions of California.[13] It is hardly surprising, therefore, that Robinson would express his belief in the general civilizing mission of the United States. The preeminence of countries like the United States and Great Britain were to him self-evident. His convictions could draw on the superiority of the new industrial methods and products just then being perfected in his native country. These material achievements added their weight to the old Puritan belief in a "chosen" people. Several centuries might have eroded the fundamentalist import of this Puritanism, but the absorption of concepts like predestination and providence proved useful to those engaged in a continuing struggle to conquer a wilderness, spread themselves across a continent, and seize and exploit its resources. The original idea that God chooses whom He wishes to save, gratuitously, through no merit of their own, helped form the sense of American (and English) superiority. This assurance was strongly reinforced by the technological innovations of industrialism. Americans convinced themselves they were chosen by virtue of the "providential" successes bestowed upon them in their pursuit of happiness, while concentration on this pursuit minimized the soul-searching and uncertain elements in the ideology. From John Winthrop to Alfred Robinson, an American's mission was to spread the benefits of a superior civilization.[14]

When Robinson generalized about the Californians, therefore, he was implicitly and probably naturally comparing them to the Anglo-

---

[12]Robinson, op. cit., xviii; see also George Tays, "Revolutionary California: The Political History of California during the Mexican period, 1822-1846" (Ph.D. dissertation, University of California, Berkeley, 1932), x-xiv.

[13]Hubert Howe Bancroft, *Works*, Vol. XXII, 698, says that Alfred Robinson was a native of Massachusetts; Adele Ogden, "Alfred Robinson...," 193, says that he was born in Boston in March, 1807.

[14]For a discussion of Puritanism and the frontier, demonstrating that the Puritans believed subjection of the wilderness to be divinely commissioned, see Alan Heimert, "Puritanism, the Wilderness, and the Frontier", in Michael McGiffert, ed., *Puritanism and the American Experience*, 163-177. For a recent

American civilization he knew. He almost always described them as indolent, the key operative word in most American assessments of the Californians' work habits.[15] They were simply incapable of making the best use of the tremendous riches and resources of their country. Robinson considered most of the governing authorities foolish and incompetent, and the institutions (except the missions) wholly inadequate. But his own self-interest apparently colored his opinions, especially about the secularization of the missions. Robinson deplored the decline and disruption of what had been his main customers and almost exclusive sources for hides and tallow. His friendship with the missionaries and his respect for the institution of the mission moved him to oppose secularization, and to criticize those whom he held responsible for the destruction of the missions. Ironically, at a time when liberalism and democracy were advancing in the United States, he even praised the dictatorial Mexican governor Manuel Victoria because Victoria counteracted the secularization decrees of former governor José María Echeandía. Robinson held Echeandía responsible for what he saw as a "work of destruction, under the name of reform." The Indians had abandoned their labors on the missions, were insulting the priests and had taken up all kinds of vices. Robinson expressed his approval of the summary execution of two Indian thieves by Governor Victoria because it "effectively put a stop to robberies of all kinds." Yet he recognized that this act went against the constitutional separation of military and political power subscribed to by most of the federalist-minded Californians, and that it hastened Victoria's expulsion.[16] He was sympathetic to Victoria even in defeat, claiming that the Californians who overthrew him "feared him even in his disabled state [he had been wounded by a sword thrust] , and kept aloof, until he had sent them word that he was willing to resign the command, and return to Mexico." When the General left, he was accom-

---

scholarly review of the literature on Manifest Destiny and mission during the 1840's, see Michael P. Malone, ed., *Historians and the American West.* The coupling of ideas of racial superiority and Manifest Destiny is treated extensively in Reginald Horsman, *Race and Manifest Destiny: The Origins of American Racial Anglo-Saxonism.*

[15]See David J. Langum, "Californios and the Image of Indolence," 181-196.

[16]See *Don Pio Pico's Historical Narrative,* 31-33, where Pico relates how he was influenced by a Mexican liberal to question the authority of the military over civilian citizens. He heard this man say "the civilians [paisanos] were the sacred core of the nation, and the military were nothing more than servants of the nation, which was constituted of the people and not of the military."

panied by the Spanish missionary Padre Antonio Peyrí who in disgust at
the political situation and attack on the missions, had given up his position as head of Mission San Luis Rey. Alfred Robinson thought the
padre had "great penetration of mind," and it was this that "led him to
forsee the result of the new theory of liberty and equality, among a people where anarchy and confusion so generally prevailed, and who, at the
time, were totally unprepared for, and incapable of self-government."[17]

Robinson's tory sentiments were reinforced by the turbulence of California politics and the seeming ineffectiveness of the Mexican system of
justice. He expressed sarcasm at the handling of a criminal case in which
a sergeant of artillery who cut the throat of one of his comrades was sent
to San Blas: "There being no constituted tribunal here to take cog-
nizance of the deed, the villain was sent to Mexico, where, the probability is, he was promoted, and will be ordered back to commit more
murders!" This was the usual way in California, he thought; the local
authorities did not have the power to deal with capital cases. Robinson
expressed his astonishment that the Indians were as docile and pacific as
they were, when California law seemed so ineffectual. He gave credit to
the missionaries for being the restraining force upon the Indians, and
the implications were clear. Without them, California was destined for
even greater anarchy.[18]

Secularization was Robinson's main example of the incompetence
and short-sightedness of the Californians. A process that was begun in
1826, secularization continued until the final disposal of mission properties by Pío Pico on the eve of the Mexican War. In fact, the missions
had never been intended by their founders to hold the vast acreages of
California in fee simple. They were designed to be trustees for the Indians until such time as the neophytes were considered to be prepared to
own and work the land for themselves. Yet this time never seemed to
come. The missions had held almost all of the arable land from San
Diego to San Francisco, and any Californians who wanted to obtain land
or expand their holdings had to deal with the missionaries, who were
usually opposed to having any acreage withdrawn from their control.
They were consistent opponents of any policy that encouraged settle-

---

[17]Robinson, op. cit., 69-70, 83-85.
[18]Ibid.,105-106.

ment on lands under their jursidiction.[19] But in a halting fashion, succes-
sive California governments managed to break the padres' control and
parcel out the former mission lands for private development. The Indians' claims, however, were almost always lost in the scramble to get mission lands as the Californians (or at least select families[20]) jockeyed for
the opportunity to get rich. In Robinson's opinion, however, they sought
wealth without having to do any of the hard labor of carving farms and
vineyards from a wilderness. The frequent revolutions in California were
really "aimed at the removal of certain governmental officers, not so
much for the desire of reform, as for the division of the spoils!" According to Robinson, when the missionaries saw what was happening, they
were determined that the Indians would benefit in spite of the apparent
greed of the Californians, so they gave orders to slaughter the cattle and
sell the hides and tallow before the government could appropriate them,
though it is difficult to see how this could have benefited the Indians.
The missionaries then contracted out the slaughtering, but the contrac-
tors hired for the job "secretly appropriated *two* hides for their portion,
to one on account of the Mission." Thus the riches of the missions were
laid waste.[21]

Such behavior by the Californians does not appear much different
from the opportunism that Americans typically exhibited in this period
when presented with a chance to get land, but according to Robinson the
Californians were operating under the influence of an odious set of
"ungovernable desires." A marked characteristic of a superior civilization, for a Boston Yankee such as Robinson, was the training of its citizens to master their own baser impulses. The Californians' character
deficiencies in this respect could be

> traced to their education, and to the indolent manner in which they have been
> reared. Thus we may trace its origin to the time when Spain held sway over the
> American republics! to the old Spaniards who, whilst rolling in wealth,
> indulged in excessive indolence. This trait of character still exists among their

---

[19]See John Walton Caughey, op. cit.,108-109; W.W. Robinson, *Land In California,*13-61;
Manuel P. Servin, "The Secularization of the California Missions: A Reappraisal,"133-149.

[20]George Tays, op. cit., 418, listed them. "The Alvarados, Arguellos, Bandinis, Carrillos, Castros,
Estudillos, Martinez, Osios, Picos, Rochas, del Valles, Vallejos, and other families, each had at least one
member connected with or as mission administrator."

[21]Robinson, op. cit., 99, 110-111.

descendants, and you might as well expect a sloth to leave a tree, that has one nick of bark left upon its trunk, as to expect a Californian to labor, whilst a real glistens in his pocket.[22]

Yet Robinson contradicted this assessment of Californians in several specific instances. For example, on one of his trips to Los Angeles, Robinson stayed with an old Ranchero, Don Tiburcio Tapia. He described Don Tiburcio as a soldier of modest means who had risen "by honest and industrious labor" to become " one of the wealthiest inhabitants of the place. His strict integrity gave him credit to any amount, so that he was the principal merchant and the only native one in El Pueblo de los Angeles."[23] But the greatest exception to Robinson's portrait of Californians was his own father-in-law, Don José de la Guerra y Noriega. In a short biography of his father-in-law, Robinson called him "a man of unspotted integrity, patriotism, humanity and wealth, he wielded immense influence in California." Here was precisely such an "old Spaniard...rolling in wealth" as Robinson had criticized for corrupting California with his example of indolence! Perhaps a dutiful son-in-law could overlook such an ancestry, however, in a father-in-law who expressed his contempt for the government of Mexico, and who desired the success of American arms. As Robinson explained: "When the American flag was unfurled over his own home, he greeted the triumphant banner as the symbol of justice and peace."[24]

As exceptions to his generalizations about Californians, Tiburcio Tapia and José de la Guerra were not alone. Robinson seemed to exempt the entire female sex! At San José he admired the women, praising them and contrasting them with the men, who were, he said, "generally indolent, and addicted to many vices, caring little for the welfare of their children, who, like themselves, grow up unworthy members of society." On the other hand, "perhaps there are few places in the world where, in proportion to the numbers of inhabitants, can be found more chastity, industrious habits, and correct deportment, than among the women of

---

[22]Ibid., 99.

[23]Ibid., 44. Don Tiburcio Tapia had been granted the Cucamonga Rancho in 1839 and was one of the largest landowners in Southern California. He was alcalde of Los Angeles in 1844 and was, according to H.H. Bancroft, "a man of good sense, good character, and some wealth...." He may have been a merchant as well, but I can find no other corroboration for this. See Bancroft, *Works,* Vol. XXII, 742.

[24]Alfred Robinson, "José Antonio de la Guerra," in Oscar T. Shuck, ed., *Representative and Leading Men of the Pacific,* 25-27.

this place." Also in California, unlike the more "advanced" cultures of the United States or Europe, one could see the vicious (men) and the virtuous (women) freely fraternizing with one another in public places, a phenomenon which Robinson attributed to the newness and unsettled state of the country. With time he believed this would change, and "a necessary distinction will prevail among the various classes; and society will be found more select, as in places of greater civilization."[25]

In *Life in California*, Robinson never gave a clear picture of the class structure in Mexican California. He moved from speaking of class distinctions to speaking of the differences between the men and the women. This ambiguity, however, could have provided a convenient cover for him if pressed about the implications of his opinions. His American sense of superiority was unmistakable in his characterizations of the male Californians, yet his acquaintance with individual Californians and his alliance with an honorable and respected California family found expression in his praise for the women of California. He was after all married to one of them.[26] If any of his California friends questioned him closely about his portrait of the California male, he could maintain that he meant only a certain (lower) class of California man. Elsewhere, he pointed out that in California there was indeed a well defined separation between the upper and the lower classes, and only a few families were considered worthy of respect. Still, in California he maintained there were no poor people—when the rancheros killed their cattle, "the surrounding population always had their share."[27]

In fairness to the balance of Robinson's perceptions, it must be said that he did not find all of the Americans he encountered in California to be model representatives of a superior culture either. "Among our own countrymen, who had lived all their lives in the Western Prairies till a taste for emigration had brought them here, we had occasional opportunities to witness a want of experience and cultivation that in many cases

---

[25] Robinson, *Life in California*, 50-51.

[26] In a letter to Don José de la Guerra written in December 1834, Robinson asked for the hand of his daughter, Anita, in marriage. He said, "Her attractions have persuaded me that without her I *cannot live* or be happy in the world. Consequently, I am begging for her hand. My circumstances are well known, and it is not necessary to say that my principal object will be to grant *all her desires* and to *become worthy* of *her esteem.*" *The Letters of Alfred Robinson to the De La Guerra family of Santa Barbara*, 3, emphasis in original.

[27] Alfred Robinson, "Statement of Recollections on early years of California",pp. 32,35.

did not fall far behind the ludicrous behavior of the rude Californians."[28] Furthermore, in 1845 he wrote a letter to his father-in-law from New York, in which he commented on the debate in Congress over the annexation of Texas. It was opposed, he said, by a majority of Americans. But it would pass nevertheless because in the United States "the Americans do not rule but only the off-scourings of the people of Ireland and Germany so that when we have a candidate to raise to the presidential chair, these are carried by their ignorance to attach themselves to the Democratic party. The Republican party! A government for everybody! But there is no solution." His cynicism about politics and his contempt for the lower classes were not confined to California![29]

Some Californians may have appeared ludicrous and lazy to a Yankee trader, but Robinson also acknowledged their kindness and easy hospitality. If he had little respect for the Californians' capacity to develop the resources and potential of their country, he did admire and appreciate the grace and natural generosity shown to him by both the mission fathers who took him in, and the rancheros who plied him with food, drink, horses for his journeys, even guides to show him the way. He liked and esteemed most of the padres he came to know in California, and he respected the Catholic Church there, which he saw as a source of virtuous influence and learning among a population generally ignorant.[30] At Mission San Gabriel, for example, he praised Padre José Sanchez as the epitome of the hospitable missionary: "Possessing a kind, generous, and lively disposition, he had acquired, in consequence, a multitude of friends, who constantly flocked around him; whilst through his liberality the needy wanderer, of whatever nation or creed, found a home and protection."[31]

The newly emerging ranchero class, expanding its holdings in the wake of secularization, was also beginning to replace the missionaries as

---

[28]Robinson, *Life in California,* 92.

[29]*The Letters of Alfred Robinson,* op. cit.,18. See also Alfred Robinson's letters to Thomas Oliver Larkin in George P. Hammond, ed., *The Larkin Papers,* II, 308; Robinson wrote to Larkin in 1844 expressing his Whig convictions and lamenting the election of James K. Polk, which he blamed on the Irish immigrants in New York. He said that the naturalization laws ought to be modified so that immigrants had to be in the country for twenty-one years before getting the vote. He did not favor annexation of Texas or war with Mexico, which he felt would disrupt trade. Robinson closely fits Reginald Horsman's description of the New Englanders of this period who "believed passionately in the special Providential mission of the American branch of the Anglo-Saxon race, but they feared the excesses of rampant expansionism, military adventure, and the extension of slavery." See Horsman, op. cit., 186.

[30]*Life in California,* 51.

[31]Ibid., 22.

customer and supplier of hides and tallow. Robinson was a frequent guest in the homes of well-to-do ranchers like Antonio Maria Lugo or Tomás Yorba. At the latter's "Rancho de St. Ana," Robinson marveled at the immense herds of cattle grazing, and at the conspicuous consumption displayed by Don Tomás in his dress:

> Upon his head he wore a black silk handkerchief, the four corners of which hung down his neck behind. An embroidered shirt, a cravat of white jaconet tastefully tied, a blue damask vest, short clothes of crimson velvet, a bright green cloth jacket, with large silver buttons, and shoes of embroidered deerskin, comprised his dress. I was afterwards informed ... that on some occasions, such as some particular feast day or festival, his entire display often exceeded in value a thousand dollars.[32]

The shift from mission to rancho was not without its trauma for Mexican California, and Alfred Robinson was obviously pained by the ruination of institutions that he had come to know and appreciate. But he would modify his opinion as the ranchos replaced the missions in economic importance. For the Indians, however, the change further disrupted their lives and contributed to their demise. With the decline of the missions, the Indians either returned to the wilds or assumed a slavelike status on the ranchos. Robinson observed that even before secularization accelerated the process of decline and degradation for the mission Indians, they were not content with the religious and work discipline of the missions. Many tried to escape, but were almost always "pursued, and generally taken, when they are flogged, and an iron clog is fastened to their legs, serving as additional punishment, and a warning to others."[33] As much as he praised the missionaries and their institution, Robinson perhaps revealed more than he knew when he said in his statement of recollections made to H. H. Bancroft in 1878: "The missions were like a large prison, at the East ... where they [the Indians] carry on work, with workshops of all kinds."[34]

Between 1836 and 1842 all of the missions rapidly disintegrated, helped along by government-appointed administrators who were at best inept and usually venal.[35] On a trip to San Diego, Robinson could see

---

[32]Ibid., 21-22.
[33]Ibid., 19.
[34]Alfred Robinson, "Statement of Recollections on early years of California," op. cit., 9.
[35]Dallas, op. cit., 35.

that everything was in ruins. To make the return journey he had to pay $40.00 for a horse to ride, when once he had only paid $5.00 or $6.00. He summed up his feelings in two sentences: "So much for secularization! So much for the Californian Government!"[36] The disarray of the missions meant that the condition of the Indians deteriorated even more. Robinson saw the Indians' vices of gambling and drunkeness result in violence and loss of possessions (meager as these were). There were even Indians who gambled away their wives and children, a final sad comment on the destruction of their culture.[37]

Alfred Robinson was a practical man. In an article he wrote for *Fisher's National Magazine* in 1846, he explained for American readers some of the changes he had seen take place in California. "Since 1834," he said, "the priests have been deprived of their property, and the missions have been entirely destroyed, under the scandalous administration of certain hirelings of the government." He documented the decline of the Indian population at the missions, from 30, 650 in 1834, to 4,450 in 1842. The mission cattle too—previously his source for hides and tallow—had dropped from 424,000 in 1834 to a mere 28,220 in 1842. Thus he seemed to maintain a consistent point of view in his opposition to the apparently harmful effects of secularization. But he went on to explain that since 1836, when the Californians drove out the Mexicans (a reference to Alvarado's revolution against the Mexican Colonel Nicolas Gutierrez, which he treated in *Life in California* without much sympathy) numbers of new farms had been created out of former mission lands, and most importantly, "hundreds of Englishmen and Americans are scattered over the extent of their domains." In 1842, 92 ranchos stretched from San Diego to San Luis Obispo with an average of 1,000 cattle on each one; from San Luis Obispo north, the ranchos were even more numerous. He estimated that the cattle on all of the ranchos in California in 1842 were in excess of 400,000, thus putting them back to their peak number during the period of mission prosperity. Further, he pointed out that 50,000 were slaughtered each year, leaving a significant yearly increase, "so that with care and attention, in a very short time the number must overreach that ever held by the missions, even in their most flourishing condition."[38]

---

[36]Life in California, 128.

[37]Ibid., 23

[38]Alfred Robinson, "Sketch of California," 36-42.

Given his negative opinions about secularization throughout most of *Life in California,* it is interesting to note the shift that Robinson underwent as the full effects of the division of mission lands began to be felt. He was after all, like most Americans, a pragmatic man. He continued to deplore the waste and destruction visited on the missions by secularization, and he never showed quite the same respect for the rancheros as he did for the padres. Nevertheless, by 1842 it was clear that the breakup of the missions had resulted in a country flourishing because of that supreme American virtue, "individual enterprise," and now "the wealth, instead of being confined to the monastic institutions, as before, has been distributed among the people."[39]

Alfred Robinson could not bring himself to conclude that perhaps some of the policies of the California government for which he held such contempt may have turned out to be beneficial. Nevertheless, the granting of mission lands to people with "industrious habits," many of them Americans, doubtless went a long way toward reconciling him to the missions' fate.[40] The American "work ethic," spirit of industry and competitive acquisitiveness were exactly what Robinson believed was needed to realize the potential for riches that he could see for himself all around him in his travels. In fact, his narrative is laced throughout with comments on the wealth of California and its possibilities for development, if only it were in the hands of an enterprising people! Up and down California, Robinson could see the fertility of the soil, the immense herds of cattle, and the ineffable beauty of the landscape. At Los Angeles, for example, he observed that the lands, "being level and fertile, are capable of great agricultural improvement." Several Americans were already living there, he noted, and "taking advantage of the resources of the place." At San Pedro he made the prophetic observation that "with very little expense, it might be made a place of anchorage for large ships," and passing through Ventura on his way to " the beautiful vale of Santa Barbara," he remarked on the fecundity of the valleys. He thought that no part of the world yielded a greater amount of agricultural produce, especially wheat, than the immensely productive soil to be found north of the San Francisco Bay. As for the bay itself, he recognized it as "one of the largest and most valuable harbors in the world," with a narrow entrance that made it easily defensible. It only

---

[39]*Life in California,* 152.
[40]Ibid., 152-154.

remained to find the right people to develop such a land. As Robinson explained it: "A country like California requires robust and enterprising men—accustomed to labor in the field, and to a life of simplicity and economy." Such a description was obviously meant to fit the sturdy, westering American pioneers who had already made a garden of the mid-west, and were beginning to arrive with the first wagon trains to California.[41]

Robinson's practicality and business sense did not exclude an appreciation for the natural loveliness he saw all around him in California. He too valued California's unique treasure, the great natural beauty of her unspoiled landscape. A night horseback ride from Ventura to Los Angeles left a lasting imprint on his mind:

> A fine moon had risen just as we set out, and so brilliantly was the whole country lighted up, that our way lay before us as clearly as at noon-day. The clear heavens; the bright moon; the beautiful country stretching far away into the blue distance, and basking in the moonlight; the deep silence, unbroken save by the footfalls of the horses, or the cries of some wild night-bird; all formed a scene of such rare beauty that the impression still lingers in my memory.[42]

Yet Robinson was realistic in seeing that much of California was a semi-desert, and that it could, like the Presidio at San Diego, remain unfinished "on account of the difficulty of procuring water." Droughts, floods, fires, earthquakes, all of these manifestations of California's geological personality were recorded in Robinson's narrative, along with the ubiquitous California flea.[43] Still, California was a desirable prize, and the final pages of *Life in California* were devoted to a discussion of the ease with which California could be made independent of Mexico, the weakness of the latter country and its distance from California. Robinson indulged in a certain (though not flawless) prophecy. He was convinced that California would inevitably slip from Mexico's feeble grasp—but not necessarily into the hands of the United States. The British, French and Russians all had designs on California. He agreed with Alexander Forbes (who wrote the first history of California), and approvingly quoted the Englishman's conviction that "California is calculated, in an eminent degree, to become a maritime power."[44] Robinson thought that an 1842

[41]Ibid., 22, 25-28, 42-43, 116.
[42]Ibid., 44.
[43]Ibid., 11, 69-70, 77, 93, 132.
[44]Ibid., 154-155.

visit by Sir George Simpson, Governor of the Hudson's Bay Company, might portend an attempt by the Company to monopolize California's trade in advance of a British take-over. He was not too concerned, however, since he felt that California would not be in worse hands than she was with Mexico. Nor did he express much more than surprise at the mistaken seizure of Monterey by Commodore Thomas ap Catesby Jones in the same year. When it looked as if the United States was actually going to possess California, Robinson said that the Americans in town were "elated, and some of the most wealthy Californians seemed not displeased that they were to have a government more stable than that under which they had been living."[45] Robinson could not see the precise outlines of the future—that Jones' action was a dress-rehearsal for what would happen only four years later. But he continued to quote the prophetic words of Alexander Forbes, who was then British consul at Tepic, Mexico. Though British, Forbes appeared to believe as much in an inevitable United States expansion to the Pacific as the Americans did: "The northern American tide of population must roll on southward, and overwhelm, not only California, but other important states." If the United States did not immediately annex California, however, Robinson in an ironic role reversal with Forbes, was still willing to see the English get the country. In this he was consistent with his Whig political opposition to an American war with Mexico, while yet maintaining a favorable attitude toward the civilizing mission of the Anglo-Europeans. Great Britain, he felt, ought to accept California as a payment for debts owed by Mexico. California was so rich and important that "soon the whole western coast of North America would be settled by emigrants, both from this country and from Europe" (he was not a complete prophet; he failed to forsee the population influx from Latin America and Asia!). He identified the San Francisco Bay area—correctly for the nineteenth century—as "the grand region for colonization," and this before the discovery of gold. Finally, his sweeping conclusion presented an early vision of California's titanic future, by one who would help to bring it about: "All this... must come to pass," he said, "for the march of emigration is to the West, and naught will arrest its advance but the mighty ocean."[46]

---

[45]Ibid., 137-138, 146-147.
[46]Ibid., 150-157.

WILLIAM HEATH DAVIS
Courtesy California Historical Society

MARIA DE JESUS ESTUDILLO
(Mrs. William Heath Davis)
Courtesy The Bancroft Library

CHAPTER II

William Heath Davis

In his extensive and rambling memoirs of a long life, William Heath Davis claimed to be the second earliest American to reside in Mexican California. He was proud of his status as a pioneer and gave 1831 as the year of his arrival. Only Alfred Robinson preceded him, he said, arriving from Boston on the *Brookline* in 1829.[1]

Davis was nine years old in 1831, and was in fact just making a visit to California at the time. He had come from the Sandwich Islands on board the merchant vessel *Louisa,* which belonged to his step-father, John Coffin Jones. Jones was a prominent merchant at Honolulu, and had married Davis' mother in 1826, three years after the death of Davis' father. Davis appreciated his step-father, who took over the duties of a father when William was just a year old. He claimed that Jones raised him "with the love of a father, and I was endeared to him, having affection for the man who bestowed tender care on the son of his deceased associate, Captain William Heath Davis."[2] The elder Davis died in the same year that his second son, William Heath Davis, Jr., was born.[3]

This father that Davis never knew had himself been a pioneer in California. As a Boston merchant ship's captain involved in the trade for sea otter skins, the elder Davis was on the coast of California as early as 1811, and William believed his father was one of the first Boston traders in California—maybe even the first. William learned about his father from his mother, from his step-father, and from ship's captains and old rancheros who had known him. They testified that the elder Davis had been a popular and successful merchant. William Senior, who spoke Spanish fluently (his son called him a "Spanish scholar, studying the lan-

---

[1] William Heath Davis, *Seventy-Five Years in California,* 240. Davis was of course incorrect. Abel Stearns, among others, had preceded him, also arriving in California in 1829. See Caughey, *California,* op. cit., 141.

[2] William Heath Davis, "Sixty Years in California," 6.

[3] Andrew Rolle, *An American in California: The Biography of William Heath Davis, 1822-1909,* 3-9.

guage when he was at school in Boston....") used to invite the Californian missionaries, officials and rancheros aboard his ship and ply them with presents and luxuries from his larder.[4] Davis learned about his father's style as a trader from Don Ygnacio Martinez, who had been comandante of the Presidio at Santa Barbara at the time of the elder Davis' visit. Martinez told the son that he had been "overwhelmed with the kindness and entertainment he met with on board the vessel and that he could only accept half of what was proferred with such grace and generosity." Such also was to be the pattern of the younger Davis' life as a merchant. The "grace and generosity" of a father he never knew was to provide the model for the son's career.[5]

Davis' mother, too, had genealogical connections with maritime New England. Hannah Holmes Davis was the daughter of Oliver Holmes of Boston. Oliver Holmes, Davis' grandfather, could also claim credit as a pioneer, having served on one of the first ships to engage in the triangular trade between New England, China and the Northwest Coast of America, via the Hawaiian Islands. It was in the Islands that Holmes—who was eventually made governor of Oahu by King Kamehameha I—married into the Hawaiian royal family, taking Mahi, a royal princess, for his wife.[6]

William Heath Davis was, therefore, one quarter Hawaiian. As a person of "mixed blood," he must have overheard more than one disparaging comment about his ancestry, like that of Robert Semple who referred to him in a letter to Thomas O. Larkin as "Kanaka Davis."[7] The Hawaiians on the coast were—like the Indians—the common laborers, often little better than slaves, and clearly at the bottom of the social and racial hierarchy. Perhaps because of this Davis was eager to point out that his genealogy was honorable. He chose not to mention his distaff Hawaiian blood, however, and one can only assume that this was due to his sensitivity to possible slights because of it. Instead he called attention to the fact that he was named, like his father, for his great-uncle, William Heath, who had

---

[4] Davis, "Sixty Years," 3.

[5] Davis, *Seventy-Five Years*, 153-154; Rolle, op. cit., 3-9.

[6] Rolle, 3-9.

[7] Ibid., 79. "Typical of the lesser merchants who hounded Davis for goods was Robert Semple at newly founded Benecia. Semple, writing to his partner Larkin on one occasion, was not complimentary toward his principle supplier. 'Kanaka Davis, slow as he is, would leap at the opportunity' to join him, he boasted."

been one of George Washington's generals. He could also claim as a model, his step-father, John Coffin Jones, whom he described as "of a proud, aristocratic nature, an inheritance from his distinguished parents, who were among the very first families of Boston."[8]

It may be that Davis was also concerned to establish his patrilineage because he had never in fact lived in New England, or any part of the United States. His older brother Robert was sent away to school in Massachusetts, but William remained in the Hawaiian Islands, only visiting California twice before finally taking up residence in 1838.[9] But an education by New England missionaries in Hawaii, and his long association with his uncle, Nathan Spear, must have been sufficient to instill in Davis at least some of the habits of mind of his Puritan ancestors. Nathan Spear kept a store at Yerba Buena (today's San Francisco), where he had purchased land rather than give up his American citizenship in exchange for a Mexican land grant. Davis lived with and worked for his Uncle Nathan when he first came to California, and Spear's influence on the young man probably encouraged Davis' own patriotic sense of his American antecedents. He was definitely proud of his uncle for having resisted the blandishments of the California government, to remain a United States citizen. Spear could have taken a large grant of land simply by becoming a citizen of the land where he lived and operated his business. He chose instead to purchase the land for his store at Yerba Buena.[10]

Nathan Spear launched Davis on a long career as a merchant, giving him his first important assignment guiding the newly arrived Johan Augustus Sutter to the site of his New Helvetia at the junction of the American and Sacramento Rivers. Davis' description of the scene that ensued when Sutter saluted their departure with cannon fire, could stand as a symbol for the end of the old edenic California:

> As we moved away Captain Sutter gave us a parting salute of nine guns—the first ever fired at that place—which produced a most remarkable effect. As the heavy report of the guns and the echoes died away, the camp of the little party was surrounded by hundreds of Indians, who were excited and astonished at the unusual sound. A large number of deer, elk and other animals on the plains

---

[8] Davis, *Seventy-Five Years,* 153; Davis, "Sixty Years...," 6.
[9] Rolle, 9-12.
[10] Davis, *Seventy-Five Years,* 72.

were startled, running to and fro, stopping to listen, their heads raised, full of curiosity and wonder, seemingly attracted and fascinated to the spot, while from the interior of the adjacent wood the howl of wolves and coyotes filled the air, and immense flocks of waterfowl flew wildly over the camp.[11]

William Heath Davis was to be connected in some way or another with the history of California, from his first view of the coast in 1831 to his death at his Hayward home in 1909. He saw Yerba Buena on a visit in 1833 when there was only a single resident tending his potato patch; he almost became the founder of the city of Oakland; he was in fact the founder of American San Diego. As he looked back on his life in California, he seemed to have known everyone and been present at almost all of the major events of the period.[12]

Seventy-Five Years in California, Davis' sprawling reminiscence, has been extensively used by historians for information about California life before the gold rush. Not much attention has been paid, however, to the overall structure and impact of the book itself. Perhaps this is because it appears at first reading to be such a chaotic jumble. People have thus made their own selective use of it without considering the book as a whole—as William Heath Davis' "life." It was quintessentially a work of memory, preoccupied with descriptive details, but with little or no heed to any overall stylistic unity. The book is almost a "free association", with Davis placing his recollections in the order that they occurred to him. *Seventy-Five Years in California* was the product of a twenty-year effort by Davis to set down all he could remember about his life, and events and acquaintances in California. He had published articles in San Francisco newspapers in the late 1880s, and these sketches eventually formed the substantial basis of a book he called *Sixty Years in California,* which was praised by most California newspapers of the day as a rich store of anecdotes and reminiscences. The reviewers recognized that Davis was no literary stylist, but they understood the historical value of his prodigious memory. *Seventy-Five Years in California* was the final product of Davis' labors as an historian and personal chronicler of an era. Davis kept a diary; he wrote a long manuscript for H.H. Bancroft called "Glimpses of

---

[11] Ibid.,16; Rolle,12-16. For a biography of Sutter, see Richard Dillon, *Captain John Sutter: Sacramento Valley's Sainted Sinner.*

[12] Davis, *Seventy-Five Years,* 249-260; Rolle,10, 142-143.

the Past," and he worked until his death on what he chose to style his "Great Manuscript." This latter was to combine all of his earlier reminiscences with all of the additional products that could be resurrected from his memory. Unfortunately, this "Great Manuscript" was destroyed in the San Francisco earthquake and fire of 1906. Davis tried to run into the burning building on the Montgomery Block and rescue his manuscript, but he was stopped by U.S. Marines. When he returned the next day, the building was still standing, but the two boxes that contained his manuscript were gone. He had only fragments and notes left at home, which he used to begin once again to put his "Great Manuscript" in shape for publication. He had only several more years to live, an old man without the time or energy to replace again what he had lost. Not until 1929 did John Howell gather together what Davis had done over the years and publish it as *Seventy-Five Years in California*.[13]

This book, in spite of the free ranging of Davis' mind—which often resulted in apparently disparate material occurring even in the same paragraph—does have an underlying thematic thread in the personality and concerns of the man himself. Davis was interested in people: the Indians, the Spanish-Mexican Californians, the foreign merchants and traders. He was interested in events: Juan Bautista Alvarado's arrest of foreigners in 1840; Thomas ap Catesby Jones' seizure of Monterey; the revolt of the Californians against Mexican Governor Manuel Micheltorena; the American conquest of California. And everything was viewed from the very personal vantage point of Davis' own sympathies, antipathies and ambivalences. As an historian, Davis made his own on-the-spot assessments of men and events, and if these quite often ran counter to prevailing opinion, the reason could usually be found in Davis' personal involvement.

Working first in his uncle's store, then as a supercargo for Captain John Paty, and finally trading on his own account up and down California, Davis became intimate with the leading personalities of California society. He observed the decline of the missions; he was a familiar figure in the households of rancheros such as Don José de la Guerra of Santa Barbara; he knew all of the merchants and traders on the coast, from Abel

---

[13] Reviews of *Sixty Years in California*, Huntington Library Rare Book 65996; John Howell, Publisher's Preface to *Seventy-Five Years in California*, Huntington Library Ms., n.p.; Rolle, 129-139.

Stearns in Los Angeles and Henry D. Fitch at San Diego to Thomas O. Larkin at Monterey, and of course merchants such as his uncle Nathan Spear and his cousin William Davis Merry Howard at Yerba Buena. He was one of them and at home in their society. He also had great respect and love for the Californians. In 1847 he married into a land-rich ranchero family, taking María Jesus Estudillo as his wife and becoming a Roman Catholic. She was the daughter of Don José Joaquin Estudillo who owned extensive acreage at San Diego as well as the San Leandro rancho in the east San Francisco Bay area. The courtesy, hospitality and grace of these upper-class Californians combined with the examples set by his father, step-father and uncle to become the practical standard for Davis' conduct and judgements. Through marriage and business ties, he was to become a Californian. Yet he was also to remain an American in his political preference, welcoming and aiding the conquest. Davis commented on almost every aspect of life in this unhurried, long-vanished California, from the doomed Indians to the American mountain men who were trekking into the territory in advance of the tidal wave of American settlement. Perhaps more even than Alfred Robinson, Davis was a cultural nexus between the old Mexican California and the newly arriving Americans who would soon overwhelm it.[14]

For those he respected, Davis had almost nothing but kind and complimentary words. For those such as John C. Fremont, whom he did not admire,he was much more reserved; yet he almost always tried to give credit where he believed it to be due.[15] In *Seventy-Five Years,* Davis seemed to have no lasting hostility or grudges against anyone, nor did he appear to have made many enemies. His attitude toward the people of California was less colored by racial and ethnocentric biases than almost any other of the Americans who observed and commented on the mores of the Californians and the Indians.[16] Familiarity bred a certain understanding. Davis may also have felt that, like many of the Californians of all classes, he himself was a person of "mixed blood." Except in the case of the Chinese in California, class more than race was the basis for Davis' finer discriminations. Davis had little to say about the Chinese in *Seventy-Five Years.* His editor apparently chose to omit the hostile expressions

---

[14] Davis, *Seventy-Five Years,* 56.

[15] Ibid., 214.

[16] With the possible exception of Benjamin D. Wilson; see below Chapter 9.

he had made against them in his earlier work, *Sixty Years in California,* where it is clear that he had obviously succumbed to the popular agitation against the Chinese that was a prominent feature of California politics in the 1870s and '80s.[17] He thought that they had drained California of its gold, demoralized the youth, and were "injurious to the prosperity of California, morally and commercially."[18] In *Seventy-Five Years,* however, he had only one brief paragraph at the end of the book in which he said that the first Chinese to arrive in California came as a cabin boy in 1838. Then, "there was no expression of alarm from the people of San Francisco that the Chinese would overrun the city of the bay and the state of California."[19]

Davis' own origins may indeed have played a role in shaping his attitude and opinions about the society he saw around him in California. Like other Anglo-Americans in California such as Alfred Robinson, Davis approved of marriages between foreigners and the Spanish-Mexican Californians. He went even further and claimed that "the stock, as usual, was improved by the mingling of the different nationalities." Nor could he be too censorious toward relations between Indians and whites. His own grandmother was an aboriginal Hawaiian. He did not believe that marriages between Indians and whites in California were too common, but he did maintain that they resulted in some fine-looking children. The Indian women of California were, he felt, of "far better stock" than those of Mexico, so the child of Indian mothers and white fathers turned out better. Sometimes if their Indian mothers deserted them, these children were adopted into Californian families where they were kindly treated and, as he had observed, were "employed as nurses and domestics, and not regarded as common servants." Davis never mentioned any cases of Indian men marrying white women, and one assumes that, as in the ante-bellum South of that time, there were strong social taboos against it. It was probably not done and certainly not discussed.[20]

Elsewhere, Davis pointed out that the Spanish soldiers and other settlers in California married Indian women because of the scarcity of

---

[17] See Alexander Saxton, *Indispensable Enemies: Labor and the Anti-Chinese Movement in California.*

[18] Davis, *Sixty Years in California,* 571-575.

[19] Davis, *Seventy-Five Years,* 261.

[20] Ibid., 95, 108-109.

white women, even though it was "contrary to the wishes of the authorities, the intermingling of races." But these Indian women were often born and raised on the haciendas, and treated as if they had been the children of the rancheros themselves. These Indian girls were given all of the refinements of such an upbringing and therefore, according to Davis, made good wives and mothers. The children of such unions, he said, "were handsomer than the children born of Castilian parents."[21]

One of the more famous marriages between a white man and an Indian woman was that of Hugo Reid, a Scotsman living in Los Angeles. Davis visited the Reids a number of times, and Reid's biographer credits Davis' influence with helping to make Reid's marriage more acceptable among the society of white merchants and their wives.[22] Davis praised Victoria Reid, Hugo Reid's Indian wife, as a good example of an Indian girl raised by a ranchero family. On a visit to the Reids, he said he was treated well "not only by Reid himself, but by his Indian wife, who was all that could be expected. A Castilian lady of standing could not have bestowed on us any greater attention or graciousness than was extended to us at Santa Anita."[23]

According to Davis, Victoria Reid had a daughter (whose father had been an Englishman) born before her marriage to Hugo. Davis described this young lady as "English in feature, with blue eyes and auburn hair."[24] This does not seem likely, nor does Reid's biographer make any mention of such a child. Reid's Indian wife had children from her previous marriage, but her first husband, who died, had also been Indian.[25] Davis may have had a lapse of memory here, which could perhaps be taken as a caution concerning the complete reliability of some other of his reminiscences. Davis' attempt to give Victoria Reid a white child was a rather unrealistic distortion of the results to be expected from such unions. His ideas about race and breeding were clearly circumscribed by the prevailing ideology of his day, and he had his own understandable ambivalence about the whole issue of the mixing of races. He was after all an accepted member of "white" society in California, both American and Californ-

---

[21] Davis, Huntington Ms. DA 2, Box 2, Folder 25, 1-3.
[22] Susanna Bryant Dakin, *A Scotch Paisano in Old Los Angeles*, 37.
[23] Davis, Huntington Library Ms. DA 2, Box 2, Folder 45, 5.
[24] Davis, *Seventy-Five Years*, 108-109.
[25] Dakin, 33-34.

ian, and it hardly seems historically possible that he could have proudly proclaimed his Hawaiian heritage at that time. Nevertheless, his interest in the intermarriage of different nationalities, and his belief that it produced an improved "stock," had obvious personal roots.

But Davis did not idealize the Indians of California. He himself had seen and heard about the constant struggle between the Indians and the Californians. He believed that harsh measures were justified by the Indians' atrocities, and necessary in order to intimidate them, since they outnumbered the settlers. In an unpublished fragment, he even rationalized shooting women because "they themselves invited the punishment by joining the males in their attacks against the soldiers and citizens."[26] He had both commercial and friendship ties with the missionaries and rancheros, and it is to be expected that he would share their opinions about the Indians. He wrote, for example, describing the way the Indians were recruited for the missions. He said they "were captured by the military who went into the interior of the country in pursuit of them...." But Davis did not say this to condemn the missionaries. He pointed out rather that once these Indians were integrated into the mission system, where they were well treated, they "soon became domesticated and ready and eager to adopt the habits of civilized life." They no longer desired their old wild existence and they helped to influence those who arrived later.[27]

Forced recruitment of Indians for the missions by the army was one practice apparently common in California; whipping was another. Davis never explicitly defended the custom of whipping recalcitrant Indians. Instead he told a story he had heard from Captain Thomas Robbins, a transplanted Bostonian who kept a store at Santa Barbara. An old Indian cook of Robbins' came to him about every six months *asking* to be whipped. The Indian told Robbins that it must be done, "otherwise he would become lazy and negligent." Though Robbins was kind-hearted, the Indian insisted on his beating, and Robbins called in the old man himself to verify the story. Davis reported that in his own family an Indian servant had to be whipped occasionally because he would become lazy and insolent. A good whipping then made him civil and obedient again.[28]

---

[26] Davis, Huntington Library Ms. DA 2, Box 3, Folder 91, 3.

[27] Davis, *Seventy-Five Years*, 5.

[28] Ibid., 93-94.

Davis was, therefore, not a conscious champion of the Indians and he no doubt saw more than a few of them whipped, like the one at San Jose in 1839 who was beaten on the bare back "for some offence he had committed, this being one of their [the missionaries'] punishments."[29] But he undermined his own case for the contentment of the Indians and the salutary use of the whip (contradictory in themselves) with his account of an Indian uprising at San Ysidro, south of San Diego. It took place on the rancho of the Ybarra family in 1837. They had actually been warned about the possibility of an attack by an old Indian servant, but the head of the family refused to heed the warning. Davis supplied an interesting reason for this: "The Californians were a brave people, especially in opposition to the Indians... and did not fear them, but considered that three or four, or eight or ten of their number were sufficient to vanquish ten times that many Indians." This stance—not unlike that of Americans who fought Indians, and who also believed in their superiority over the Californians—cost Ybarra his life when he and several of his men were caught by the Indians near the corral. They tried to escape to the protection of the house, but an Indian boy employed by the family barred the door and they were all killed.[30]

Shortly after this, a wider Indian uprising seemed to have been planned, one having all the overtones of a slave revolt. A Californian woman overheard one of her Indian cooks plotting with another to attack the pueblo of San Diego. The leading men of the town (including the Picos) were informed and they seized all of the Indian cooks they could lay hands on. Davis described their fate: "A trench of suitable depth was then dug and the Indians made to kneel close beside it. Then, on being shot, each fell into the ditch, where he was buried. Eight or ten Indians were executed at this time." To be certain that the planned revolt was nipped in the bud, an Indian considered to be a spy was tortured until he revealed the location of his comrades. The Californians cut off his ear, and then threatened to continue the process until they had him reduced to little pieces.[31]

These were rancheros who dealt in this way with the Indians. Davis simply told about the revolt without offering any comments or condem-

[29] Ibid., 179.
[30] Ibid., 126-127.
[31] Ibid., 130.

nation of their conduct. He seemed to think the mission system's handling of the Indians, however, was "well designed" to keep order and discipline among them. The missionaries appointed Indian *capitanes* to keep their fellow tribesmen in line with the requirements of mission life and to report any violations. In 1833 at Mission Dolores, Davis observed that the Indians gathered there—some two thousand to twenty-five hundred—were admirably disciplined. It seemed to him like a military camp. A few years later in 1838 Davis saw another apparently disciplined group at the Mission San Jose.[32]

Yet this military discipline obviously concealed, or suppressed, a great deal of unrest among the Indians. Davis cited incidents that ran counter to any argument that they were uniformly happy in the missions. In fact, what he had to say about two renegade mission Indians showed that Davis had a certain admiration for the courage and pride of the Indians, and an understanding for the reasons why they would revolt. The case of Yoscolo and Stanislaus was one in which both Indians had been raised within the missions, the former at Santa Clara and the latter at San Jose. Both became rebels, joining their bands together to attack the missions and ranchos. As Davis put it, both of them "preferred the freedom of wild life and the exercise of authority over the tribes to the tame civilization of the missions." Yoscolo ran away from Santa Clara because as a *capitan* he was about to be punished for offenses committed by some of his people, for whose actions he was being held responsible. Yoscolo gathered some five hundred men and attacked the mission. They broke into the mission stores, and took with them about two hundred Indian women when they left. After several years and several abortive attempts to subdue these Indians, Juan Prado Mesa, who Davis said had a reputation as a successful Indian fighter, led the Californians against Yoscolo's band. The Indians were finally brought to bay at Los Gatos, in the mountains between Santa Cruz and San Jose. There they fought well, forming themselves into a disciplined military square; but they had only bows and arrows, and were finally defeated by the fire power of the Californians. Yoscolo was taken prisoner and beheaded. His head, according to Davis, "was affixed by the hair to the tip of a pole planted in front of the Church at Santa Clara, and remained there for several days as a warning to other Indians."[33]

---

[32] Ibid., 179.
[33] Ibid., 179-181.

The second Indian, Stanislaus, had both a river and a county named after him. Davis described him as "well educated, brave and talented," an assessment that few of his contemporaries from the United States were ever to make of any California Indians, who were typically described in almost bestial terms. Stanislaus could not abide life at the mission, and ran away from San Jose, taking with him a number of followers and joining his band with that of Yoscolo. As Davis remembered it, Mariano Vallejo led the first effort to suppress Stanislaus and Yoscolo, but he was not successful. The Californians thought they had the Indians trapped at their camp on the Stanislaus River, but the Indians were too clever. Davis' account of what happened showed his respect for the Indians, and has a humorous touch at the expense of their pursuers:

> The Californians reached the camp and prepared to attack it. As soon as the presence of the troops was known, the enemy formed an ingenious plan to evade them. A large number of bundles of grass were set afloat down the stream, and as the current took them past General Vallejo's camp, in the indistinct light of the moon the soldiers mistook them for Indians and supposed that their wily foes were getting away in a body; whereupon, the entire force set out in pursuit of the supposed aborigines, who, after being followed some distance down the stream, were discovered actually to be men of straw. Meanwhile, the real Indians had taken up their march to the interior where they were safe from all pursuit, as no white man would follow them into those well-nigh inaccesible retreats.[34]

These events took place in 1831, and though Davis was in California that year, he was just nine years old. Perhaps he heard later stories and discussions about the exploits of Stanislaus and Yoscolo, stories which clearly stayed in his mind. These Indians had demonstrated their intelligence and bravery against a climate of opinion that saw them as particularly primitive and therefore inferior.[35] On some level, Davis might have identified with them, since Hawaiians, though not seen as quite so primitive a people, were nevertheless also viewed in a similar light.[36] He was

---

[34] Ibid., 180-181. See also James J. Rawls, *Indians of California: The Changing Image,* 89. where he says that "The Vallejos had been notorious in the 1830's and 1840's for their raids on native villages and seizure of laborers."

[35] See Rawls, 28-33, 39-41, 46-51, 53-54.

[36] See below Chapter 11 for a contemporary view of Hawaiians by Lieutenant Henry Wise of the United States Navy.

certainly horrified when he heard of the massacre of Indian men, women and children perpetrated upon the Indians of the Clear Lake region in 1841 by the forces of Salvador Vallejo. These Indians had apparently been committing "depradations" [sic] against the surrounding ranchos, and soldiers were sent to deal with them. They caught the Indians in their camp, just emerging from their *temescales* (sweat houses used for cleansing and rituals). As they came out singly and in pairs, in Davis' words "they were barbarously shot or cut down, until about a hundred and fifty men, women and children had been slaughtered." This, in Davis' judgement, was unjustified butchery, though he did not question that the Indians deserved some punishment for their raids.[37]

Elsewhere he softened the implied criticism of Salvador Vallejo by pointing out that Vallejo had in the past shown great clemency to these same Indians from whom he suffered substantial losses. The killing of the women and children, Davis said, "might have been avoided, but the men deserved the fate inflicted upon them." Davis knew Salvador Vallejo well, and felt that the Californian really wanted to "preserve" the Indians, and "inculcate habits of industry as farm hands and other labors [sic]."[38]

Davis was not about to stray too far from what he considered to be the main stream of respectable opinion, and he went on in *Seventy-Five Years in California* to say that when the news of the massacre reached Yerba Buena, the people there were sickened by it too. Men like his uncle Nathan Spear, and the officers of the Wilkes expedition who were in port at the time, were alike in their criticism of the unnecessary harshness meted out to the Indians, and Davis thus kept his place within the circle of his peers concerning the matter.[39]

Davis, in fact, so appreciated the lifestyle and mores of Mexican California, that he made significant efforts in his reminiscences to bring to life again what he considered to be a vanished "Golden Age" of hospitality and gracious living that were the hallmarks of pre-conquest California society. Davis' own fortunes had declined by the time he began work on his "Great Manuscript," and he may have looked back on his past with

---

[37] *Seventy-Five Years*, 182.

[38] Davis, Huntington Library Ms. DA 2, Box 3, Folder 92, 2.

[39] Davis, *Seventy-Five Years*, 182.

considerable nostalgia.[40] His friends the Californians had also sadly suffered from a reversal of their fortunes by the time of Davis' writing
(1889). He considered that their children were "a good deal degenerat-
ed, as compared with their fathers," and he blamed this on the "unjust
treatment they received from the American government in the matter of
their landed property." The rancheros had been forced to prove title to
their lands in American courts, where they did not speak the language or
know the procedures. Lengthy and expensive litigation, and unscrupulous lawyers, drained their savings. Land-rich and cash-poor, the Californians, "who were honest and simple hearted," were forced to pay for
legal services with promissory notes backed by their land as collateral.
They were bankrupted; their land was taken from them and their sons
and daughters grew up in poverty. "Thus," said Davis, "the old stock
rapidly deteriorated and went into decay."[41]

The old Californians, Davis thought, lived simple and idyllic lives.
They were respectful and always civil, hospitable as a matter of course,
temperate in habits and generous by instinct. Their uncomplicated and
healthy existences resulted in a ripe old age for many of them. Davis
remarked on the number of Californians who had reached advanced age
while retaining their health. Though not without some minor flaws of
character or custom, generally they were, as Davis put it, "about the happiest and most contented people I ever saw...."[42]

It is not clear, however, that Davis meant to include in this idyllic picture all of the people who had resided in California before the conquest.
He was talking rather about those people he knew best, the upper class
of merchants and rancheros. These people were proud of what they considered to be their noble Spanish lineage, and according to Davis "did
not associate freely with the humbler classes...."[43] No doubt this meant
that Davis himself associated very little with the lower classes, especially
after he had married into ranchero society and become an accepted and
respected member of the California aristocracy. In *Seventy-Five Years*
Davis did not have a great deal to say about the class structure of Mexi-

---

[40] See Rolle, 105-128, for a discussion of Davis' later career.

[41] Davis, *Seventy-Five Years*, 144-146; see also Leonard Pitt, *The Decline of the Californios*, for a
book-length discussion of this process.

[42] Davis, ibid., 31-32, 47.

[43] Ibid., 50.

can California, but in an unpublished fragment he gave a fuller picture of the stratification that existed at the time. "Probably half of the people lived by their daily trades," he thought, doing such jobs as making shoes and boots, tending stock as vaqueros, even playing musical instruments. The women of this class did the laundry

> for those who were more fortunate in this world's goods, and also did sewing for those aristocratic families of Spanish blood. The women of humble positions in life were always treated by the former class with kindness and generosity, and were put at ease and on friendly social relations when in the sewing-room, chatting and laughing as if one of the family.

The ranchero also treated his help, while with the herds, in an easy and informal manner, laughing and joking with them at the noon meal.[44]

The ranchero's life and livelihood centered around his herds of cattle, which he handled with ease and relative efficiency. Davis said of them that they were "systematic and methodical in regard to the management of haciendas." This was a characterization that was not exactly in line with the general impression of indolence and implied mis-management conveyed by many other contemporaries who wrote about these Californians. Much of their lives was spent outdoors and on horseback. Their work was seasonal, a period of really intensive effort being required at *matanza* time, usually in the fall when the cattle were slaughtered for their hides and tallow, though even then the vaqueros and Indians did most of the physical labor. The cattle were trained early to go to the rodeo grounds, by salting the area and by herding them there periodically, and tame cattle were used to subdue the unruly ones. Little use was made of the meat of the slaughtered animals, except what was needed for home consumption, so large quantities of beef became food for bears, wolves and other carrion eaters. Davis did not fault the rancheros for this waste; there was little else that could have been done with the meat then, since there was almost no market for it. He did criticize them for their lack of attention to selective breeding methods (apparently a particular interest of Davis', for people and animals), which he said would have improved their stock of cattle and horses. He also had a clearer picture of the limitations of the market for agriculture at that time than

---

[44] Davis, Huntington Library Ms., DA 2, Box 2, Folder 4, 1-7.

some of his contemporaries who visited California and took the
rancheros to task for not growing more crops. They were interested in
agriculture, Davis maintained, and would have engaged in it more
extensively had there been a market for their produce. On his advice,
farmers at Yerba Buena began planting potatoes, pumpkins, cabbages
and onions to trade with the whalers who came into the bay, and others
would have done the same given a similar opportunity to sell what they
grew. Nowhere does Davis call these people indolent, and he therefore
stands as a significant exception to the many observers of Mexican California who used this term like a refrain. Their frame of reference was the
"work ethic," and the Industrial Revolution which was changing the
work-habits of Europeans and Americans. Davis had only lived in the
Hawaiian Islands and California, but as a merchant he was well
acquainted with the options available to the Californians for making a
profit. He never considered them to be lazy.[45]

California may have been a "backward" society in comparison to the
bustle and drive that marked the beginnings of industrial development
in the United States, but to Davis this pastoral, slow-paced character of
the country had a certain appeal. He was American and patriotic
enough, however, to hail the signs of industry and growth evident at San
Francisco after the conquest, and he welcomed the arrival of Sam Bran-
nan and the Mormons. They had among them mechanics, carpenters
and house builders, and they set right to work to construct American-
style houses. "From every direction in the village," said Davis, "the signs
of progress under the change and that of the American system became
apparent."[46] Yet there was a charm and utility to the adobe dwelling that
Davis was compelled to recognize. It may have been modest, but it was
roomy, warm in winter and cool in the summer, and generally quite comfortable. Furthermore, the California women who kept them were
"exceedingly neat and clean in their houses and persons and in all their
domestic arrangements."[47]

---

[45] Davis, *Seventy-Five Years*, p. 118; see also, David J. Langum, "Californios and the Image of Indolence," for a listing of all the observers, American and European, who called the Californians 'indolent.'
Langum, 195, said this criticism was "a more generalized *European* critique of an undeveloped Latin
country which had indeed developed an especial depth to the *mañana* habit because of the ease of living,
bountiful nature and climate, cheap labor, and political and geographical isolation." Emphasis in original.

[46] Davis, ibid., 238.

[47] Ibid., 44.

In fact, Davis agreed with Alfred Robinson in his respect and admiration for the women of California. He felt that they were the most virtuous women he had ever seen, and made faithful wives. But unlike Robinson, he thought that the men too were kind fathers and husbands, generally moral and true to their women. Only the single men were excepted, because they associated to some extent with Indian women. Davis said that the women of all classes were faithful and the unmarried ones chaste, though he excluded the Indian women who were still tribalized. But there were occasionally cases that did not fit Davis' overall picture of Californian fidelity and morality. For these lapses the Californians reserved special punishments: "So great was the horror of the older Californians to any exception in this respect that the guilty parties, when discovered, were dealt with severely." The men were imprisoned for several years at hard labor and the women were publicly shamed by having their heads shaved.[48]

Davis was not to be any more specific about the sexual mores of the Californians. He did not discuss those of the lower class women who may have been part Indian, and perhaps it is not unfair to conclude that Davis did not care to touch on a subject that was so close to home. The sexual mores of the Hawaiian Islanders whom Davis had known as a youth were probably much closer to those of the California Indians than the puritanical New England component in Davis' make-up cared to confront. Davis himself might have been sent to California because of an unfortunate marriage to a native girl at Honolulu, and the sexual practices of his mother and sister were known to have disturbed and upset him.[49]

In comparison to what he had seen in the Hawaiian Islands, the virtue of the women of California may indeed have impressed Davis. He was certainly convinced that they were smarter and more talented than the men, with "natural dignity and self-possession" in spite of limited opportunity for education. He also approved of the California customs regarding courtship and marriage. The period of courtship was lengthy and couples were almost never permitted to be alone together. Nevertheless, Davis believed the lack of haste was beneficial, allowing young people enough time to get to know one another and to ponder such an important step as marriage. Davis' own experience was of an engage-

[48]Ibid., 45, 160.
[49]Rolle, 12, 34-35.

ment that lasted over two years. As was expected of him, he became a Catholic at the beginning of his courtship, and he persisted in spite of opposition from an older Estudillo sister, who was jealous that the younger woman should marry before her.[50]

It will probably never be entirely clear to what extent Davis idealized the early Californians. He lived almost his entire life among them as a member in good standing of their society. It is also less likely that he would have experienced any of the undertones of racial discrimination from them as he did from Americans like Robert Semple. The elite of Santa Barbara who attended Thomas O. Larkin's wedding in 1833 may have been "all of Castilian extraction" as Davis affirmed, but many Californians, possibly a majority, were, like Davis himself, of "mixed blood." If the upper class Californian discriminated, it was more on the basis of class. In any case, Davis' assessment of their character was almost uniformly positive. They were honest, honorable, and almost never uncivil. As he put it, "They regarded their verbal promise as binding and sacred, relied upon their honor and were always faithful.... They were too proud to condescend to any thing mean or disgraceful." Their vices—if they were to be considered as such—were few and harmless. One seldom saw a drunken Californian. They were not naturally gamblers, though the lower classes liked to play a little cards for small amounts of money. The rancheros, however, only indulged themselves on special occasions such as feast days. At those times they would bet heavily on horse races, "not for the gains but simply for the pleasure." The young people had immense respect for their parents. Young men would cease smoking and remove their hats when approached in the street by an elder. The vaqueros and servants of the ranchos also showed this kind of respect to the rancheros. A sixty-year-old man on a visit to his eighty-year-old father at San Jose, stood until his father told him to be seated.[51]

As a merchant, Davis was ready to trust the Californians for whatever goods they wanted. He knew that they would always pay their debts. He could not say the same, however, for the foreign residents, some of whom were "of doubtful financial responsibility. Men of this character would come to me and ask for credit which I was compelled to refuse."

---

[50]Davis, *Seventy-Five Years*, 44-46, 52-56.

[51]Ibid., 45, 61, 138-139.

Davis was quick to point out that these types were mostly runaway sailors and not the hunters and trappers. The latter, "though lacking in the graces of civilization," were honest and industrious, and could be relied on to pay their bills.[52]

Davis' concern for strict probity in his business relations did not extend as far as the Mexican customs laws. The duties on imports into California were often as high as one hundred percent, and merchant ship's captains commonly resorted to smuggling, said Davis, "whenever they saw an opportunity to outwit the customhouse authorities...." Davis himself engaged in such practices and told of bribing a guard placed on his ship at Yerba Buena. He entertained the customs official with liquor and cigars and slipped him a twenty dollar gold piece. Meanwhile the ship's crew unloaded the more valuable half of their cargo before proceeding to Monterey where they would have had to pay duties on it. Davis rationalized such activities by maintaining that they benefited the people of California as well as the merchants. The latter were not considered criminals by the community, but members in good standing who were doing a service. Customs officials required no oath from the merchants as to the truth of their cargo lists, and the practice was therefore to prepare fictitious invoices and pay duties on only one-fourth of the actual cargo. To have paid full duties would have destroyed the merchant's profits from the voyage, and customs officers themselves admitted duties were too high; the government would have collected more money had they been lower. The job of the officers was also made more difficult by the lack of enforcement means. They had neither the personnel nor the revenue cutters to police incoming ships, nor were they overzealous about upholding the customs laws since the rancheros themselves encouraged the merchants to get in as many duty free goods as possible; they knew that duties paid would be added to the price of the merchandise. It was therefore concealed behind false linings in ships' holds and numerous other hiding places; the Channel Islands were also used to stash cargos. The merchant thus had almost no incentive to obey Mexican customs law. In Davis' words: "If he defrauded the government, he was helping the people."[53]

---

[52]Ibid., 147-148.
[53]Ibid., 78-82.

Other than the customs laws, which were so easily evaded, Davis made no complaints (like those of Alfred Robinson) about Mexican justice in California. He actually appreciated the *alcalde* system, where the *alcalde* was judge, jury and lawyers all in one. Plaintiff and defendant stated their respective cases before the *alcalde*, who made his decision right on the spot. In capital cases, the governor and his cabinet had full power to condemn, discharge or pardon, which was fine with Davis. He was used to making his way in California through his personal relationships, and he liked the personalism of the Mexican system. To him, the *alcaldes* were mostly good men and respected by the people; the governor and cabinet too were just and satisfactory. "I believe," he asserted, "that more substantial justice was done in this way than in the courts of the present day [1889], with all their elaborate machinery and prolonged course of proceedings." As he saw it, the American rule of law and not of men had not helped his Californian friends and in-laws.[54]

In a small, tightly-knit society such as pre-conquest California, where everyone knew everyone else, the key to success as a merchant was the cultivation of personal relationships. Like his father, Davis carefully nurtured his business connections and acquired the habit of friendly, courteous intercourse that comes through in his writings, where he seldom has anything derogatory to say about anyone. When he began in 1845 to go up and down the coast as a trader on his own, his tact and interpersonal skills stood him in good stead. At Monterey, for example, he saw that the port headquarters needed paint, so he gave General José Castro the necessary supplies from his ship's stores to do the painting. He had the General and his wife aboard the ship, along with Pablo de la Guerra who was the port collector at the time, and he served them champagne and complimented the General's wife on her beauty, about which he could see the General was proud. He then borrowed several cannons and fired a salute to the Mexican flag. "Thus," he said, "my introduction to the port of Monterey as a merchant in my own behalf was happily accomplished and everything made smooth for future trade."[55]

Davis valued his friendships and connections with the prominent men of his time. He paid homage to many of them in *Seventy-Five Years In*

---

[54]Ibid., 63.

California. His own father-in-law, José Joaquin Estudillo, was mentioned in almost a score of instances throughout the book, most often being included in Davis' lists of important people in attendance at some social event. But once Davis described a wrestling match at the tavern of Jean-Jaques Vioget in Yerba Buena—"a sort of exchange or meeting place for comparing notes on business matters," where also "a little amusement was perhaps indulged in." William Rae of the Hudson's Bay Company challenged Estudillo to a match, and was most surprised when the latter threw him, not once, but three times. As Davis related it with obvious pride in his father-in-law, Rae was compelled to confess that a Spaniard was as good or better at wrestling than a Scotchman, "whereupon the crowd burst into loud laughter."[56]

Davis enjoyed telling anecdotes about his friends, even if sometimes they seemed to contradict what he had elsewhere said about California customs. In 1842, for example, Davis made the acquaintance of José de la Guerra, to whom he sold merchandise. Unlike many of the rancheros, de la Guerra generally paid cash for his goods. Davis expressed some surprise at the large amount of money the old gentleman had on hand in such a cash-poor economy. He kept it in baskets in the attic of his Santa Barbara home where apparently his sons discovered a way to climb out on the roof and reach into the attic with a pitchfork to pilfer some of it. (Davis claimed they would never have taken a large amount.) De la Guerra eventually found out what was going on and put a stop to it, though according to Davis the old Californian never knew how much his sons had gotten away with, because he did not know how much money he actually had in the baskets. Davis was more concerned with his story telling than he was attentive to maintaining the consistency of his opinions. He insisted that José de la Guerra was a good businessman and "knew how to take care of money." Nor was Davis disturbed that the activities of de la Guerra's sons may have eroded his case for the depth of filial piety evinced by the Californians.[57]

As a merchant, Davis' affiliations were widespread, yet he does not appear to have actively participated in the politics and intrigues of his times. He was acquainted with most of the principals on both sides of

---

[56]Ibid., 18, 69, 85.
[57]Ibid., 185-186.

any controversy and probably considered it wiser not to take sides himself, though in certain cases he clearly leaned a little in a particular direction. Factional strife was endemic to Mexican California, sometimes pitting the north against the south in a struggle over the seat of government and the customs revenues. Foreign residents, including Americans like Isaac Graham, were often drawn into these contests. In 1840 when Graham and some of his cohorts were arrested on orders from Governor Alvarado and sent to Mexico, Davis too was briefly incarcerated. He spent twenty four hours under arrest, and was during a part of that time treated to a dance party![58]

Years later, Davis said he was told by Manuel Castro that Alvarado and José Castro had been unduly alarmed by fears of an American takeover in 1840. Davis thought they were prompted by secret instructions from Mexico to be constantly on the alert for any plans or moves by Americans to seize California. Such fears made sense given the continuing influx of Americans into the territory (many of whom never bothered to get passports from the California government), and the recent history of American activities in Texas. But to Davis there was no cause for alarm. He said there were no such American designs at that time, even though

> for a long time it had been the common talk among the Americans when among themselves or in company with the rancheros that at some future time the United States would hold possession of California and that our government would never permit any other nation to be the possessor of this territory.[59]

Davis had his characteristically personal explanation for the arrests: the officials of the government were "jealous and inimical." The rancheros, on the other hand, were "exceedingly friendly to the Americans and the United States Government." Davis believed the ranchero class hoped for United States governance because "they could not fail to perceive the American superiority in intelligence, education and business ability." Now sounding like other American observers at that time, Davis further maintained that the rancheros were tired of "the constant

---

[58]Ibid., 35-37.
[59]Ibid., 36.

revolutions to which the Mexican people were addicted...." Only the
women were patriotic, he said. They hated the idea of any change and
refused to listen to the suggestion that the U.S. or any foreign power
should assume control of their country.[60]

One of the "constant revolutions" to which Davis alluded took place in
1845. Davis was an observer of this revolt which resulted in the expulsion
of Governor Manuel Micheltorena. Micheltorena had offended the Californians in several ways. First of all he was not one of them, but had been
sent up from Mexico. Secondly, he brought with him as troops the off-
sweepings of Mexican jails and prisons. These people were alleged by
many contemporary observers to have stolen everything and anything
they could get their hands on, a practice perhaps somewhat mitigated by
the fact that their pay depended on the collection of customs revenues
and was usually in arrears.[61] Davis, however, was one of the few Americans who took Micheltorena's side, at least in retrospect. According to
Davis the revolt was not due to the mis-rule or bad government of
Micheltorena, or to the thievery of his troops, which Davis downplayed.
It was the turbulent and ambitious nature of the California politicos that
was at fault, men such as José Castro and especially Juan Bautista Alvarado. It was these men and not the depredations of the troops—who Davis
admitted might have stolen a chicken or two—that stirred up the people
to revolt against Micheltorena. In Davis' opinion, there was really no
greater evidence against Micheltorena, and the responsible men of the
country (obviously Davis included) had nothing against him.[62]

---

[60]Ibid., 36-37. See also H.H. Bancroft, *Works*, Vol. XXII, 758, where Mariano Vallejo is described
as "an open friend of the U.S. as against the schemes for an English protectorate."

[61]On November 14, 1844, the American Consul, Thomas Oliver Larkin, wrote to Governor
Micheltorena complaining about the depredations of his troops. A servant of one Señor Antonio
Mendez, "in the peacefull [sic] occupation of his business, in the open day has been in a most violent
manner assaulted wounded and robbed by Soldiers under the command of your Excellency...." Larkin
said he hoped the culprit would be punished. He claimed it was the same person who had committed
several robberies previous to this one but had suffered no consequences for them. *Larkin Papers*, II, 283.
The Spanish merchant José Arnaz suffered personally from Micheltorena's *cholo* troops. While at a ball
in Monterey in September 1843, his room was broken into and his trunk robbed. In 1844, he was
robbed again in Los Angeles. He had the *alcalde* help him to recover his belongings from some of
Micheltorena's soldiers, who he said were never punished. See José Arnaz, "Memoirs of a Merchant,"
38.

[62]Davis, *Seventy-Five Years*, 95. Davis did not seem to be aware of, or at least concerned with, a possible
source of merchant hostility toward Micheltorena, the fact that in 1844 he arbitrarily forbade the introduction of foreign goods in Mexican vessels without full duty payment. See Sherman F. Dallas, 223-224.

Davis was in Los Angeles when Alvarado and José Castro arrived to plead their cause and gain support for a final confrontation with Micheltorena. Calling attention to the "jealousy between the sections of the country north and south," Davis identified Alvarado as the leader of the northern faction and the Carrillos and Picos as leaders in southern California. Alvarado, who was nothing if not eloquent, managed to persuade the southerners to join him against Micheltorena by promising to support Pío Pico for governor. Davis felt that José Antonio Carrillo and Pío Pico were intelligent men, but that "Alvarado was superior to them all."[63]

In Davis' account of the affair, Micheltorena was supported by foreigners (led by Sutter) who expected land grants as rewards. He did not say what prompted the foreigners in the south (mostly Americans) to support Alvarado, but when they went out to fight, one of them, Los Angeles merchant Alexander Bell, left Davis in charge of his store. Davis had managed to avoid actually having to take sides, but he professed to be nervous nonetheless. The ruffianly reputation of the Angelinos made him concerned about being left alone at the store. Turning the tables on the Californians with their accusations about Micheltorena's troops, Davis had this to say about Alvarado's supporters:

> As there were a good many doubtful characters about Los Angeles, I feared that some of them might break in and take possession of the funds. I was not disturbed however. Perhaps Alvarado had taken all this class along with him as part of his army.[64]

As for the Mexican General, Davis concluded that Micheltorena had never been compelled to surrender, since his forces were superior to those of Alvarado and his allies. He only did so because he did not want to hurt the people of California, for whom he had warm feelings. Davis said he was told by Sutter that Micheltorena had ordered his command not to injure the Californians, but to fire over their heads. Why did William Heath Davis side with Micheltorena against the Californian leaders? His opinions in the matter were not the prevalent ones, then or later. Perhaps he still carried a grudge against Alvarado for having him arrested in 1840. Davis believed that there would probably never have been any trouble at all, had there been no Alvarado to stir it up. The lat-

---

[63]Davis, ibid., 97.
[64]Ibid., 97. See below Chapter 9 for Benjamin Davis Wilson's account of Micheltorena's defeat.

ter aroused grievances that were largely imaginary, and used them in an effort to regain offices for himself and his followers. After Micheltorena's expulsion, in fact, Alvarado did become the collector of customs at Monterey. But a more likely reason for Davis' support of Micheltorena may have been the circumstance that it was Davis who took Micheltorena back to Mexico aboard his ship. And given Davis' personable style, on such a voyage anyone who was at all civil and agreeable to him would have won him over. This Micheltorena appeared to have done; moreover, Davis was loyal to his friends, and the ex-governor clearly made a very positive impression on him. According to Davis:

> Micheltorena stood nearly six feet in height, was straight, of handsome appearance, with a military air and bearing. He spoke the French language correctly and fluently, and his own language so finely that it was a pleasure to listen to him. He was a good diplomatist as well as a good general and was liked by the solid men of the department. He tried to serve the people well and to please them.[65]

Davis certainly ranked himself among the "solid men" of California. He was almost always at pains to show that his own opinions marched in step with theirs, and since he could usually find people he respected on both sides of any issue, Davis often performed a kind of balancing act. For example, his apparent distaste for Alvarado is misleading. Though not mentioned in *Seventy-Five Years in California,* Davis owed Juan Bautista Alvarado a debt of gratitude for testifying on behalf of his wife's family in their legal dispute with squatters in the 1850s. The ex-governor did not buckle under a difficult cross-examination, but in Davis' words "showed the true statesman and soldier under fire," impressing everyone who heard him in the courtroom that day. Davis continued to respect and appreciate Juan Bautista Alvarado in spite of the latter's high-handed actions as governor, about which Davis had his reservations.[66]

Another whose precipitous action might have given Davis pause was United States Navy Commodore Thomas ap Catesby Jones, but Davis had no such circumspection when it came to the Commodore. In 1842, Jones seized the port of Monterey in the mistaken belief that the United States and Mexico were at war. Davis was at pains in giving his history

---

[65]Ibid., 99-101.
[66]Davis, Huntington Library Ms., DA 2, Box 5, Folder 275, 2.

of the affair to absolve Jones of any charges that his action had been foolish, unnecessary or dishonorable. He was as usual also personally interested in and connected with this event, though he was not an eye-witness to the surrender of the town. As Davis told it, the two United States ships under Jones—the frigate *United States* and the sloop-of-war *Cyane*—on entering Monterey Bay had encountered the Mexican barque *Joven Guizpocoana*, on its way out to sea. Commodore Jones ordered this vessel to return to port. On board were Davis' future wife and father-in-law, who were briefly held as prisoners of war. The women became agitated and frightened at the news that they were pris-oners, so the captain of the Mexican ship asked Jones if he would allow the ladies to be put ashore. Jones granted this request. Then he sent an officer to shore demanding the surrender of the port. In Davis' version, the townspeople were "horror stricken, especially the officials and the women, the latter going about the streets or looking from their win-dows with their hair hanging loosely about them and tears streaming from their eyes, bewailing the loss of their country, the humiliation of their flag, and fearing that their lives and property might also be sacri-ficed." Having first instructed a subordinate to comply with the demand for surrender, since the Californians did not have the forces to defend the town, Governor Alvarado fled to avoid the humiliation of having to hand over the port himself.[67]

Later, after Thomas O. Larkin helped him to discover his mistake, Commodore Jones attempted to make amends by returning the port to the Mexican officials and honoring them aboard his flagship. Davis arrived at the port several days later and called on Jones, and became convinced that the Navy man was both a gentleman and a far-sighted patriot. Davis was certain that the United States Government could not have selected a better man to watch over American interests in Califor-nia, "not only because of his superiority as a naval commander, but on account of his intelligence, sagacity, diplomatic talent and courage, these qualities rendering him peculiarly fitted for an undertaking requiring delicacy and tact in its management."[68]

Delicacy and tact are perhaps not quite the words one would chose to describe a Navy Commodore who seizes the port of a country with

---

[67]Davis, *Seventy-Five Years*, 83-86.
[68]Ibid., 88.

which his government is not at war. But Jones felt he was doing what he had to do given his instructions and the climate at the time. British-American rivalry in Oregon, British intrigue in Texas, and wide-spread American opinion concerning British designs on California were all contributing factors, along with the United States' developing conflict with Mexico over Texas, and U.S. efforts to purchase California. These combined to persuade Jones that movement of the British fleet from Callao was aimed at pre-empting the United States in California. Davis was certain that Jones had acted in good faith when he grabbed Monterey. Davis also offered as evidence of Jones' rectitude in the matter, an account written by Stephen S. Culverwell, who had been a sixteen-year-old ship's powder boy on board Jones' flagship. Culverwell wrote his account in 1889 and gave it to Davis. In it he maintained that "the commodore's instructions were to keep watch of the British fleet, and, if anything should occur which looked suspicious, he was to get ahead, and take possession of Monterey." Jones himself gave Davis a firm rationale for what he did, which Davis quoted: "Although I was doubtless hasty in my action, it was better to be a little too soon than an hour too late. The delay might have been fatal."[69]

Jones went on to tell Davis how impressed he was with California, that the territory was destined to be of great importance to the United States, which must insure its possession, and that only the British were to be feared as rivals in this. Jones was proud of having been the first to raise the American flag on California soil, and he believed that act to have established the priority of American claims to the country—never minding the fact it was still a part of Mexico! Davis was definitely a Jones partisan, and no doubt the Commodore's kind treatment of Davis' future bride, María Estudillo, had helped to insure this.[70]

---

[69]Ibid., 83-87. Specifically, while in the Port of Callao, Jones learned that a French fleet had sailed from Valparaiso in March 1842, to an unknown destination. Then, after returning to Callao from a training cruise and before receiving any new instructions from Washington, he saw the English fleet leave on a secret mission. At the same time, he received a message from the U.S. consul at Mazatlan saying that war with Mexico over Texas was imminent. He talked the situation over with his officers who agreed that if war had been declared they had to act immediately and seize every port in California. They would be upholding the Monroe Doctrine in keeping out the English. See Charles Roberts Anderson, ed., *Journal of a Cruise to the Pacific Ocean, 1842-1844, in the Frigate 'United States,'* 78-80, where Jones' letter to his officers is reprinted. See also Neal Harlow, *California Conquered: War and Peace on the Pacific, 1846-1850,* 4-5.

[70]Davis, *Seventy-Five Years,* 87-88.

Sailing again into Monterey in 1846, Davis saw the American flag floating over the town, this time for good, and chided the English ship's captain about the United States having beaten the British. When he landed, he was welcomed to American soil by Commodore John D. Sloat, whom he called "an agile, nervous little man." His subordinate, Captain William Mervine, however, appeared energetic and decisive in contrast to the irresolute Sloat. "Mervine was outspoken and frank, unquestionably a better qualified officer than Sloat."[71] Mervine was impatient with the latter's slowness and vacillation, and Davis believed it was Mervine's comprehension of the situation and his pressure for action that was responsible for American success at Monterey. In Davis' eyes, Mervine was a hero even if he did fail to retake Los Angeles after the revolt in the south. But at Los Angeles, the decisiveness that Davis considered such a positive trait of Mervine's character, has had a different light cast on it. Mervine's failure against the Californians has been attributed at least in part to his hasty and ill-prepared attack on them, in which he failed to take the needed artillery.[72]

Nevertheless, Davis wanted to believe the best of those Americans he thought deserved the credit for the conquest of California. At the same time he wanted to show his friends the Californians in the best light, both the ones who had joined the forces of the United States and even those who had opposed themselves to American arms. Heading Davis' list of creditable Americans was Commodore Robert Stockton, whom Davis got to know at Yerba Buena. Davis was almost immediately impressed by Stockton: "He was fine-looking, of dark complexion; frank and off hand in manners and conversation; active and energetic. There was nothing weak or effeminate about him. He at once impressed us as a strong man and of decided ability."[73]

As military governor, Stockton later denied Davis and his associates permission to construct a dock at San Francisco, and Davis' biographer says that Davis took this as a personal rebuke.[74] But this did not prevent Davis from venerating Stockton, even titling one section of *Seventy-Five*

---

[71]Ibid., 206.
[72]See Neal Harlow, 167-170.
[73]Ibid., 208.
[74]Rolle, 60.

Years in California, "Stockton, the Real Conqueror in California."[75]

Perhaps Davis elevated Stockton, in spite of the Commodore's later thwarting of Davis' business plans, as a way of lowering John C. Fremont, whom he did not care for at all. While at Yerba Buena, Stockton asked Davis to purchase small arms for him in preparation for the Commodore's campaign to pacify the rebellious south.[76] Davis delivered these weapons and supplies to Stockton at San Diego, where he was cordially treated and promptly paid by the Commodore.[77] In contrast, he sold supplies to John C. Fremont at Santa Barbara, for a large part of which he never received reimbursement. As Davis told it, he was peremptorily summoned by Fremont, who insisted on seeing him at once, even though Davis was otherwise engaged in business at that moment. Davis said he "surmised that the colonel wished to obtain supplies, and while I wanted to assist the government, and to do everything I could toward making the men under Fremont comfortable, at the same time I did not care to become his creditor."[78]

This must have been hindsight speaking, for at the time Davis had no reason to believe that he could not trust Fremont to see that the debts he contracted were paid. He could see that Fremont's men looked "ragged and dilapidated" and he remarked on the difficulty of their march, the severity of the weather and the hardships they had so obviously endured. These men had nothing but praise for Fremont's leadership and nerve in taking them over the Santa Ynez mountains at night, during a storm and on a steep and treacherous road, and Davis acknowledged this. He refrained from describing Fremont's appearance and character, however, which he usually did when he liked someone. Instead, in a matter-of-fact tone he told of Fremont's desire for supplies. Fremont assured him that though he had no money at the moment, he would "doubtless capture Los Angeles within six weeks, and I could depend on getting my money then, and he pledged his word he would pay for the supplies within that time."[79]

After Fremont's arrival in Los Angeles, Davis called on him to collect

---

[75]Davis, *Seventy-Five Years,* 215.
[76]Ibid., 210.
[77]Rolle, 54.
[78]Davis, *Seventy-Five Years,* 213.
[79]Ibid., 215.

the money owed him. He was met by Colonel William H. Russell, who put Davis off for a week, claiming that Fremont's duties as governor made him too busy to see his creditor. Russell worshipped Fremont as a hero, and carried his admiration, in Davis' opinion, "to a ridiculous extent, thinking Fremont appreciated him." Davis was convinced that Fremont was deliberately avoiding him. He finally just sent in his bill and got Fremont's endorsement, but he had harsh words for the soldier: "If he was not prepared to redeem his promise, he could at least have said so in a fair, square, and manly way."[80]

To William Heath Davis, the only contribution to the conquest of California made by Colonel John C. Fremont, was accepting the surrender of the southern Californians at Cahuenga. Fremont was supposed to have linked up with Stockton as the latter approached Los Angeles. Davis said the plan was for Fremont to halt outside the town and send word to Stockton at San Diego. Word never came; Stockton grew "impatient at the long and mysterious delay" and moved on Los Angeles without waiting any longer for the Colonel.[81] Davis goes no further than innuendo here, but his estimate of Fremont's character was clear. It was reinforced in an unpublished fragment, in which Davis discussed the Bear Flag revolt. In it he claimed that Fremont ended up with an expensive, double-barreled German gun taken by some of the Bear Flaggers from Jacob Leese, the brother-in-law of Mariano Vallejo. Fremont neither returned the gun, nor compensated Leese for its value.[82]

General Stephen Watts Kearny did not rank much higher than Fremont in Davis' estimation. According to Davis' history, before the Battle of San Pasqual, Stockton sent Lieutenant Edward F. Beale to guide Kearny and his dragoons into San Diego. The Lieutenant could see the condition of Kearny's men, weak and fatigued from their long march. He

---

[80]Ibid., 223-224.

[81]Ibid., 215.

[82]Davis, Huntington Library Ms., DA 2, Box 4, Folder 174, 6. In a letter to Thomas Oliver Larkin dated May 24, 1847, Jacob Leese asked the Consul to try to collect from Fremont money owing to Leese in the amount of $5609.00 for supplies given to Fremont and his men. Leese told Larkin to convey to Fremont that "I wish nothing moor [sic] of him, nor do I wish to injure him in any weigh [sic] whatever about what is passed [sic] between himself and me. All I want is to secure through him the value of my property as pr. the following list." On the list, in addition to horses, livestock and equipment, Leese listed "One double barell [sic] silver mounted German stoplock rifle" worth $125.00. See *Larkin Papers*, VI, 171, 172.

could see that the troops, many of them mounted on pack mules, were no match for the superb cavalry skills of the Californians, on well-rested horses and led by Andrés Pico. These Californians were, in Davis' words, "numerous, as well as brave, and not to be despised as enemies." But this was not the judgement of other Americans with Kearny, who were contemptuous of the Californians. Kearny, spoiling for a fight, refused to listen to Beale's plea to avoid the Californians and come in to San Diego. He insisted on attacking, with disastrous results.[83]

When Kearny and his men were finally rescued by Stockton's relief column and escorted with their dead and wounded into San Diego, Kearny (according to Davis, the Stockton partisan) immediately demanded to be commander in chief. Stockton refused to accede to this, however, vowing that he, not Kearny, had done all the training and made all of the preparations to prosecute the war against the rebellious Californians. Kearny could do nothing but "quietly submit" and volunteer to join Stockton on the march to Los Angeles. At the Battle of San Gabriel, it was Stockon whom Davis praised for his "great skill, coolness and bravery." The Commodore took over an artillery piece and used it masterfully to break up a mass of charging Californians.[84]

Davis had nothing more to say about Kearny in connection with the fighting. But he had plenty to say about his friends the Californians. Many of them had participated in a procession honoring Stockton at Yerba Buena when he first arrived in California. To Davis this was straightforward evidence that they regarded the Commodore—and the United States—as a friend. Furthermore, many Californians chose to join Stockton's forces, serving bravely on the march from San Diego to Los Angeles. Davis extolled their contribution:

> During the march, and afterward, the natives in Stockton's army were mounted as cavalrymen and were assigned to picket duty, a very responsible

---

[83]Davis, *Seventy-Five Years*, 216-217. Kearny also lost the element of surprise when he overruled Lieutenant Archibald Gillespie's suggestion to use his mountain men to reconnoiter. Kearny sent his aide-de-camp and six dragoons who made so much noise they were discovered by the Californians. Nevertheless, Kearny went ahead, perhaps on the assurances he had received from Gillespie and Kit Carson that the Californians were cowards and would run away; perhaps also on his recent experience in New Mexico, which he had occupied without resistance. See Neal Harlow, *California Conquered*, 182-183. See also below Chapter 7, for a discussion of Kit Carson's role.

[84]Ibid., 218-219.

service—which showed the confidence the commodore placed in them. They were specifically adapted for this duty, being genuine horsemen and knowing the country thoroughly. They were, moreover, faithful and trustworthy.[85]

Davis may have wanted to give special recognition to the Californians who threw in their lot with the Americans, but he was far from hostile to those who fought against the United States. One of the more successful of these was clearly Andrés Pico, who inflicted the worst losses of the war in California on Kearny's dragoons at San Pasqual. As with some of his other judgements, Davis ran against the grain of that American opinion which denigrated the Californians' courage. In speaking of Pico, he said:

> Don Andrés Pico, who was brave and honorable, displayed so much courage and coolness as to excite the admiration of the Americans. He never did an act beneath the dignity of an officer or contrary to the rules of war, and was humane and generous. If he saw one of the enemy wounded he instantly called upon his men to spare the life of the wounded soldier. Kind and hospitable, Pico was held in great esteem by the Americans who knew him.[86]

Thus Davis sought to counterpoise his friendship and regard for the Californians—his wife's people—with his patriotic support for American arms and his satisfaction in seeing California come under the control of the United States. In fact, Davis' life was a kind of balancing act. He held many different elements within himself: his Hawaiian blood; his American citizenship and New England ancestry; his friendships and marriage ties with the Californians. He respected gentility and social standing, and at his best, he appreciated the qualities of intelligence, honor and bravery in people of whatever class or race.

Davis lived well into his eighties. He saw his beloved California transformed under a tidal wave of immigration and development. He spanned two epochs, yet seemed to prefer the earlier, simpler and perhaps purer, surely less complicated California. He himself experienced a certain decline from the height of his social and financial successes. He saw the lands of his wife and father-in-law occupied and engrossed by squatters, and he became much less sanguine about the vaunted benefits

---

[85]Ibid., 209, 218.
[86]Ibid., 217.

of American civilization. Experiencing the kind of lawlessness that the gold rush, and after it the land rush, ushered into California, Davis would question the costs of progress:

> ...who will deny that what we exultantly commend as the glorious onward march of "modern civilization" is indeed much like the triumphant tramp of invading hosts... it heeds little the discord and destruction, the doom and despair, which marks its onward and often rueful march, o'er the prostrate fallen and crushed beneath its resistless tread.[87]

As an old man, Davis turned increasingly to the past, his memories, his "Great Manuscript." He had seen tremendous changes, but perhaps even he would have found it difficult to imagine the magnitude of industrial and population growth that California was yet to experience. He had made his own pioneering contribution to California's evolution as a dynamic, trend-setting society—as a merchant, as a land developer and builder, as a founder of cities. Moreover, he stood out in this nascent period of California's history as a person with the sympathies and broadness of vision to embrace disparate cultures that were and continue to be an important part of our American heritage. He should thus receive additional credit for being one of California's first and most important autobiographers, blending his life with that of an era, and illuminating both.

---

[87]Davis, Huntington Library Ms. DA 2, Box 5, Folder 276, 23.

WILLIAM DANE PHELPS
By permission of the Houghton Library, Harvard University

CHAPTER III

William Dane Phelps

Captain William Dane Phelps, writing under the pseudonym "Web-foot," published his autobiography in 1871. California had been a posses-sion of the United States for twenty-five years and Phelps gave himself a prominent place among the American pioneers in Mexican California, and in the events which secured California as an American province. *Fore and Aft; or, Leaves from the Life of an Old Sailor* was Phelps' retrospective of his years at sea, including his experiences as the captain of merchant ships plying their trade up and down the California coast.[1] He was acquainted with many of the men who would play leading roles in this early history of United States penetration of California, and he himself was an eyewit-ness to some of the military engagements of the Mexican War as it was fought there. He had friends on both sides of the war, though he was a definite American patriot who also on occasion displayed his belief in the inferiority of the Californians while seeking to explain away those instances when American honor in arms appeared tarnished. Like Alfred Robinson, Phelps had his ambivalences about the character of the Cali-fornians. He too was impressed with the beauty and fertility of Califor-nia, and certain about the territory's destiny: it would inevitably belong to a people who could truly appreciate and develop it.

In his youth, Phelps was already eager to go to sea as a privateer in the War of 1812. His parents, however, insisted that he was too young and instead sent him from his Gloucester, Massachusetts, home to learn the printing business in Boston. To please them he complied with their wishes, but as he explained, "at the expiration of a year [I] went to sea to please myself." He was only thirteen when he shipped as a cabin boy, and from this lowly position he worked his way up to command his first ship in 1831. He endured more than his share of the hardships of life at sea—

---

[1]William Dane Phelps, ("Webfoot"), *Fore and Aft; or, Leaves from the Life of an Old Sailor* (Boston, 1871).

short rations, thirst, flogging and shipwreck. Once while still a boy, he was left with six others on desolate Prince Edward's island in the Indian Ocean to collect seal skins and sea elephant oil. The men had provisions for nine months, but it was twenty-eight before the ship returned for them. They survived on seal meat, sea birds and their eggs. Phelps summed up his experiences by saying that "our past lives had been thus far past [sic] in scenes of hardship and suffering without much respite therefrom. Hunger, thirst, and almost nakedness, we were familiar with, and the peltings of the pitiless storm we were not strangers to."[2]

His life at sea did not shake Phelps from his strong New England Protestantism, nor undermine a certain self-righteous, even arrogant, moral tone that comes through in his autobiograpy and in the sea-journals that he kept during his sojourns in California. Perhaps his faith, in spite of some of its more negative elements, was what helped to sustain him through such rigors and perils.

His first trip to the coast was in 1840, on board the Bryant and Sturgis hide trader the *Alert,* the same ship that had carried Richard Henry Dana home to Boston after his "two years before the mast." Phelps had read Dana's book and acknowledged that he "was impressed with the correctness of his [Dana's] description of the manner of collecting and curing a cargo of hides...." He also acknowledged the contribution made by Alfred Robinson's friend and companion, William Alden Gale, to the opening of the hide and tallow trade in California. Gale, he said, first sailed the coast in 1809 as a fur hunter, taking 73,000 fur seals from the Farallone Islands. He said Gale had been responsible for beginning the hide trade, which Phelps maintained had helped lead "to the acquisition of California, at the close of the war, by our Government, at a cost of fifteen million dollars in gold—money well spent." Furthermore, Phelps believed and stated in a passage that reveals his conviction of American superiority and nineteenth century faith in progress, that the hide trade and the gold rush had resulted in "an extension of civilization unprecedented in the history of the world, and a marvel of the nineteenth century, to be ranked with the invention of steam and telegraphic machinery." He credited certain Americans with being important pioneers of this process. Alfred Robinson, he said, "early identified his interests with those of California" through marriage. Thomas O. Larkin was another

---

[2]Ibid., 11, 43-60, 124.

who helped win California for the United States, and whose child was "the first born in California of American parents.[3]

In *Fore And Aft*, Phelps offered a description of the state of trade in California in 1840. Since there was very little hard cash available—a situation that was common on the American frontier generally—the Boston firm of Bryant and Sturgis had established themselves successfully on the coast through the use of credit. This firm, Phelps' employer at that time, furnished most of the trade goods purchased by the Californians, and also most of the cash with which the Mexican Government paid its employees, troops and revenue officers. This economic leverage was obviously beneficial when it came to dealing with some of the government's more onerous trade restrictions. Moreover, as Phelps pointed out, the use of credit allowed Bryant and Sturgis to dominate the trade, whereas companies such as the Hudson's Bay Company could not compete because their system used exclusively cash or immediate barter. "The people of the country had no money; they had been accustomed to buy their goods of the Boston ships on credit, and to pay for them in hides and tallow when they could." American economic predominance was therefore already evident in California, and this fundamental relationship between the merchants and the missions and rancheros must have helped reconcile the Californians to American rule, at least during the brief period immediately after the conquest, before the great gold rush migrations swamped the old Californians. The American merchant ship's captains like William Dane Phelps brought news and provided essential communication for the local residents, carried passengers, even served local government by transporting its officials and its political exiles, as William Heath Davis had done for ex-Governor Micheltorena.[4]

Twenty-five years removed from his experiences, Phelps in *Fore And Aft* was mainly concerned with being an historian, but one who put himself at the center of many of the historical events he discussed. He was not in Monterey in 1842 when Thomas ap Catesby Jones seized the port for the United States, but he heard news of it in San Diego. He also

[3]Ibid., 242-243. Bancroft, *Works*, XXI, 706, states that Larkin's wife "was the first American woman to live in Cal., [sic] and her son Thomas O., born in April, '34, was the 1st [sic] child born of American parents in Cal."

[4]Phelps, *Fore and Aft*, 250; Briton Cooper Busch, ed., *Alta California, 1840-1842, The Journal and Observations of William Dane Phelps, Master of the Ship "Alert,"* 19-20, henceforward referred to as *Journal, 1840-42*.

picked up a rumor that Governor Micheltorena was heading his way with a large force and the aim of seizing all American property. In his autobiography, he said he had $30,000 worth of hides at San Diego, which he was determined not to give up without a fight.[5] But in his journal covering the years 1840-1842, he appeared quite a bit more cautious. Alfred Robinson had advised him to put off for the northern ports, and Phelps himself related that he would "rather run than fight. I have no fears of them taking my ship."[6]

In his journal, Phelps had been sarcastic about General Micheltorena; he displayed the stereotypical American view of Mexican bravery when he said that Micheltorena was reputed to be a gentleman, but had "served against Texas, and can probably run as fast as any Mexican soldier, or he would not have left Texas alive." His opinion of Micheltorena's troop reflected the consensus of most of the foreigners and Californians. They were "the sweepings of the Mexican prisons... I fear California will rue the day she permits these ragamuffin freebooters to set foot on her soil."[7] Phelps might indeed have taken Robinson's advice, however, if the sea otter hunters and dead-shot American mountain men George Nidever, Isaac Sparks and their companions had not arrived on the scene, all armed and eager for a fight. Phelps was happy to have them stash their furs on the *Alert* and prepare to defend them. He claimed they all had "a mortal hatred to Mexicans," even though Nidever at least and probably several others were married to local women, and he admitted that "with the addition of nine hunters and their rifles, I feel quite secure."[8]

In fact, it appears that Phelps really had little to fear, from the local people at least; the San Diego Presidio sent out a bullock to provision his ship. As he put it, "we have friends among our enemies." This reassurance did not suffice, however. Phelps still felt he had to take action; so he went to Point Loma and spiked the old, rusted cannons of the fort there. He was a man with no connection to the military, and he undertook his act of hostility on a rumor of war. After spiking the guns, the crew of the

---

[5] Phelps, *Fore and Aft*, 263.

[6] *Journal, 1840-42*, 331-333.

[7] William Dane Phelps, "Journal, 1841-43," Bancroft Library Microfilm, 92-93; henceforward referred to as "Journal, 1841-43."

[8] *Journal, 1840-42*, 333-334. See below Chapter 8 for a discussion of George Nidever's life in California.

Alert continued to load hides as usual. Phelps commented in his journal: "Our situation is certainly a rather singular one (laying in an enemy's camp taking in a cargo in time of war)." Finally, on November 2, 1842, news arrived that Jones' seizure had been a mistake. There was no war. This disappointed Phelps at the time. "I hope this is not true," he said, "but that the American Govt. will hold on to this country and will take ample satisfaction of Mexico for her oft repeated insults & aggressions on our flag." What, exactly, these insults and aggressions were, Phelps did not say.[9]

After the "Commodore Jones War" as he called it, Phelps returned to Boston on what was to be "the last voyage fitted out by Bryant, Sturgis & Co.", a voyage which he proudly proclaimed he "had reason to believe...was conducted to their satisfaction."[10] The pioneering firm was retiring from the trade, but William Dane Phelps would be back. In his autobiography, he had little more to say about his experiences on the coast from 1840 to 1842, but his sea-journals fill in the gap. They reveal a religious man, convinced of the righteousness of his beliefs and his culture, and equally persuaded that the benighted peoples of California, with few exceptions, were "the most ignorant indolent and vicious population of any country I have ever visited." He believed that the Catholic missionaries had dragged the Indians to the missions by force, and "amidst much abuse...compelled them to master a Latin prayer of which neither priest nor Indian knew the import...." The Indians were pronounced to be Christians, "and consequently slaves to the church." Generally, he believed the Indians were treated like cattle by the rancheros, who he said lassoed them and dragged them to a corral where they were branded. The padres also caught the Indian and "branded him with the mark of Holy Mother Church and then employed him to entrap his fellows."[11]

He contrasted this treatment of the Indians by the Californians with what he saw of John Sutter's system when he visited the enterprising Swiss in 1841. Phelps went up to New Helvetia, he said, because he wanted to see for himself if what Sutter had told him about the beauty

---

[9]*Journal, 1840-42,* 336; *Fore and Aft,* 263.
[10]*Fore and Aft,* 268.
[11]"Journal, 1841-43," 4, 23.

and superiority of the region was true. Phelps was indeed impressed with the "beautiful, gently undulating country, abounding with rich feed and agreeably diversified with trees and wild shrubbery." He enjoyed Sutter's hospitality, and was impressed when Sutter told him that his great-grandfather had been one of the Knights of Malta. Apparently, Sutter was an excellent self-promoter, and knew just what to say to a Yankee Puritan like Phelps. He told Phelps that he had come to the Sacramento Valley to escape the despotism of Europe, and as Phelps described it, Sutter was "now creating a colony, building houses, raising cattle, civilizing the Indians, and trapping beaver...." Phelps inspected Sutter's fortifications, which the Swiss had built because, in Phelps' words "experience has shown that neither the Californians nor Indians are to be trusted." Yet Sutter had tamed the Indians in his area, most of whom had been won over, according to Phelps, by "acts of kindness and also intimidated by punishments." Phelps praised the Indians of the Sacramento. He thought they were handsome, and more intelligent and warlike than those of the sea coast. They were, however, also much afflicted with "that horrid disease which Europeans & Americans generally introduce wherever they go."[12]

Phelps did not maintain a strict consistency in his opinions about the Californians. In another place in his journal he praised the missionaries for their fidelity and humanity to travelers, and he said that the mission Indians (those who had apparently been rounded up and branded?) displayed toward the padres "unbounded affection and devotion." Most of the padres, he felt, were honest men and did their best, but—good Protestant that he was—it was the system in California that was to be lamented. He blamed Catholicism's "withering baleful influence" as the "root from which springs ignorance and everything that is *Ante* to the best interests of man." But he thought it fit well with "the native indolence of their character and total defect of all independent spirit." Still, he could see in the Californians no real discontent with their lot, even though in his opinion the men were in thrall to the priests. The latter made of them "superstitious, ill-blooded scoundrels" who beat and abused their wives, and were completely unable to think for themselves. These California

---

[12]Ibid., 21-29; Phelps did not specify what the disease was, but the implication was that it was venereal. See also Richard Dillon, *Captain John Sutter*.

men were all addicted to gambling and liquor. Moreover, Catholicism encouraged their vices. As Phelps put it: "They indulge freely in all licentiousness and crime, confess to the Priest, receive absolution, and are ready to repeat the same." The women reminded Phelps of those he had seen in Greece. They "lavish all they can get to decorate their bodies, while their minds are as barren of knowledge and comprehension of what relates to housewifery as the rooms of their mud-built huts are destitute of furniture, or the most simple comforts of life." Overall, Phelps thought the population of respectable women in California was small. Only those who were married to foreigners seemed to make good wives, and these lacked the education to put them on an equal footing with respectable women in the United States. Yet Phelps too could succumb to the charm of California women. In his autobiography, he described two "graceful young ladies with regular features, symmetrical figures," whose dark eyes "flashed with all the intelligence and fire characteristic of Spanish women."[13]

Like Alfred Robinson, Phelps seemed to view the lower classes,(those who lived in mud-built huts, destitute of furniture), with a more jaundiced eye. When he enjoyed the hospitality of wealthier Californians, he softened his judgements. Ships' captains like Phelps, and the Californians who were their customers, spent many sociable hours together. Phelps recalled in his autobiography the time when he was a guest of Don Carlos Carrillo in Santa Barbara. Don Carlos had five daughters, all married to Americans "of respectable, even distinguished, positions." The leading Californians, besides showing their wisdom by allying themselves with Americans through marriage, were also men of the utmost probity and integrity in business and religion. Phelps illustrated this with an anecdote about Don José de la Guerra y Noriega, the father-in-law of Alfred Robinson. In pre-conquest days, as Commandante of the Santa Barbara Presidio, Don José captured an American ship's captain engaged in smuggling. The captain was given the choice of either being sent to prison, or being confined a prisoner at Don José's house. He chose the latter, where according to Phelps "the best room, with the best bed in the house, was his place of incarceration. A servant every morning brought to his bedside...a bowl of rich chocolate...after which he was

---

[13]*Journal, 1840-42*, 127-129, 147-148; *Fore and Aft*, 342.

politely invited to breakfast with the family." The captain was allowed to go where he wanted as long as he returned to dinner. His ship was sent off for three months, then returned for him. He was set free, paid for the goods that had been confiscated, and told not to engage in smuggling again. Phelps said further of Don José: "And this was a man whom I have heard named as a bigoted Catholic. Perhaps he was: he was also a Christian gentleman...."[14]

William Dane Phelps could overcome some of his religious prejudice when it came to "respectable" people who were also good customers, just as no doubt José de la Guerra could overlook a little smuggling in order to keep getting the Yankee goods he desired. In spite of (or perhaps because of) a long life at sea, and the cosmopolitan influences of the world's great ports, Phelps remained a genteel New Englander, a sociable person who enjoyed what he considered to be good company; but in California he was continuously being affronted by the "baser" habits of the natives, especially, in his opinion, their intemperance. He thought that the people of California "consumed more liquor than in any country on the globe," and he blamed this for what he saw as the laziness and vice all around him. He offered as an example the case of one "Don Abelard" in San Luis Obispo who did nothing with the rich soil in his possession. He blamed this on the Don's own penchant for drink, and on the fact that for the price of a bottle of rum, the Don could get all of the Indian labor he needed. The Californians, then, were crippled by their fondness for liquor and by a reliance on Indian labor that sapped their own incentive to work hard. They were thus in possession of a fertile land, with a salubrious climate, yet they seemed to make so little of their opportunities. "It is astonishing," he said, "that these people can content themselves with the spontaneous production around them...when by a very little labour they could obtain immense quantities of fruit and vegetables." Phelps never seemed to speculate about why the Californians did not just put their Indian laborers to work improving the land.[15]

Phelps clearly had less understanding of the agricultural options available to the California rancheros than did William Heath Davis. Yet Phelps' attitude toward the Californians and their seeming inability to

---

[14]*Fore and Aft*, 348-351.
[15]*Journal, 1840-42*, 166.

take full advantage of their country was conveniently balanced by the thought that "a few years will see this beautiful country in the possession of a people who can appreciate its natural advantages." This was obviously meant to apply to his own countrymen, though Phelps (like Richard Henry Dana) feared that the California lifestyle might corrupt the Americans with some of the same bad habits the Californians had. On a Sunday visit to Santa Barbara, his Puritan soul was outraged to find the American residents there, even New Englanders, playing cards! They greeted him with "blasphemous expressions of joy as one that would join them in their impious pastime. I need not say that I soon left them...." He had assumed that the Americans would be a good influence on the Californians, but he was disappointed. Rather than "infusing among the degenerate inhabitants of this country somewhat of the correct and sterling principles which they had imbibed or at least been taught at home," the Americans seemed to have plunged into the customs of the country, "and willingly whirled round in utter recklessness of their better feelings and more enlightened education." But this apparent cultural betrayal by his fellow Americans was not to shake Phelps' conviction of American superiority. When he returned again to the California coast in 1846, he was ready to render any assistance to, and justify any activities of, the American forces—military and settler —who were about to wrench California from the weakened and divided Mexican regime.[16]

If we accept H.H. Bancroft's assessment of Phelps' "history" of the Mexican War in California, the captain was not always an accurate witness, and comparing his journal accounts with his reminiscences of almost thirty years later in *Fore and Aft*, it is clear that Phelps had a tendency to exaggerate his own importance in events. Yet Phelps was there on the scene and could not resist turning the spotlight on his own role. He himself asserted that because he was there, "it is fair to assume that my observations of those times are worthy of credit...."[17]

As would be expected of an American patriot, Phelps was a consistent apologist for the American forces. He scrupulously avoided taking sides in any internal disputes between members of those forces, such as the

---

[16]Ibid., 59, 129-130.
[17]Bancroft, *Works*, XXI, 775-776; *Fore and Aft*, 287.

celebrated disagreements between John C. Fremont, Robert Stockton and Stephen W. Kearny. He also took some pains to present the American war effort in California in the best possible light, while denigrating the Californians. His account opened with Fremont's movements in northern California before any official news of war had reached the territory. According to Phelps, General José Castro had given Fremont and his men permission to camp in California and proclaimed his friendship. But, said Phelps, "notwithstanding his repeated protestations of friendship (which in a Mexican are very wordy, but mean nothing)," Castro proceeded to raise a force to drive the Americans out. At this point, Phelps himself became an actor, sending a note to Fremont offering to take him and his men on board the ship if necessary. Phelps did not record Fremont's response to this offer. The latter issued his defiant proclamation and from his position on Hawk Peak prepared to repel attack. Phelps indulged in a bit of romantic jingoism as he described the Americans in action. Even though he did not actually see what Fremont and his men were doing, he nevertheless maintained that "a fine bead was drawn along the tubes of fifty four deadly rifles, by eyes that never quailed at danger." Phelps of course exonerated Fremont of any responsibility for this confrontation and praised him as strictly a gentleman.[18]

The following June, Phelps was in Los Angeles where he was to be an observer-participant in the early events of what had not yet become a shooting war in southern California. In conversation with then-Governor Pío Pico, Phelps was informed that war would soon be declared and that Pío Pico had orders to treat all American ships as enemies. Pico, however, aware of his own difficult situation, told Phelps that without money and troops there was little that could be done to prevent an American take-over. In Phelps' words, which show that his commercial and friendship ties with leading Californians could sometimes overcome his prejudices, he characterized Pío Pico as "an honorable, well-meaning man, not favorably disposed to the occupation of his country by Americans...."[19]

Prior to his visit with Pío Pico, Phelps had been in the Bay area when

[18]Ibid., 279-283.
[19]Ibid., 284.

the Bear Flag Revolt took place. He called it a defensive measure against General Castro's threat to force Americans out of California. In his journal kept at the time, he said Castro's proclamation called all the foreigners in California thieves and vagabonds and ordered them to leave immediately on pain of death. "Self-preservation compelled the settlers to take up arms against the Govt. whose laws they had heretofore respected."[20] Phelps also seemed to justify the killing of three unarmed Californians by Fremont's men, because as he claimed, they were Castro's scouts and carried orders to "kill every foreigner they found, man, woman, and child." He mentioned as a further mitigating factor that previous to this incident, Castro's forces had captured two Americans who had been "tied to a tree, shot, and cut to pieces with knives, and their bodies thrown into a ditch." In contrast to this barbaric treatment at the hands of the Californians, the settlers under William B. Ide "surprised and took possession of Sonoma...but not the least violence was offered to the inhabitants."[21]

While all this was happening, there had as yet been no official word that war existed between the United States and Mexico. Nevertheless, Fremont told Phelps that war did exist, and that he (Fremont) was, in Phelps' words, "acting in obedience to the orders of the United States Government." Then for the second time in his career in California, Phelps helped to spike the guns of a fort, this time at Fort Point in San Francisco. Accompanied by some of Fremont's men, including Kit Carson, Phelps used his ship to transport the war party to Fort Point. He added a bit of spice to this adventure (and no doubt credit to his own

---

[20]Briton Cooper Busch, ed., *Fremont's Private Navy: The 1846 Journal of Captain William Dane Phelps*, 29-30; henceforth cited as *1846 Journal*. Bancroft, *Works*, XXII, 81-83, stated that Castro never issued such a proclamation, nor did he order the settlers to leave the country or organize an army against them. Bancroft thought the proclamation was a forgery. In fact, in early March, 1846, Castro had written a proclamation in response to Fremont's presence near Monterey, but this proclamation made no threats against the settlers. At that time also, according to Thomas O. Larkin, José Castro had gone to Sacramento to meet arriving settlers, "and bade them welcome to California." However, in a dispatch sent to Fremont by Larkin around March 8, the latter said that Castro told him "that Capt. Fremont was driven away and that in May all other americans [sic] would be." Perhaps this communication was the source of the settlers' fears? See *Larkin Papers*, IV, 237, 240-241, 272-273.

[21] *Fore and Aft*, 285-287. For a discussion of the killing of the three Californians by Fremont's men, see below Chapter 7. Kit Carson appeared to have been responsible, under orders he said he received from Fremont.

profession as a sea captain) by having Kit Carson say to him, "Cap., I'd rather ride on the back of a grizzly than on this boat."[22]

The mobility of a merchant ship's captain apparently allowed Phelps to be on hand for a number of actions in the war. Arriving in San Pedro in the summer of 1846, he learned that General Castro had fled Los Angeles at the approach of Commodore Stockton's forces. Phelps then rode out "about ten miles from the Pueblo," where he found Stockton's army hidden by "the high, wild mustard, which at this season (July) covered the plain...." Still no official declaration of war had reached California, and Phelps stated that "it was not certain that war would ensue." But this did not inhibit Commodore Stockton from taking action. In Phelps' laudatory description of him, Stockton was "a man not unwilling to assume great responsibilities, and where there was a doubt in the case, to give duty the benefit of it, especially when inclination and warlike propensity led in the same direction."[23]

Stockton's total force numbered only about 350 men, who were obviously unfamiliar with California, because while camped at Temple's Rancho they were alarmed by yelling, which they took to be Castro's forces preparing to attack. Their fears were calmed, however, when an old Indian informed them that the sounds they heard came from coyotes![24]

Stockton's little army was reinforced by Fremont and 200 more men, and on August 17, Fremont started in pursuit of Governor Pío Pico who was at his rancho with his government's archives. That same day, the U.S. ship *Warren* arrived with the official news that the war had begun. Meanwhile, Phelps, on his own business, had started for San Diego on horseback. On the way he ran into some Californian soldiers whom he knew and who were "my debtors for goods." They could easily have killed him, thus ridding themselves both of a creditor and an enemy of their cause. Instead, as Phelps related it, he was well-treated by them. Obviously, these Californians had never heard of, or were not obeying General Castro's bloodthirsty orders to kill every foreigner.[25]

---

[22] Ibid., 289-290. Bancroft, *Works*, XXII, 177, discounted the importance of this action, saying that, "In the absence of a garrison, with no powder, it is not surprising that...not one of the ten cannons offered the slightest resistance."

[23] Ibid., 297-299. Bancroft, *Works*, XXII, 280, stated that Phelps' account of Stockton's march into Los Angeles on this occasion was "the only one extant, so far as details are concerned."

[24] Ibid., 301.

[25] Ibid., 302-304.

Clearly Phelps, as an American merchant ship's captain, might play an especially useful role as an intermediary between the Americans and the Californians, and this was what he claimed to have done with Pío Pico. Phelps said it was he who carried Fremont's message to Pío Pico, assuring him that if he would come to Los Angeles and give his parole, the Governor would not be molested. Phelps maintained that he convinced Pico. The latter "seemed satisfied that entire submission, under the circumstances, was best, and that to keep good faith in dealing with the American officers was the best policy for him to pursue."[26] But Pío Pico told a different story. In his own account of these events, Pico, who said that he favored a British protectorate for California, credited Juan Bandini and Santiago Arguello with procuring from Fremont a safe conduct for him. However, Bandini and Arguello, who were according to Pico "in alliance with American forces," failed to persuade this last governor of Mexican California. Pico went into hiding until September 7, when he retreated to Mexico.[27]

Perhaps Phelps' memory failed him here, and he was carried away by his own desire to be more of an historical actor than he actually had been. He even gave himself some credit for Stockton's (temporary) pacification of Los Angeles with music. Stockton used his band to play for the people of the Pueblo. This helped to calm them and ease their fears about the consequences for them of an American regime, and the concerts were generally greeted with enthusiasm. Phelps claimed that it was he who suggested these sunset band concerts. As an additional proof of how much he was valued, Phelps also said he received from Stockton an offer of a commission as a privateer. He turned this down, pleading his "coast business" as an excuse. In his journal kept at that time, however, he maintained that he was more afraid of

> our own countrymen privateering under the flag of Mexico than of the enemy. There are not wanting those who would readily avail themselves of a commission to plunder defenceless merchant Ships if they could have the opportunity.... I have determined to keep my vessel in port until the war is over.

But when he came to write his autobiography, time and patriotic feelings

---

[26]Ibid., 306-311.
[27]Martin Cole and Henry Welcome, eds., *Don Pío Pico's Historical Narrative*, 123, 138-140.

had eliminated any negative references to his own countrymen, and the historical center gravity had shifted more to himself.[28]

Southern California was not to remain pacified. Lieutenant Archibald Gillespie was left in charge of Los Angeles. Phelps wrote in his journal that he thought Gillespie was "a secret agent of the U S Government." But in his autobiography, Phelps omitted any references to mistakes or poor judgement on the part of Archibald Gillespie. Heavy-handed and foolish, the Marine Corps Lieutenant antagonized the Angelinos with a series of burdensome and absurd restrictions. He did not allow two or more persons to talk together on the street; he forbade any of the Californians, who had grown up in the saddle, from galloping their horses through the town; he prohibited any parties or gatherings in homes. Gillespie made himself so unpopular with the natives that some peaches given to him ostensibly as a gift had been rolled in the spines of the prickly pear cactus! Things finally came to a head when a group of young Californians attacked Gillespie's headquarters. They did no real damage, but Gillespie ordered his men to arrest the leading citizens of the Pueblo, and these proud men were dragged from their homes. It was the last straw, and threw the country into revolt.[29]

News of the revolt reached Phelps in the north and he was once again on hand to observe the responses of the principal American actors. Stockton sent for Fremont and then took the ship *Sterling* to go to the relief of Gillespie. He also had a further mission to San Diego. There, according to Phelps, Stockton was supposed to "save the hides which I had at that place, and was fearful of losing, consisting of over 20,000 dried and cured, packed away in a hide-house on the beach." The was not the first, and would scarcely be the last instance of the American military being deployed to protect American business. In his autobiography, Phelps maintained a respectful tone towards Stockton, but at the time, he was critical of the Commodore for withdrawing all his forces from San Diego where there was "more American property than all other parts of the coast together. This seems strange."[30]

Stockton's plan, as Phelps recounted it, was for Fremont to land at

---

[28] *Fore and Aft*, 306-311; *1846 Journal*, 65.

[29] *1846 Journal*, 34; Remi Nadeau, *Los Angeles, From Mission to Modern City*, 22-23.

[30] *Fore and Aft*, 311-312; *1846 Journal*, 62.

Santa Barbara (which along with San Diego had also been retaken by the Californians), seize it and proceed south to "fall on the Californians before they knew he was advancing on them." Stockton was to reoccupy Los Angeles and relieve Gillespie. Fremont, however, was forced to land at Monterey and proceed overland, and Stockton found that Gillespie had already surrendered.[31] In his journal, Phelps told how Stockton had landed at San Pedro, attacked the Californians there and "killed over a hundred men and a larger number of horses." Then a few pages later Phelps was forced to report that Stockton's alleged fight at San Pedro,"which seemed so plausible and authentic turns out to be utterly false." This so easily accepted rumor, which turned out to be so wrong, might have provoked Phelps to a bit more caution and uncertainty of tone in his reminiscences thirty years later. He did not repeat this error, but he was still persuaded that his memory of the events was one of unquestionable accuracy. After all, he had been there![32]

Stockton gathered more forces at San Diego for his march on Los Angeles, while Fremont slowly and cautiously made his way south from Monterey. General Stephen Watts Kearny had also arrived in San Diego, battered and wounded after the disastrous "Battle of San Pasqual" in which the Californians inflicted a sharp defeat on the Americans. This ignominious performance by American arms ran drastically counter to Phelps' efforts to portray the valor and superiority of American forces, and immediately before he discussed Kearny's defeat he tried to leave the reader with a sharply contrasting image by telling the story of Lieutenant Theodore Talbot's exploits in Santa Barbara. Surrounded by over one hundred Californians, Talbot and his ten Americans refused to surrender, made good their escape with no losses, and crossed the mountains of the Coast Range to return to Monterey.[33] Phelps could not explain away the Californians' victory at San Pasqual, however, and he was forced to confess that "This time the Californians made a good fight,

---

[31] *Fore and Aft*, 312.

[32] *1846 Journal*, 68-69.

[33] *Fore and Aft*, 313-314. Bancroft, *Works*, XXII, 316, called Phelps' account of Talbot's withdrawal from Santa Barbara, "purely imaginary....Evidently some of Talbot's men on arrival at Monterey indulged in the trappers' propensity for story-telling." Neal Harlow, *California Conquered*, 170, stated, however, that Talbot and nine men, "spurning surrender...made an arduous thirty-four-day flight through the wilds to Monterey.

in which the Americans suffered severely; and but for a relief party sent by Commodore Stockton from San Diego to meet them, they could scarcely have maintained themselves." Phelps sought an explanation for this debacle, and talked to the leader of the Californians, Andrés Pico, who told him that he found Kearny's men straggling along without any apparent discipline. Pico took advantage of the situation, "an opportunity for attack which he could not resist." Phelps recounted some of the factors contributing to his countrymen's defeat at the hands of a people generally considered indolent and cowardly. The men were worn down by a long march; they had heard that California was already secured and therefore were not on their guard—but finally he admitted that "certainly it was a discredit to American arms."[34]

Phelps was not quite finished discussing the American military performance in California. He had one more encounter to explain, the repulse of Captain William Mervine's attempt to relieve Gillespie in Los Angeles. Mervine had arrived at San Pedro on the frigate *Savannah* and found Gillespie surrounded. He made an effort to advance on Los Angeles, but was turned back by cannon fire from General José María Flores and some 300 Californians. Mervine and his men retreated to their ship unpursued by Flores, for the Californians' one and only cannon had run out of ammunition, but not before several casualties had been inflicted on the Americans. Phelps defended Mervine. He said:

> Captain Mervine of course, could not know this, and took what seemed to him to be the only course to save his men. Captain Mervine, in this affair, would have been blamed, had he not made the attempt to aid Gillespie: his zeal and courage impelled him to the rescue; he cared nothing about the enemy, if he could only get at them; this he expected to do, but was disappointed. The mistake was in not having the carriage gun.

Phelps could not imagine that such a "mistake," in a military man, might raise serious questions about his judgement and fitness to command troops.[35]

Phelps' ending for the war in California reserved all of the glory and

---

[34]*Fore and Aft*, 312-315.

[35]Ibid., 316. Neal Harlow, 167, accepts Lieutenant Archibald Gillespie's criticisms of Captain Mervine. There were no field pieces on board the *Savannah*, but the merchant ship *Vandalia*, anchored nearby, had two six pounders that could easily be mounted, and Mervine was advised by Gillespie to use them. Harlow quotes Gillespie's statement that "no attention was paid to either our advice or information...indeed! he [Mervine] was without reason."

honor for the heroic Commodore Stockton and Captain Fremont. At "Rio San Gabriel," Stockton's men crossed the river under fire, charged, and "routed General Flores and his entire force." But it appears that this was not quite decisive, for the next day the struggle resumed. Flores, concealed in a ravine near "La Mesa," opened up with his artillery on the American flank, and charged their front and rear. In Phelps' description of the action, "The Commodore silenced their guns, repelled the charge, and the enemy fled. The next morning the amphibious army [because made up of so many sailors] entered and reoccupied the town [Los Angeles] without further molestation." Flores, meanwhile, managed nonetheless to get away from Stockton. He turned the command over to Andrés Pico and headed for Sonora. The Californians were persuaded by another Pico, Jesus, to surrender to Fremont who got them to sign the famous "capitulation of Cowenga," as Phelps called it.[36]

It is interesting to note that, though General Kearny was with Stockton at San Gabriel and La Mesa, Phelps failed to mention him. Instead he emphasized that "in the history of California...to Stockton and Fremont, with their respective forces, belongs the honor of the capture and conquest of California." Perhaps Phelps could not bring himself to include Kearny after the General's disgrace at San Pasqual. He did not discuss the feud between Fremont and Kearny over who was the legitimate military governor of California either. Rather, he left the subject of the war by saying that he was "omitting many details of events which at this late date might fail to interest." Yet a more judicious assertion here might be that Phelps was in fact omitting details that might have undermined his case for the glory and good judgement of both "fighting Bob" Stockton and John C. Fremont. Stockton, for example, may have been able to end the war earlier had he agreed to General Flores' terms at the time of Gillespie's ouster, rather than letting it be known that he would have Flores shot at the first opportunity. Furthermore, Fremont and his California Battalion had arrived too late to participate in any of the fighting around Los Angeles. But since he was judged by the Californians to be more sympathetic than the stern Stockton, it was Fremont with whom they entered into negotiations and Fremont to whom they surrendered.[37]

[36]*Fore and Aft*, 318-319.
[37]Ibid., 319-20. See also Remi Nadeau, 32-37; Neal Harlow, 231-32; Ferol Egan, *Fremont: Explorer for a Restless Nation*, 361-405.

As an old man, Phelps had transformed memories of events he had either experienced or been close to, into a generally positive and nationalistic picture of the American conquest. Even palpable American errors were excused or explained away. In his journal written at the time, Phelps was not so laudatory toward some of the American leaders, the "great naval gentlemen" as he called them. In fact, he felt that their war operations had been "conducted badly." They did not know enough about California, he felt, "and though they sometimes condescend to ask the opinion of Capts [sic] of Trading Ships who know every part of it, they seldom act on the information received." Phelps believed that it was because they were jealous of any share in the merit. But his reminiscences insured that he would share in the glory. Both the Phelps of the 1840s on the scene, and the autobiographer of the 1870s looking back continued to have a measure of egotism in common, even if the latter, now more conscious of himself as an historical personage, became less rigorously accurate in his role as an historian.[38]

Phelps, like all of us, was a product of his age and culture. When we reflect on his pride and prejudices, it may be too easy to overlook some of his better qualities. He had a feel for the beauty of the landscape that would be called "transcendental" by some of his New England contemporaries. In the early 1840s, returning from a visit to Sutter, he floated down the Sacramento to the Straits of Carquinez. There he went on shore and, captivated by his surroundings, climbed to the top of a small mountain. As he took in the view, he said he felt "more in the presence of my creator...in such an elevated situation. Man feels more his own littleness, and consequently the unbounded power and wisdom, and goodness of the Almighty, than he is apt to do in the every day walks of life."[39]

Phelps closed his autobiography with a description of his last voyage round the horn to California, with an inexperienced crew eager to get to the newly-discovered gold fields. Six years absence from Los Angeles had seen great changes—new buildings, vineyards, old ranches cut up into smaller farms, many new immigrants from the United States and elsewhere. In fact, the new arrivals now outnumbered the natives, so that the latter appeared, in Phelps' words, "as pilgrims and strangers in their

[38]*1846 Journal*, 70.
[39]"Journal, 1841-43," 32.

own land." Now that the old Californians were being displaced, Phelps found himself sympathizing with their plight. He deplored the land policies of the United States Government and the "sharp practices" of the new migrants. He explained how the old California rancheros, many of them undoubtedly old friends and customers,"were compelled to employ lawyers to defend their property, in some cases giving one-half the property to secure the other. In all cases a large retaining fee was demanded, secured by mortgage of cattle and land." The discovery of gold had spelled doom for the old California way. It was now missed and appreciated as only that can be which is gone forever. Phelps recalled how he knew "the principal people of the country, and every house was a home to the stranger, the latch-string outside, and the entertainment to be found within, furnished without money and without price." Still, Phelps did not entirely lament the passing of the old life. He lingered lyrically on his final visit to San Pedro, that "well-remembered spot," and brought California's past and future together in a single image:

> The hills were clothed in green, the plains were waving with an immense sea of wild mustard, in full blossom. The colored patches of earth in the far distance marked out, as in former years, the gardens of San Gabriel. The old bluff point of the harbor, known as "Don Abel's nose," was still there, its proportions unchanged by winds or rains. The one adobe house and its wooden frame companions, were, as in former years, the sole tenements of the past. The cattle and horses had disappeared from the hills; all else seemed as in olden times. But the days of "hide drogging" were past. Since those days a mighty people had possessed the country, and though no sign of progress was perceptible at San Pedro, cities and towns with wealth, luxury, and civilization were fast spreading over the land.[40]

---

[40] *Fore and Aft*, 328.

PART II
Before the Mast

RICHARD HENRY DANA, JR.
From a daguerrotype at Craigie House, Cambridge, Mass.

CHAPTER IV

Richard Henry Dana

While the merchants and traders were traveling up and down the California coast in the summer of 1834, another young employee of Bryant, Sturgis and Company was embarking from Boston as an ordinary seaman on a voyage that would make him famous. Richard Henry Dana's "two years before the mast" would result in a classic of American literature, and turn the world's attention to the little-known Mexican Pacific province of California.

Like many millions of people after him, Dana came to California in pursuit of improved health. A bout with the measles, and the "medicines" of the times (bleeding, purgatives, blisters), had so reduced him in body and spirit that he felt listless and without his customary ambition. A sea voyage would be just the thing to restore his health, and remove from his father the financial burden imposed by an invalid son on his hands. The Danas were an old and aristocratic New England family, Federalist in their political principles and proud of their ancestry, but in reduced financial circumstances at the time of Richard Henry Dana, Jr.'s, illness. So rather than lie around at home being "a useless, pitied and dissatisfied creature," as he described it, Dana decided "to relieve myself of ennui, to see new places and modes of life, and to effect if possible a cure of my eyes...."[1] He could not afford a gentleman's tour, and he did not want to embark as a passenger without books (which he would have been tempted to read despite his eyes). Instead, "aided very much by the attractiveness of the romance and adventure of the thing, I determined to go before the mast, where I knew that the constant occupation would make reading unnecessary, and the hard work, plain diet and life in the open air...would...make a gradual change in my whole physical system."[2]

---

[1] Richard Henry Dana, Jr., *An Autobiographical Sketch*, 63-64.
[2] Ibid., 64.

Even then, California had begun to gain a reputation as an ideal place to go for one's health, with a good climate and, for a young sailor, plenty of hard, invigorating labor.[3] The dual aspect of the practical and the romantic could not help but sway this young Boston Brahmin and former student of Ralph Waldo Emerson. In California, Dana was to find the grinding practicality of New England enterprise and the exotic flavors of a foreign land and peoples. He was to have a first-hand education in direct interaction with what one of his biographers characterized as the ferocity and grandeur of men and nature in a primitive state.[4]

Another biographer considered it fortunate that *Two Years Before the Mast* had to be written almost entirely from what Dana could remember. When he returned from California, he had given his sea-journal to his cousin, who lost it, leaving Dana with only a twenty page notebook and his memory. He was therefore forced to fulfill Wordsworth's criterion for transforming emotions into poetry.[5] He had to reflect on the turbulent events of his voyage in the relative tranquillity of his Boston home, concentrating the force of his mind on distilling the essence of his youthful adventure.[6]

In *Two Years Before the Mast*, young Richard spoke of his experience as an interlude, a holiday from what he felt should be his real ambitions—a Harvard education and a career in law or letters as was befitting a Dana. He knew that the cruise meant "separating myself from all the social and intellectual enjoyments of life."[7] Yet in his *Autobiographical Sketch* he expressed some contempt for those who he felt merely "talked about life rather than lived it."[8] And twenty years later he would confide to his journal: "I believe I was made for the sea, and that all my life on shore is a mistake...."[9] His book and memories of his two years before the mast

---

[3]Ibid., 66.

[4]Samuel Shapiro, *Richard Henry Dana, Jr., 1815-1882*, 8.

[5]Wordsworth had been a favorite of both Richard Henry Dana, Sr., and his son. Young Richard wrote a speech for his Harvard commencement on a text from Wordsworth. See James D. Hart, "Richard Henry Dana, Jr." (Ph.D. dissertation, Harvard University, 1936), 17, 122-123.

[6]Robert L. Gale, *Richard Henry Dana*, 117.

[7]Richard Henry Dana, Jr., *Two Years Before the Mast: A Personal Narrative of Life at Sea*, two vols., John Haskell Kemble, ed., (Los Angeles, The Ward Ritchie Press, 1964), p. 8. All quotations from this edition, henceforward refered to as *Two Years*.

[8]*An Autobiographical Sketch*, 3.

[9]Quoted in James D. Hart, "Richard Henry Dana, Jr.," 167.

THE BRIG *PILGRIM*
From an original oil painting by William S. Thompson
Courtesy Collection of Santa Barbara Historical Society

would always remain for Dana, sometimes regretfully, as reminders of
the life he might have lived.

Richard Henry Dana's trip to California in the forecastle of a Boston
hide ship was a special opportunity for the young man to meet and live
on terms of intimacy with people he would not ordinarily have associated with had he remained at home in his circle of upper-class Cambridge
connections. Sharing the hardships of a sailor's life with the men before
the mast, and with the Sandwich Islanders on shore at San Diego,
allowed Dana to see these people in a deeper, more humane way. Unfortunately, he was to fall short of this when it came to the Spanish-Mexicans and Indians of the coast. His contacts with them were much more
casual. In forming his opinions of them, he accepted appearances
framed in stereotypical terms, something he would probably also have
done with the sailors and Sandwich Islanders, had he not been pushed to
a more profound understanding by shared experiences. His portraits of
his fellow sailors can be revealingly contrasted with his often typically
New England, and American, opinions of the Californians and Indians.
It was evident in his case that familiarity bred understanding in place of
contempt. Richard Henry Dana's brief life at sea, and in California, was
an educational experience which, if it did not completely transform the
young New England aristocrat, at least permitted him to experience at
first hand a far different and harsher world, one that would stir his sympathies and stimulate his sense of *noblesse oblige*.[10]

When he was on the coast, the hard work and hardships of a sailor's
life made California seem anything but an idyllic place. The young man
was soon treated to the primitive nature of man, and his ferocity, in the
form of the captain of the *Pilgrim*, Frank Thompson. Dana was a reluc-
tant witness to the infamous and sadistic flogging of two of his fellow
sailors.[11] The event shocked and sickened him. He may have been
reminded of his own childhood "flogging" by an autocratic schoolmas-

[10]As a lawyer in Boston, Dana fought the Fugitive Slave Law in the 1840s and defended fugitive
slaves "when to do so meant a serious jeopardy to his legal and social standing in Boston." Ibid., 155.

[11]As Dana described the incident in *Two Years*, 102-106, Captain Frank Thompson took a dislike to
one of the sailors, Sam the Swede, who was clumsy and slow of speech. The latter had dropped a marlin
spike from the rigging, an accident which Captain Thompson "set down against him." Thompson
accused Sam of talking back to him, which the Swede denied. Sam was then tied up for a flogging, when
another sailor, John, an American, asked Thompson why Sam was being flogged. For this offence, John
too was tied up and flogged.

ter. In his *Autobiographical Sketch*, where he described this incident, he said that he was "a boy of tender feelings. I well remember shedding tears alone at imaginary cases of suffering suggested by something I had accidentally seen." He had a strong sense of the injustice witnessed and experienced at the hands of several schoolmasters; yet in his own case, he had the backing of his family and his father to rely on. One teacher who went too far in his punishment found himself without a job at the insistence of Richard Henry Dana, Sr.[12]

There was no one to protect the two sailors from the wrath and power of a Frank Thompson, however, and upset as he was by the sight of this brutality, young Dana must also have been aware that his own class and political connections made him immune to such treatment. His ambiguous position and feelings were strongly expressed at this episode. He saw both a sailor under a certain regime, and as he put it "a human being, made in God's likeness—fastened up and flogged like a beast. A man, too, whom I had lived with and eaten with for months, and knew so well." But what could be done? The sailors were at the mercy of the ship's captain who had the law on his side, and Dana's own conservative background would hardly have allowed him to go too far in questioning this. He knew that "If a sailor resists his commander, he resists the law, and piracy or submission is his only alternative." As disgusting as it was, Dana and the poor sailors saw that it had to be endured. Yet Dana's New England conscience was aroused by this brutal scene, and he vowed that he would do something to help the suffering sailors.[13] In fact, his first publication when he returned to Boston and Harvard College, was an article in the *American Jurist* entitled "Cruelty To Seamen." In it he disagreed with the decision of one of his Harvard law instructors, Judge Joseph Story. Dana felt the Judge had been too lenient on a ship's captain and first mate who had beaten a sailor to death. Dana argued that a captain should not be let off for cruel acts just because his friends testify to his good character. He might act well at home, Dana pointed out, but at sea, "far from all the restraints of friends and superiors and public opinion, possessed of despotic power, and with none to see or hear him but those who stand to him in the relation of slaves, [he] may show himself a very fiend."[14]

---

[12]*An Autobiographical Sketch*, 40-47.

[13]*Two Years*, 103-106.

[14]Richard Henry Dana, Jr., "Cruelty To Seamen," 6.

Such clearly was Dana's opinion of Frank Thompson. He learned from this episode just how little power over their own existences sailors actually had. He also discovered something else about these men: they behaved toward each other, as he could see, with "a consideration and delicacy which would have been worthy of admiration in the highest walks of life." He observed at first hand that, despite their lowly positions in life, certain members of the crew displayed decency, intelligence and strength of character. Dana was an eyewitness to the results of brutal treatment inflicted upon people who were basically powerless to do anything about it, and he saw what this could do to the human spirit. He also observed that human spirits differed in their capacities and responses. Of the two men who had endured the flogging, one of them was angry and spoke chiefly of revenge. He was an uneducated foreigner, and as such Dana considered his emotional range to be limited. The impact of the beating on him was less affecting. The other, however, was an American who had some education. This made him feel more deeply, in Dana's words, "the degradation that had been inflicted on him, which the other man was incapable of." Ironically, the American sailor was also from Washington, D.C., where slaves were sold openly in the market places, and the beating seemed to have broken his spirit. He appeared to Dana to care only that the voyage should be over.[15]

Such passages as these reveal the extent and limitations of Dana's sympathies. With one noted exception (considered below) he responded with more interest and attention to those who were closer to him in class and education. Not surprisingly, he was also more judicious in his opinions of those people with whom he had the longest and closest contact. Life in the forecastle was harsh and often brutal. The sailors learned to make a joke of the many brushes with death they endured almost every day, and they had little sympathy for a man who could not pull his weight, even if he was sick. Dana explained it this way: "A thin-skinned man could not live an hour on board ship. One would be torn raw unless he had the hide of an ox. A moment of natural feeling for home and friends, and then the frigid routine of sea-life returned."[16]

Though it was indeed an opportunity to observe men (and himself)

---

[15] *Two Years*, 109, 132.
[16] Ibid., 248.

under trying and primitive conditions, Dana worried that the life before the mast would deaden his sensibilities and make him fit for little else but the existence of a sailor. At one point he even accepted this as a probability, and began to plan for it by working to qualify as a ship's officer.[17] Nor were the floggings the worst of what he had to witness or endure on the coast. Elsewhere he explained that "most of my reflections, and much of the wickedness which I was placed in the midst of" had not been permitted to be made public in *Two Years Before the Mast*.[18]

It was with great relief, then, that Dana was able to turn away from such events as the floggings, to find a kind of romantic renewal in the California scenery. Loading hides at Santa Barbara, his first port of call, brought forth comments on the famous California climate. It was January, yet "It was a beautiful day, and so warm that we wore hats, duck trousers, and all summer gear." There were no profound changes in the seasons there, and the temperature never dropped below freezing. The surf at Santa Barbara was also rendered in an accurate image that vividly pictured "the great seas...rolling in in regular lines, growing larger and larger as they approached the shore, and hanging over the beach upon which they were to break, when their tops would curl over and turn white with foam, and beginning at one extreme of the line, break rapidly to the other, as a child's long card house falls when a card is knocked down at one end."[19]

Much of Dana's time was indeed spent getting knocked about by this surf, trying to land a boat through it, or wading into it with a hide on his head. Picturesque though it was, California was also the hated scene of much drudgery and discomfort, and there were times when Dana professed a profound distaste for the country. Yet so much of *Two Years Before the Mast* was taken up with the sights, sounds, look and feel of California, so much to detailing the people encountered and the friendships that made the life of a "hide drogher" bearable, that Richard Henry

---

[17]Ibid., 95-96.

[18]*An Autobiographical Sketch*, 65-66; Dana's editor, John Haskell Kemble, pointed out in his introduction, *Two Years*, xiii-xiv, that Dana omitted profanity, sexual references and accounts of dodging Mexican customs officials. The former material was left out because his publisher, Harpers, intended to issue the book to the New York School District Library, and the Family Library; the latter was left out in deference to Bryant, Sturgis & Co. who in 1840 were still in the hide business in California.

[19]*Two Years*, 62

Dana's California possesses an attraction that easily overrides his own labelling of it as "the hated shores" or "the hell of California."[20]

Dana astutely observed the geographical division between southern and northern California, which he placed around Point Conception:

> As you go to the northward of the point, the country becomes more wooded, has a richer appearance, and is better supplied with water. This is the case with Monterey, and still more so with San Francisco; while to the southward of the point, as at Santa Barbara, San Pedro, and particularly San Diego, there is very little wood, and the country has a naked, level appearance, though it is still fertile.

He commented on the San Francisco Bay area, recognizing that it would be the center of California's future prosperity because of its wood, water, climate and anchorage. He also had a more emotional reaction to certain features of the California landscape. Immediately after the flogging, which happened at San Pedro, the sight of the grave of an English sea captain on a "small, desolate looking island" in San Pedro Bay reinforced Dana's own sense of isolation and helplessness, but also revived his "poetic interest" which he was happy to discover had not been wholly suppressed by the degradation of his circumstances.[21]

Later at San Juan Capistrano, which he called "the only romantic spot in California," Dana was impressed with the "grandeur in everything around, which gave a solemnity to the scene, a silence and solitariness which affected every part. Not a human being but ourselves for miles, and no sound heard but the pulsations of the great Pacific!" The beauty of the setting and the chance to observe it "free from the sense that human beings were at my elbow," helped Dana to regain satisfaction in the responses of his "better nature." California may have been the site of too many days of grinding labor for Dana to have expressed unqualified admiration for it, and he also seemed to have grown a bit weary of the close quarters and what he called—lapsing into his Brahmin mode—the "paltry, vulgar associations" of the forecastle. But he could still turn to the lonely land and seascapes for relief. Such as it was, to him "This was the romance of hide droghing!"[22]

---

[20]Ibid., 252.
[21]Ibid., 76, 106-107, 224-228.
[22]Ibid., 141-143.

Dana may have grown momentarily weary of their company, but he could scarcely escape for long the close quarters and intimate contact with the ship's crew; nor did he desire to do so. He was eager to be accepted by the crew, doubly so since among the ordinary sailors who had little education and few other choices in life, he was privileged and different. He was anxious to do a good job and, like the young man that he was, to prove himself. When he had accomplished a particularly skillful act of seamanship, he listened to the praise he received "with as much satisfaction as I ever felt at Cambridge on seeing a 'bene' at the foot of a Latin exercise." In a fit of youthful exuberance, he even hazarded his life at "Dana Point," scaling some cliffs to dislodge hides that had failed to fall all the way to the beach when thrown. He was called a "damn fool" for volunteering to risk his neck for a dozen hides.[23]

Among the ship's crew were many ignorant and superstitious men, but there were also several individuals who were sources of fascination, insight, even romantic inspiration. Living and working with them on a daily basis, Dana got to know them well. One who stood above the rest, in Dana's estimation, was the English sailor Tom Harris who was his messmate aboard the *Alert*. Harris had a powerful mind and an almost photographic memory that strongly impressed Dana. Harris had ruined several opportunities to advance himself because of his addiction to alcohol, and he had had little incentive to stop until he saw a drunken shipmate injure himself seriously in an alcoholic stupor. Harris resolved at that moment never to drink again, and as Dana reported it, he never did. From Harris, Dana received a broader picture of the habitual life of a sailor—stories of conniving ship owners and brutal ship's captains, tyranny and toil. His sympathies were stirred and his respect for Harris, whose "reasoning powers were striking," was considerable. He knew that Harris' lack of formal education was a misfortune, but he nonetheless felt that Harris' intellect was superior to "all the young men of my acquaintance at college...." Harris became a kind of mentor to Dana, teaching him seamanship, expanding his knowledge of his fellow sailors, and adding to Dana's growing insight into the complexities of the human character under the stress and deformation of a variety of novel and unusual circumstances. He said of Harris: "Such was the man, who,

---

[23]Ibid., 77,198-200.

at forty, was still a dog before the mast, at twelve dollars a month." Dana could think of no one else with whom he would have preferred to spend his time, not even his society friends in Cambridge.[24]

Dana's "democratic" impulses were further strengthened (at least while before the mast in California) by another member of the crew, George Marsh. Marsh too was an Englishman who had come aboard the *Alert* in California. He showed signs of an education beyond that expected of an ordinary seaman. Dana was immediately attracted to him, suspecting that he was of more genteel birth than his present circumstances would indicate. Marsh also had his story to tell. He had been captured by South Sea Islanders, narrowly escaping death, and had kept a journal of his experiences. Marsh did not impress Dana as being in quite the same league with Tom Harris, however. Harris had developed his mind and character despite the considerable handicap of low birth. Marsh, in Dana's view, had the good fortune to have been born into a higher social rank, yet he had done little with himself. Nevertheless, George Marsh provided another occasion for Dana to add to his education about human nature, and to reveal his own self-expectations. When Marsh got the job of second mate aboard a different merchant vessel on the coast, and bade his farewell to the crew, he singled out Dana, "as much as to say, 'We understand each other'." Dana was then sorry he had not probed Marsh further for his whole story. He seemed to be someone extraordinary, like Tom Harris, someone who came to represent the surprising intricacy and human depths which were so easily overlooked by those who never strayed from the safety of their homes; in Dana's words, they "never walked but in one line from their cradles to their graves." Dana saw no Providential Hand here to account for the lowly status of these remarkable men, but rather the actions of an adverse fortune on characters of varying strengths. He was prompted by his experience with these men to give some advice, perhaps intended for his peers who had stayed at home:

> We must come down from our heights, and leave our straight paths for the byways and low places of life, if we would learn truths by strong contrast; and in hovels, in forecastles, and among our own outcasts in foreign lands, see what has been wrought among our fellow-creatures by accident, hardship, or vice.

Many an American would follow Dana's (and Horace Greeley's) advice

---

[24]Ibid., 191-196.

and leave the well-trodden path for the byways of the west, though motivated more by a desire to get ahead than by any puritanical impulse to probe the mysteries of the human heart. But later American writers, the realists and naturalists, were to take Dana's counsel to their own hearts.[25]

Then as today, California was a melting pot of cultures and nationalities. Dana had plenty of opportunities to observe a variety of people from around the world. On the coast were Russians, Englishmen, Frenchmen, Italians, Spaniards, Hawaiian Islanders and the native Californians of both the upper and lower classes. Many foreigners, including Americans like Alfred Robinson, were proud and happy to marry into an upper class California family like the de la Guerras, though Robinson doubtless had little occasion (and probably less inclination) for intimacies with the lower classes. He balanced his opinion of the Californians between the elitism of the patriotic Yankee, and the respect owed to his personal friends and in-laws among the Californians of social prominence. Richard Henry Dana's background arguably gave him as much or more of a claim to mix on a level with the elite of California, but his position as a common sailor placed him in far different circles. Still, he seemed to have been present at some important social events, such as the wedding in Santa Barbara of Alfred Robinson himself. Robinson, he said, was marrying the daughter of "the grandee of the place, and the head of the first family in California."[26] Dana did not particularly care for Robinson, and perhaps part of his antipathy was due to Robinson's pretensions to a social prominence that the young man felt was really eclipsed by his own. The agent was also responsible for seeing that the hides were collected and the merchandise sold, and no doubt he could be short with the sailors who had to do the heavy work. Dana said he was "very much disliked by the crew, one and all", and even took particular pleasure in drenching Robinson in the surf one time.[27] Observing the dancers at the wedding, Dana compared the Yankee stiffness of agent Robinson to the "grace and spirit" of the Californians, particularly Don

---

[25]Ibid., 201-204, 251.

[26]Ibid., 236.

[27]Ibid., 213; in a letter of Frank Thompson's, reprinted by Kemble in ibid., 399, the Captain of the *Pilgrim* and the *Alert* criticized "the capricious temper of Mr. Robinson," and said that "it is impossible for a man to put up with some of his *would be* dignified ways at all times." Emphasis in original.

Juan Bandini. Yet he was both attracted and repelled by the dancing of the Californians. It was "to me, offensive....Indeed, among people of the character of these Mexicans, the waltz seemed to me to have found its right place."[28]

During his time in California, Dana never seemed to have reached the level of intimacy and sustained close contact with any of the native Californians or Indians that he experienced with certain members of the ship's crew, and especially with the Hawaiians who shared his interlude on shore at San Diego as a hide curer. No Californians of whatever caste were discussed in the way that he mentioned such fond acquaintances as Tom Harris, or Hope, the Hawaiian. In fact, the only Californian identified by name at all was Don Juan Bandini. To Dana he was a "decayed gentleman" who had squandered his fortune and was "living upon the charity of our agent."[29] Though this may have accurately foreshadowed the fate of the California landowners as a class, Dana clearly had misunderstood Bandini's position. In 1835, at the time Dana saw him, Bandini had returned from Mexico and was indeed without a lot of ready cash (as were most of the rancheros in California). But he was the vice-president of the Hijar and Padres Colonization and Commercial Company and supercargo of the company's vessel, the *Natalie*, as well as Inspector of Customs for California. The latter position was one of particular importance to the merchants and ship captains trading in California where customs duties could be up to eighty percent of the value of the trade goods.[30] Bandini's later career would also seem to contradict Dana's image of him as a decayed gentleman, having his vitals eaten out by one whom Dana identified as "a fat, coarse, vulgar, pretentious fellow of a Yankee trader," feeding off of the Bandini's, and "grinding them in their poverty, having mortgages on their lands, forestalling their cattle, and already making in-roads upon their jewels, which were their last

---

[28]Ibid., pp. 236-239. Just exactly what "the character of these Mexicans" was Dana never spelled out in this instance, but he seemed to be implying that they were altogether too sensual and intimate for his reserved New England tastes.

[29]Ibid., 233.

[30]See H.D. Barrows, "Juan Bandini," in *Historical Society of Southern California Publications*, IV, (Los Angeles, 1900), 243-246. Samuel Eliot Morison, *The Maritime History of Massachusetts, 1783-1860*, 267.

hope."[31] Bandini served in numerous positions in the Mexican government of California, including administrator of San Gabriel Mission
from 1838-1840.[32] He was granted several large tracts of land during his
time, and was considered a capable and popular man. He was an early
supporter of American power in California. His daughters were married
to Americans (including Abel Stearns, a prominent Los Angeles merchant), and he continued to prosper until his death in 1859.[33]

When he arrived in California, Dana borrowed a Spanish grammar
and a dictionary from the ship's cabin and began to learn Spanish. He said
that he soon got a reputation as a linguist, and was sent to shore on
errands which gave him "opportunities of seeing the customs, characters,
and domestic arrangements of the people...." Later, he also took advantage of Juan Bandini's secretary to improve his Spanish and to learn more
about Mexican politics. Yet his generalizations about the Californians
lack the sympathetic closeness that he showed himself capable of with the
ship's crew and his friends the Kanakas. His assessment of Californians as
a class was in line with that of many American observers at the time.
They were "an idle, thriftless people, and can make nothing for themselves." They had to buy everything from the American merchants,
including "bad wine made in Boston," in spite of the numerous and productive grape vines to be seen everywhere in California. The Indians did
all of the hard work, "two or three being attached to each house; and the
poorest persons are able to keep one, at least, for they have only to feed
them and give them a small piece of coarse cloth and belt, for the males;
and a coarse gown, without stocking, for the females." Doubtless, as in
the American South of this period, the low-caste status of the Indian in
California contributed greatly to attaching a stigma to any sort of manual
labor, though Richard Henry Dana did not draw such a conclusion.[34]

---

[31] *Two Years*, 233-234; William Dane Phelps in his *Journal, 1840-42*, 267, claimed that the "fat, vulgar Yankee" was Henry D. Fitch of San Diego. Phelps maintained that Fitch was "fair and honorable in
all his dealings." Dana's only motive for so characterizing Fitch, Phelps said, was that Dana had entered
his house "intoxicated and using offensive language," and Fitch threw him out!

[32] He was one of the few administrators who did not fit Dana's later characterization of them as
grasping after the spoils of the missions. See Susanna Bryant Dakin, *The Lives of William Hartnell*, 225.

[33] Barrows, "Juan Bandini," 243.

[34] *Two Years*, 82-88, 234.

Dana clearly identified a caste system in California. He claimed it was based on the amount of Spanish blood one possessed, "which also settles their social rank" and relegated the Indians to the bottom. Those with the most Spanish blood were the aristocrats of the country. As Dana described it:

> They can be told by their complexions, dress, manner, and also by their speech; for calling themselves Castilians, they are ever desirous of speaking the pure Castilian language, which is spoken in a somewhat corrupted dialect by the lower classes. From this upper class, they go down by regular shades, growing more and more dark and muddy, until you come to the pure Indian, who runs about the country with nothing upon him but a small piece of cloth, kept up by a wide leather strap drawn round his waist.[35]

Though he was conscious of their humble position in California, and indeed might have been expected to sympathize with them as fellow "slaves," Dana's Calvinist work-ethic heritage made him bridle at the Indians for failing to lend a helping hand. Near Los Angeles—"a fine plane country, filled with herds of cattle...and several of the wealthiest missions"— Dana and some other crew members had been forced to roll heavy barrels full of trade goods up a slippery hill. Having exhausted themselves at this, they tried to persuade the Indians who were there with ox-carts full of hides for trading, to help them unload the carts. But in Dana's words, the "lazy Indians" refused.[36]

Yet Dana was aware of the abysmal condition of the California Mission Indians, and, like Alfred Robinson and others, blamed it on secularization. The Indians remained, in Dana's perception, "virtually slaves, as much as they ever were", and "the missions are given over to be preyed upon by the harpies of the civil power" who exploited them ruthlessly and to the general detriment of the country. The "administradores" were opportunists who were only interested in plunder, and missions and country in general were better off under the priests.[37]

---

[35]Ibid., 84.

[36]Ibid., 100.Twenty years did not change his opinion of the Indians. On his 1859 return visit to California, he observed the Indians at Clark's Camp near Yosemite and noted in his Journal: "Indians lazy, sleep in open air, with fire & plain cooking coals, & gather acorns & sugar-pine cones etc. Chief do [sic] servile work for Clark, to get food." Robert F. Lucid, ed., *The Journal of Richard Henry Dana, Jr.*, III, 853.

[37]Ibid., 168.

Dana also had his comments to make about the Californian propensity for revolutions. The government of the country under Mexico was, as he saw it, "an arbitrary democracy, having no common law, and no judiciary." The laws were "made and unmade at the caprice of the legislature," and revolutions were organized by those with the least to lose and the most to gain by a new division of the spoils. Only "will and fear" operated to provide what little justice existed in such a seemingly lawless process. But if the Californians' political practices did not merit Dana's respect, neither did he think too highly of comtemporary American politics, which had its own spoils system. The Californians may have lacked the commercial expertise and shrewd business sense of the Americans, but their political methods were certainly more direct. When they wanted a change, according to Dana "instead of caucusing, paragraphing, libelling, feasting, promising, and lying, as with us, they take muskets and bayonets, and seizing upon the presidio and custom-house, divide the spoils, and declare a new dynasty."[38]

This might sound like a bold and forceful way to prosper, and indeed the vigilante justice of California's early American period was at least as lawless. Americans in general, however, seem to have considered themselves braver than the Californians, and their society more just. Certainly Dana, like so many of his fellow Americans (especially the frontier types) had a low opinion of the Californians' courage and their commitment to justice. He cited as evidence the story of a Yankee who was murdered by a "Spaniard" in Los Angeles. The latter was caught, tried and shot by some local vigilantes who had no faith that the California government would ever bring the murderer to justice. Included in their ranks were some forty Kentuckians. California's governor at the time issued threats about punishing the perpetrators of this high-handed action, but did nothing. Dana believed this was because, as he put it, "forty Kentucky hunters, with their rifles, were a match for a whole regiment of hungry, drawling, lazy half-breeds." A few months later, there was another murder in San Diego. Dana heard conflicting versions of what had happened. Some said that the foreigners had pursued and shot the murderer. Others said nothing had been done about it. Dana

---

[38]Ibid., 168-169.

remarked that when a crime was committed by an Indian, however, "justice, or rather vengeance, is not so tardy."[39]

Dana's contempt for California justice was consistent with his generally low opinion of the men he encountered in California. They were, he thought, "thriftless, proud and extravagant and very much given to gaming," which was an echo of Alfred Robinson's opinion. Unlike Robinson though, his portrait of the women of California was decidedly less delicately handled. He agreed with William Dane Phelps. The women were beautiful—but ignorant and not overly moral. Married women "have but little virtue," and only the jealousy and vengefulness of their husbands kept them in check. Unmarried women were watched carefully by the older women in their families, and their honor upheld by fathers and brothers. The result was that infidelity was much less frequent than might be supposed. Yet Dana pointed out that "the very men who would lay down their lives to avenge the dishonor of their own family, would risk the same lives to complete the dishonor of another." With the Indians, of course, the situation in Dana's eyes was even worse. Their morality was not upheld by any sense of family honor or fear of vengeance for its violation. In fact, Dana frequently observed Indian husbands playing the pander for their wives.[40]

Dana's New England upbringing strongly colored his opinions. In the absence of more extended contacts with the Californians, his cultural preconceptions prevailed. His ingrained habits of discipline and respect for hard work were polished at sea and stayed with him all his life. Twenty years later, Henry Adams described his father's friend Dana, as a "man of rather excessive refinement trying with success to work like a day laborer, deliberately hardening his skin to the burden, as though he were still carrying hides at Monterey."[41] Most men would have considered themselves at least modestly successful to have written and accomplished what Dana did in his life. But Dana looked upon himself as "a

---

[39]Ibid., 169-170.

[40]Ibid., 171. Dana may have done more than observe during his time in California, and his opinion of the morals of California women was probably arrived at first hand. In his journal of his return to California in 1859, he visited Mariposa where he remarked that "A woman here is cook who lived with me sev. months, named Mary Collins." See *The Journal of Richard Henry Dana, Jr.*, III, 854.

[41]Quoted in the introduction to *An Autobiographical Sketch*, 6-7.

failure compared to what I might and ought to have done."[42] As a man, his accomplishments were considerable; as a Dana they would never be enough. Dana may not have spared the Californians, but neither did he spare himself. Hard work was always the necessary foundation for any successes, and Dana liked to compare the work-habits and ingenuity of his fellow sailors (and by implication Americans, or Anglo-Saxons in general) with the way other groups in California conducted their business and pursued their various callings. Dana judged people in the typically American fashion, by what they did and how hard they worked at their callings. This no doubt accounts in part for his lack of respect for the Californians in this regard, and Dana was quick to note that the Americans in California had "more industry, frugality and enterprise than the natives." Because of this they "get nearly all of the trade into their own hands." Even the Californians seemed to recognize the business and organizational skills of the Americans, and made several of them alcaldes of Santa Barbara and Monterey.[43]

Dana could also see how valuable a possession California might one day be. It had, he exclaimed:

> four or five hundred miles of sea coast , with several good harbors; with fine forests in the north; the waters filled with fish, and the plains covered with thousands of herds of cattle; blessed with a climate than which there can be no better in the world; free from all manner of diseases...and with a soil in which corn yields from seventy to eighty fold. In the hands of an enterprising people, what a country this might be....

This grand vision was spoiled for Dana only by the thought that later generations of Americans living in California under the influence of the prevailing relaxed life-style, would catch the "California fever"—laziness! Little did Dana imagine how thoroughly and completely the Yankees would one day replace the old Californians, nor what the development of California would mean for the peace and wild beauty of the landscape. The easygoing life-style, however, remains as one of a repertoire of enticing images of California that continues to induce millions to move there.[44]

---

[42]Ibid., 21-22.
[43]*Two Years*, 88.
[44]Ibid., 171-172.

Dana was not familiar enough with the Californians to have identified any exceptions to his rule of thumb about California habits of labor—for example, someone like Alfred Robinson's friend from Los Angeles, Tiburcio Tapia. In fact, Dana's pride in the work ethic was such that there were few in California of any nationality (other than Americans or English) who he felt could measure up. He contrasted the crews on the English and American ships with some Italian sailors he encountered off San Juan Capistrano. The Italians had a crew of thirty men, nearly three times that of his own ship (he had transfered from the *Pilgrim* to the *Alert* in preparation for the voyage home), yet, he said, "the Alert would get under weigh and come to in half the time, and get two anchors, while they [the Italians] were all talking at once, jabbering like a parcel of Yahoos, and running about decks to find their cut block." On the other hand, the Italians had one advantage over the Americans, "and that was in lightening their labors in the boats by their songs. The Americans are a time and money saving people, but have not yet, as a nation, learned that music may be 'turned to account'."[45]

Like the appeal of the Italians' songs, certain of the Californians' customs must have had their attraction for a sailor whose time was ever at the disposal of the ship's captain. On all of the Catholic holidays, the locals (and the Catholic Italian sailors) had time off to attend the bull and bear baiting, cock-fighting and horse racing indulged in at every opportunity by the fun-loving Californians. Dana joked that there was "no danger of Catholicism's spreading in New England; Yankees can't afford the time to be Catholics."[46]

Despite his own obvious belief in the necessity of hard labor, as a sailor Dana could also see that there had to be some limits and some rewards, the latter coming even in the form of leisure time. He noted the results of harsh treatment and lack of appreciation on the work discipline of the *Pilgrim*'s crew after the floggings. They were listless and slack in their work. No one put out any extra effort despite the exhortations of the mate. A day's "liberty" on shore, however, was almost a cure for this. It revived the spirits and made the hard life of a sailor once again

---

[45]Ibid., 139.
[46]Ibid., 137.

bearable. A Sunday's liberty in San Diego (a town that would become famous for sailors' shore leaves) prompted Dana to rhapsodise:

> I shall never forget the delightful sensation of being in the open air, with the birds singing around me, and escaped from the confinement, labor, and strict rule of the vessel—of being once more in my life, though only for a day, my own master. A sailor's liberty is but for a day; yet while it lasts it is perfect. He is under no one's eye, and can do whatever, and go wherever, he pleases. This day, for the first time, I may truly say, in my whole life, I felt the meaning of a term which I had often heard — the sweets of liberty.[47]

Dana must have been pleased to be assigned to the hide-houses on shore at San Diego. There, though the duties of a hide-curer were hard and dirty, he had about three hours each afternoon in which to read, write or develop his friendship with the native Hawaiians (Kanakas) who were also assigned to hide curing duties, and who had their own ideas about work.[48]

One of Dana's biographers accuses him of being "too quick to ridicule all natives."[49] If this criticism is restricted to his attitude toward the native Californians, perhaps it is true. But his close friendship and high regard for the native Hawaiians with whom he shared several months of his life while curing hides at San Diego, is strong evidence against such a blanket assertion. The key to his differing attitudes about these two groups is, I believe, the fact that, as with the ship's crew, he lived and worked with the Hawaiians and really got to know them. In contrast to this level of intimacy, his contact with the Californians was brief. He was just beginning to learn Spanish, and did not become thoroughly acquainted with their character and customs. As we have seen, he failed to completely understand Don Juan Bandini's position, and in fact never really had a chance to arrive at the kind of sympathetic feeling for the Californians that someone like William Heath Davis would acquire in a lifetime spent with them. Dana was in California during the period when the United States was only ten years away from making it an American possession and displacing the rule of Mexico. He

---

[47]Ibid., 117.
[48]Ibid., 146.
[49]Robert L. Gale, *Richard Henry Dana*, 125.

had absorbed the same rationale as thousands of other Americans who believed that their destiny was to extend United States rule across the continent. Thus, his Yankee work habits contrasted greatly with the apparently easygoing life in California, and his real lack of intimacy with them contributed greatly to his generally negative opinion of the Californians.

For the Kanakas, however, he had the greatest affection. He would, he said, have entrusted anything he had, including his life, to these intelligent, kind-hearted people, and here at least was an instance where he did not allow his overly developed work-ethic to negatively influence his opinion. The Hawaiians had their own ideas about work, and like the "lazy" Californians and Indians, they had their own labor rhythms. Captain Frank Thompson, for example, could not persuade them to work at all, not even by offering them a month's wages in advance. Dana explained their philosophy: "So long as they had money, they would not work for fifty dollars a month, and when their money was gone, they would work for ten." Meanwhile, they would lounge around, smoke, get drunk and do anything they felt like doing. For Dana, who had harsh words for both the Indians and Californians' work habits, those of the native Hawaiians could be tolerated because of his understanding of their characters and his appreciation for their spirit of brotherhood and open-handed generosity. He was adopted, in fact, as a particular friend (an *aikane*, almost like a brother) by one of them, called Hope. "I do not believe I could have wanted any thing which he had that he would not have given me," Dana said. Indeed, he valued these people more than some of his own countrymen. As he put it, to ask for a favor or an "act of sacrifice," he would have applied to the Sandwich Islanders before going to any of his fellow Americans on the coast, "and should have expected to have seen it done, before my own countrymen had got half through counting the costs."[50]

The generosity of the Hawaiians was not infrequently contrasted with the mean-spirited behavior of some of the Americans in California. Hope was wasting away from a disease, evidently venereal, which he would never have contracted but for the Europeans and Americans. Like the

---

[50] *Two Years*, 146-151.

Indians of North America, propinquity to civilized nations spelled doom for the native Hawaiians, who were being decimated, as Dana pointed out, "at the rate of one fortieth of the entire population annually." Dana tried to help his friend, but could get no assistance from the hateful Captain Thompson who would not trouble himself for a "d——d Kanaka." Dana's concern for the plight of the Hawaiians strikes the reader as quite modern—a sympathetic reaction to the devastation visited upon a native tribal people by an expanding European and American business civilization. But Dana's attitude toward commerce and the people who were its representatives and products was always one of ambivalence—a mixture of aristocratic contempt (or puritanical revulsion) for its lax morality and sharp business practices, and an admiration for its efficiency and genuine accomplishments. It was, after all, his civilization. And his preference for the Hawaiians in California was perhaps understandable when he described at least one type of American living there, a "good specimen of the California ranger" whom he met in San Pedro. This gentleman was a tailor who went trapping, ended up in Los Angeles where he frequented the numerous places where liquor was sold, and was now at San Pedro trying to dry out and remove himself from further temptation. Dana pointed out the fellow's failure in this regard, and characterized his existence in California as "a specimen of the life of half of the Americans and English who are adrift over the whole of California."[51]

Nor did he spare the merchants and sea captains (of whom perhaps, after Frank Thompson, he had had enough) who traded along the coast. Smuggling and other sharp practices were commonplace along California's shores, as we have seen. Alfred Robinson demonstrated awareness of it without any of the moral judgement that accompanied Dana's reflections. William Heath Davis looked upon it as a positive good. They both knew that often getting around the Mexican customs rules could mean the difference between profits and losses for the ship's owners, and their own shares were wrapped up in it too. They also knew that it was of benefit to the Californians. Dana on the other hand, when noting the way that extra cargo was slipped ashore without being subject to the Mexican duties, and the cheating on ballast that took place "in ports of

<hr>

[51]Ibid., 244-246.

inferior nations" as he phrased it, remarked that such practices bred "an indifference to the rights of others."[52] Both points of view are characteristically American, and have been in tension in our society since its inception, a legacy of the "Puritan dilemma" that put at odds the practical and the ethical. It is fitting that a son of the Puritans should once again call attention to it in a California that was on its way to becoming the end point for the American dream.

---

[52]Ibid., 253.

CHAPTER V

William Henry Thomes

Nearly all of the Americans (and Europeans) who came to California during the Mexican period faulted the Spanish-speaking Californians for making such poor productive use of the rich lands that they possessed.[1] It was, these observers believed, a kind of moral failing: the Californians were simply too indolent. It was assumed that herding cattle was something less than genuine labor. Furthermore, the actual work was usually done by Indian peons or part-Indian vaqueros who knew nothing of the kind of industrial discipline and "work-ethic" upon which the foreigners' judgements were grounded. Even so intelligent and incisive an observer as Richard Henry Dana believed the Californians were not capable of developing their own lands. Two cultures possessing contrasting ideas about work were meeting in California. Manifest Destiny, a puritanical sense of superiority, economic and technical advantages—all of these combined to shape the attitude of Americans toward the Californians who were still locked into a semi-feudal, hacienda-based agriculture. It was clear to most American residents and visitors that California was languishing under the rule of Mexico, and that it was only a matter of time until a more "enlightened, civilized" power would establish a protectorate. White foreigners also viewed the part-Indian Californians through the lens of a racial Anglo-Saxonism which was then a prominent part of many an American's mentality. No doubt another visitor to California, William Henry Thomes, shared all of these sentiments in a vague way. In fact, Thomes would take the cultural differences he saw in California and give them an overtly racist "explanation."[2]

---

[1]See David J. Langum, "California and the Image of Indolence," 181-96. See also, James D. Hart, *American Images of Spanish California*.

[2]Criticism of the Mexican government in California was not confined solely to American residents. In 1828, José Bandini, the father of Juan Bandini, published "A Description of California in 1828." In it he

William Henry Thomes was clearly inspired by the success of Dana's *Two Years Before The Mast*, and decided to produce a book chronicling his own "adventures" in California as a young sailor. Like Dana ten years prior, Thomes had sailed "before the mast" to California at age eighteen, arriving in 1843. He too was on a hide and tallow ship out of Boston— the *Admittance*, belonging to William Appleton & Company, successor to Bryant & Sturgis. His first book, *On Land and Sea*, was an autobiographical account of his experiences, which Thomes attempted to enliven by some crudely fictional interpolations particularly expressive of adolescent libido.[3] The latter may indeed have had a real basis in Thomes' experiences while in the ports of California, but it had to be sufficiently disguised and made "innocent," even comic, in order to be acceptable to Thomes' Victorian audience of the 1880s. The book can therefore be divided into two categories: a straightforward account of Thomes' experiences in California which relied on his memory and on a diary kept by the Captain of the *Admittance*; this constituted the greater part of the narrative.[4] The second category consisted of those elements which Thomes believed (correctly, if intuitively) would give his book a popular appeal: some "love interest," a racist, stereotypical view of Mexicans (Thomes used this term throughout when he spoke about the Spanish-speaking Californians), and name-dropping—placing his alter ego in positions of intimacy with important people in the history of Mexican California.

The second category was to become a formula for success as Thomes went on to publish many more books of adventure designed to appeal to the day-dreaming or self-aggrandizing fantasies of an "adolescent" audience. In his next book, which continued his California adventure

criticized the policies of the Mexican government for restricting trade and for allowing the missions to continue to tie up productive land. He too viewed the Indians as "by nature slovenly and indolent," and the Spanish-Mexican Californians, he thought, "live in idleness; it is a rare person who is dedicated to increasing his fortune." He blamed this on the lack of available private land. 7-9, 24. For a discussion of American racial Anglo-Saxonism, see Reginald Horsman, *Race and Manifest Destiny*, 208-248.

[3]William H. Thomes, *On Land and Sea, or California in the Years 1843, '44, and '45*, henceforth cited as *On Land and Sea*. The book was originally serialized in *Ballou's Monthly Magazine*, in 1883. *Ballou's* was one of the first "penny publications" to popularize and exaggerate western heros like Kit Carson. See Henry Nash Smith, *Virgin Land*, 94-98.

[4]See George Stewart, *Take Your Bible in One Hand: The Life of William Henry Thomes*, 9, "...in spite of Thomes' incredible romancing...the general accuracy of this book cannot be doubted."

through the Mexican War, Thomes put himself and his young shipmate and friend, a French lad named "Lewey," at the center of a series of picaresque "heroic" adventures.[5] Thomes' books are puerile and superficial, and justifiably forgotten today. Yet the autobiographical content of the first two—the fact that Thomes was actually on the scene during the time about which he writes—and the popularity of books which purveyed negative stereotypes of the Mexican Californians, make the works of interest as artifacts of American culture.[6]

Thomes was unquestionably in California from 1843 through 1845, and almost certainly also afterwards for some months spanning at least part of the American conquest. *On Land and Sea* can be usefully compared to *Two Years Before The Mast*, particularly since Thomes explicitly invoked Dana throughout the book, and his experiences paralleled those of Dana in a number of instances. Thomes was by no means a skillful writer, nor was he highly educated or insightful. He was a middle-class person of rather ordinary intellect who reflected as well as reinforced the popular prejudices displayed in his books. By the time he published his second California "novel"in 1885 (he called them novels, which doubtless thus permitted his romantic extravagances), forty years had passed since California had come into American hands, and the state was on the eve of another great immigration boom. Thomes could validly present himself as a pioneer "explaining" California to a new generation of Americans headed there. The California themes others had expressed, Thomes would also play upon, but with an additional facet that by the 1880s the old widespread view of the Californians as lazy and unfit had now hardened into a racist caricature, and Thomes helped to "innocently" legitimize this bigotry.[7] In terms of the perpetuation of prejudice,

---

[5]William H. Thomes, Lewey and I; or Sailor Boys' Wanderings: A Sequel to "On Land and Sea," henceforth cited as Lewey and I.

[6]H. H. Bancroft, Works, XXII, 746, says that Thomes, age 16 at the time, came to California on the Admittance in 1843, returned east on the schooner California in 1846, and came again to California in 1849 on board the Edward Everett.

[7]Thomes cannot be solely blamed for views that were widely expressed in the 1840s. In addition to the writers dealt with in this book, such as Thomas Jefferson Farnham (see below Ch. 10), see also for example, Phillip St. George Cooke, The Conquest of New Mexico and California: An Historical & Personal Narrative, 20, where he states that when he led the Mormon Batallion against the New Mexicans in Santa Fe during the Mexican War, they "became panic-stricken at once on the approach of such an imposing array of horsemen of a superior race...."

Dana's work can be seen as a lost opportunity to extend the same sympathy and understanding he had for the sailors and Kanakas, to the Californians and Indians. Thomes on the other hand seemed to have spent much more time than Dana on shore and among the Californians. Yet he almost never ceased to portray them negatively—at least, the men. Both Dana and Thomes had certain experiences with women in California. Dana chose not to discuss his. Thomes featured his own amorous adventures, but in a way that would not compromise his pose of innocence and naivete.

On Land and Sea told the story of a couple of mischievous and fun-loving boys out to have a good time in California by playing practical jokes and flirting with any young women at every opportunity. Thomes and his friend Lewey were indeed "like hornets, always stinging and buzzing, and making fun where fun was possible."[8] Yet Thomes described scenes of California life with a great deal of accuracy in addition to his romancing.[9] He recorded the voyages of the *Admittance* up and down the coast from San Diego to San Francisco, and he recreated dialogues with people who lived in California at that time. The major "characters" in his book are almost all historical figures. The book was essentially an autobiography in which the author (consciously, and almost always recognizably) tried to enliven his narrative with what George Stewart has called "a tawdry gilding easily separable from the really genuine material beneath."[10]

William Henry Thomes commented on most of the people and places that Richard Henry Dana had found of interest in California, though everything was treated much more lightly. Dana had his Frank Thompson, the Captain of the *Pilgrim* whose sadistic flogging of several crew members so profoundly affected him, but the Captain of Thomes' ship the *Admittance* was kind-hearted, treated the ship's boys gently and overlooked their mistakes and adolescent pranks. Captain Peter Peterson, who continued as Thomes' friend for forty years after Thomes served

[8]Thomes, *On Land and Sea*, 13.

[9]James D. Hart, op. cit., 31, says of Thomes: "By the time that Thomes wrote of his adventures they were forty years in the past, and a man near sixty recalling his teen-age life is more likely to be given to some romancing, even though Thomes could also recall sharp and unattractive details of daily life."

[10]Thomes, *On Land and Sea*, 9.

under him on the *Admittance*, was a Dane, thirty three years old, tall and muscular and "strong as a mule, and, like a mule, inclined to kick when things did not go just as he thought they should...." But the boys never tasted his wrath, and he treated the rest of the crew well—as long as they did their jobs. Only once was there any trouble between the Captain and the crew. Stirred up by a single malcontent, the men began to complain about the amount of work they had to do, and about the food. Thomes said they were dissatisfied with the fresh beef so readily available in California, and were demanding salt pork or beef instead! Captain Peterson quickly quelled this would-be mutiny by singling out the ring-leader, one Charley, also a Dane by birth. The Captain threw Charley to the deck then clapped him in irons, and for the rest of the voyage Charley was hazed and given all the worst jobs. Thomes did not see this as an injustice. Rather it suited him and his friend Lewey just fine. Charley had tried to bully them, and they had little sympathy for him.[11]

While on board the *Admittance* Thomes did witness a flogging, but not of anyone in his crew. They were anchored next to the USS *Dale* at Monterey Bay, and Thomes saw two sailors from this American navy ship tied up and beaten. He was told by some of his shipmates not to look at this, but out of boyish curiosity he watched anyway. The first sailor to be beaten was a young American. This fellow begged and cursed as he was being lashed, and because he had cried out, he was jeered contemptuously by his mates. The other one was an older man who Thomes said had been on a British man-o'-war. When they removed his shirt Thomes could see on his back the evidence of previous beatings. This veteran endured the punishment without uttering a sound, not even flinching. Thomes claimed he was made "dizzy and sick at heart, after witnessing the scene on the Dale."[12]

But from this incident Thomes drew no profound lessons about human nature or men in adversity. It did not happen aboard his ship, and he was sufficiently distanced from it so that it simply took its place among the myriad other impressions of life in California—most of them pleasant or amusing, a few horrifying, but none that were seriously

---

[11]Ibid., 12-13, 163-169.
[12]Ibid., 93-96.

threatening to the moral equilibrium of a young man who could observe
them all in safety. Dana had been only too conscious that his class and
connections protected him from the excesses of a Frank Thompson, yet
he was deeply affected by the flogging he was forced to witness, and it
influenced his life. Thomes on the other hand, though good at capturing
the surface excitement and color, and momentarily disgusted with such
scenes, remained basically unaffected by them. On the way to California, for example, the *Admittance* was chased down by a slave ship in need
of water. Thomes happened to be among the crew that rowed Captain
Peterson and the first mate over to the slaver, which was armed to the
teeth and had virtually compelled the *Admittance* to "heave to." Again
out of curiosity, Thomes peered through an iron grate at the slaves below
in the hold and described what he saw:

> The steam and the stench that came up those hatchways were so terrible that
> I could only give a glance, and saw that the unhappy slaves were all seated,
> chained, handcuffed, and crowded together so that there was not an inch of
> spare room, as the negroes were dovetailed together, and when one swayed by
> the motion of the vessel, the others were obliged to do the same, or feel the
> rough grating of the iron rods that passed through their shackles, and pre-
> vented them from tearing each other in their rage and despair.

This moving description might have become the basis of a transforma-
tion and development in Thomes' outlook. To a Dana it would have
been a contributing factor in a process of maturation, but not for
Thomes. Thomes imitated Dana in a number of places, but the imita-
tions were all superficial. He was never to draw on his experiences
for some of the deeper personal insights that make *Two Years BeforeThe
Mast* an enduring masterpiece. Perhaps the forty years that separated the
events of his youth from his writings about them denied him this wisdom.[13]

Seeing the slaves was a shock at the time, but the effect was temporary. Prior to this encounter, Thomes and Lewey had been talking about
running slaves from Africa themselves, and soon after it they thought
nothing of playing a practical joke on the ship's cook, a black man who
kept them awake at night with his nightmares.[14]

[13]Ibid., 30-39.
[14]Ibid., 29, 49-51.

If *On Land and Sea* lacks the literary merit or humanistic depth of Dana's classic, it is nonetheless an entertaining young sailor's-eye-view of California in the early 1840s, and it adds some interesting brush strokes to any picture of pre-conquest California society. Though Thomes did not have Dana's gifts—or his Brahmin perspective—his attitudes are useful for what they can tell us about a rather ordinary middle-class American of the nineteenth century. Thomes came originally from Portland, Maine, where he had been born on May 5, 1824. Both his parents died when he was a young man, and he was taken to Boston by an uncle and left in the care of a guardian. He was indifferently educated, first in a private school then in the public schools, which his biographer surmised to mean that his family was neither rich nor poor, but of the middling sort.[15] Thomes himself said that going to sea had been an excellent alternative to remaining in school where he did not excel and was not happy, or to staying in Boston as "a nuisance to all my relatives and guardian...."[16]

Perhaps it was more for his mental health (and that of his family) that William H. Thomes went to sea. But once there, he quickly adjusted after an initial bout of homesickness. In three months he learned to laugh at the kind of storm that frightened him on his second day out of Boston; the waves that made him seasick then "were not more than potato hills as compared to the seas we encountered off Cape Horn...." While struggling off the stormy Cape, Thomes "looked long and earnestly" at one of the bleak Diego islands where an older brother he had never known was buried. His brother had been killed there while sealing many years before. Like Dana staring at Dead Man's Island off San Pedro, Thomes indulged in a moment of melancholy. It was to have no permanent significance, however, a mere interlude on the way to California. [17]

The first sign that the *Admittance* was approaching California was an immense floating redwood log sighted while they were several days away from the coast. Then on March 4, 1843, they rounded Point Pinos and sailed into Monterey Bay. They were met by a cutter from the USS *Dale*, whose crewmembers were markedly uncomplimentary about California

---

[15]Stewart, op. cit., 1-7.
[16]Thomes, *On Land and Sea*, 6.
[17]Ibid., 59-60.

and its inhabitants. Monterey, Thomes quoted them, was "a bloody hole anyway, and not worthy of a sailor's notice," and the adobe building visible on the rock ledge of the shore they pointed out as "the bloody greasers' custom house." Thomes was thus duly introduced to California.[18]

Such ethnocentric comments run as a kind of refrain through both of Thomes' works on California. Immediately after hearing the sailors' assessment of California and its people, Thomes himself chimed in with his own appraisal of their habits. The Mexican, he said, was basically afraid of water. He knew that it was good to drink, but it was "useless to him as an article to cleanse the hands, the body, or wash the face." He found the Californians (with the usual upper-class exceptions) backward and lazy. But he also now added a more overtly racist element to his characterizations. This he applied to the lower classes with whom a young sailor would be most likely to associate in California, and whose admixture of Indian blood—and in some cases also African—made them darker and even more "different."[19]

Thomes' attitudes were a curious blend of his own middle-class New England origins and his subordinate position as a common sailor. As a young man in California, and himself in a lower social position, the issue of his status must have been frequently made evident to him. Dana had resented what he perceived to be the supercilious behavior of Alfred Robinson, and embraced the lower-class Sandwich Islanders. But Dana's social position in the world was secure. For William Thomes, perhaps the only thing that set him off from the lower class Californians was a white skin. In retrospect, Thomes may have perceived that he too was destined for better things than being an ordinary seaman all his life. Yet unlike Dana, whose experiences in California caused him at least partially to grapple with the varieties of the "human condition," Thomes in his autobiography never got beyond or behind his stereotypical views. He did, however, in an 1887 interview with one of H. H. Bancroft's researchers (a sure badge of his pioneer status in California) present a more restrained

---

[18]Ibid., 73. The term "greaser," which Thomes used here, did not come into common use until after the gold rush. See Leonard Pitt, *The Decline of the Californios*, 48-68.

[19]For a discussion of this process of racial stereotyping, see David Weber, ed., *Foreigners in Their Native Land: The Historical Roots of the Mexican Americans*.

picture of the Californians he had known in his youth. On the whole, Thomes admitted that he had grown to like the Mexican character as he knew it in California (he used no racial slurs here). People were courteous and hospitable. They would welcome a stranger into their homes, where he could stay as long as he liked, eat when he wanted, and no one bothered him or bothered about him. Evenings were devoted to fandangos and musical entertainments. There were few books and few people who could read them, though there was an oral tradition carried on by the older generation, who would tell stories and relate events of the past. Sexual mores were strict, he maintained; ladies were never allowed to see a man alone (except a brother or father) "until the very day that they were married, and even then the fathers exercised a supervision over their daughters...." Adopting the merchants' point of view, Thomes' only complaint was that certain Californians would at every opportunity "cheat" the American businessmen who sold them goods. The merchants compensated for this by raising their prices and passing shoddy goods, so that, in Thomes' words, "it was an even thing all round."[20]

But the people who would or could not pay their debts were not the "best" people in California. At Santa Barbara, which Thomes called "the pleasantest happiest quietest handsomest [sic] little place that we had seen on the Coast," lived some of the oldest and wealthiest families in California. These people always paid their debts. Those who did not had often made promises they were unable to keep, which Thomes said was " the custom of the Country and the people." In his retrospective for Bancroft, Thomes idealized the "most beautiful girls and the most courteous and able Spanish Mexican gentlemen" that he met in California, while in his autobiographical novels he presented consistently stereotyped images of the poorer classes. His overall assessment of life in California, from the vantage point of his success forty years later, was of

> a simple Arcadian sort of life with a happy contented people who were rich in lands and cattle, cared nothing for wealth, firm in their friendships, bitter and deadly in their hostilities, not always truthful, and the lower classes not always honest, but the upper classes gentlemanly, polished, with a natural born courtesy that seemed to be innate.[21]

---

[20]William Henry Thomes, *Recollections of Old Times in California or, California Life in 1843*, 13-16.
[21]Ibid., 17-24.

This makes it clear that Thomes by no means lumped all of the Californians together in his judgements, though sometimes, like Dana and Alfred Robinson, he attributed certain qualities to the Californians in general without specifying a particular class. No confusion existed, however, about that quintessentially upper class Californian, Don José de la Guerra y Noriega of Santa Barbara. In *On Land and Sea*, Thomes called him "one of the best-hearted and most honest grandees of the country....He always paid his debts very promptly, and it was a pleasure to sell his family goods, for he didn't ask for six years credit, and then repudiate his obligations."[22]

Reflecting the perspective of his business-oriented employers (and no doubt his business-oriented society), Thomes' judgements of the Californians—ones he seemed to have carried throughout his life—centered significantly on their commercial behavior. Honest trade transactions and responsible fulfillment of contract obligations were virtues Americans could understand and respect. California, however, possessed no working judicial system which could settle disputes about business transactions. Local *alcaldes* tried to mediate disagreements, but they were not authorized to hear cases involving more than $200.00. Furthermore, if no agreement could be reached between differing parties, all that an alcalde could do was issue a certificate saying conciliation had been tried! There were no higher appellate courts, and recourse could only be had to the Governor, whose decision could be based as much on personality as on law.[23] Thomes, therefore, appreciated the reliable business practices of Don José de la Guerra (several of whose sons-in-law were themselves astute businessmen such as Alfred Robinson), while pointing out that it was dangerous to refuse even "the meanest ranchero what he desired," because he might boycott the merchant ship, or worse, threaten the life of the ship's agent. Such people obviously operated with a different set of standards, and though Thomes cited no actual examples of any Californians menacing a supercargo, he did say that the *Admittance*'s agent (Henry Mellus) would not take any chances. Mellus just charged the rich for what the poor took.[24]

---

[22]Op. cit., 107.
[23]See Woodrow James Hansen, *The Search for Authority in California*, 46.
[24]Thomes, *On Land and Sea*, 107.

Thomes spoke well of Henry Mellus, who as a young man had come to California with Richard Henry Dana in the *Pilgrim*, and he liked Mellus well enough—except when the supercargo seemed to be putting profits ahead of the crew's welfare. Then Thomes threw over his employer's outlook and took Mellus to task. At Santa Cruz the sailor's were obliged to "raft off lumber and shingles...up to our necks in water twelve hours a day, for a week at a time, owing to the greed of our agent, who cared nothing for the health of the crew, if money could be made for some one." At such times as these, the men would curse Henry Mellus and California.[25]

Thomes also encountered and commented on many other personalities in California who would have prominent places in the history of this period. In fact, Thomes became a bit of a "name dropper" and felt obliged or compelled to recount his own relationships with several of the individuals whom Dana had spoken of in *Two Years Before The Mast*. One of the first people he saw when he arrived at Monterey in 1843 was Thomas Oliver Larkin, who had just been made United States Consul. Larkin was ferried out to the *Admittance*, and Thomes was able to observe this influential businessman. According to Thomes, Larkin at first appeared deaf, cupping his hand to his ear when spoken to. But on further evidence, Thomes could see that this was a tactic on Larkin's part, and that the Consul heard just fine when it suited his purposes. Thomes credited Larkin with foiling every British plot to seize California, and said that it was by Larkin's advice that American warships looked in at California ports frequently to "let the Mexicans and English agents see that we were a power at that time on the ocean." The Monterey merchant had also apparently absorbed the customs of California, because he was hospitable to strangers, and even lent books from his library to Thomes while the *Admittance* was at Monterey.[26]

Business had been slow on the coast, so Larkin informed them, due to a serious drought that had destroyed the grasses on which the cattle fed; thus the Californians were short of their major export items, hides and

---

[25]Ibid., 178.

[26]Ibid., 75. I could find no reference to Thomes in the *Larkin Papers*. Whether Thomes actually knew Larkin, or was expanding his own historical connections forty years later, we have no way of knowing for certain.

tallow. It is probable that this was behind Thomes' complaints about Californians who did not meet their financial obligations. But it was business as usual in terms of getting around the Mexican customs duties. To illustrate the laxity of the customs officials themselves, Thomes said that a Mexican officer left on board the ship at Monterey to prevent smuggling, drank a bottle of their Boston sherry and passed out on deck until the next morning. During the night, a sailor accidentally broke a customs office seal over one of the hatches. The ship's crew simply re-sealed the hatch and the sleeping officer never knew. The *Admittance*, like every other merchant ship in California, resorted to smuggling to avoid the bulk of the customs duties. Thomes pointed out that there were, stowed away under fifty or sixty tons of salt, "valuable articles, kept out of sight until brought to light at San Diego, where we landed the salt, and took in stone ballast in its place." No customs officials had bothered to dig beneath the salt in their inspections.[27]

While at San Diego, Thomes met another prominent American who had linked his fortunes with those of California, Captain Henry Delano Fitch. Thomes and his shipmate Lewey went with Captain Peterson to dinner at Fitch's house, which Thomes called "one of the largest in the town." Here he discovered that Fitch, whom Dana had called a fat, vulgar Yankee, was indeed rather stout, and obviously a Yankee, but nevertheless, echoing William Dane Phelps' opinion, "one of the most generous, whole-souled Americans on the coast." Thomes claimed that Fitch always laughed at Dana's estimation of him, but that he was a sensitive man and must have felt hurt by it. If Fitch confirmed Phelps' assertion, that Dana was thrown out of his house intoxicated, Thomes made no mention of it. Fitch would return in the sequel to give the boys some advice about their love lives.[28]

The *Admittance* called at San Pedro at the end of June 1843, and while at this port of Los Angeles, the Captain brought on board "Don Juan Bandini, and Messrs. Woolskill [Wolfskill] , Pryor, Carpenter, Temple, and Stearns," the leading businessmen of southern California. Of all these gentlemen, Thomes was most interested in Bandini because of Dana's description of him. In contrast to the latter, Thomes found Ban-

[27]Ibid., 87.
[28]Ibid., 263.

dini "ordinary." He was "thin and dark, with eyes that were heavy, a face that showed age, and...deep wrinkles around his temples." He had a stoop to his shoulders and a narrow, weak chest. Apparently Thomes could see none of the graceful qualities in him that had impressed Richard Henry Dana.[29]

Much more impressive to the young William Henry Thomes were the mountain men he saw, starting with Isaac Graham at Santa Cruz. He met Graham, he said, when he was entrusted by Henry Mellus with a message for that notorious character. He took it to Graham's sawmill in the Santa Cruz Mountains. Graham had also owned a still that was a gathering place for the more unruly foreign elements in California. His deportation by the California authorities in 1840 may have suppressed some of his more objectionable activities, however, because Thomes made no mention of Graham's still or any of his unsavory acquaintances. Instead, he glorified Graham as a prominent player in "all the various revolutions." Thomes claimed that Graham was so feared by the Californians, that just the mention of his name would cause an entire company of them to flee, so deadly was he with a rifle, and so courageous against his foes.[30]

More and more American mountain men were coming into California to settle in the mid-1840s, and Thomes seemed to have accurately registered this. He also did his part to reinforce the growing legend of their ruthless bravery and prowess with the rifle. At Santa Barbara in 1844, Thomes noted few changes from the ship's last visit, except to say that "we found a dozen more trappers from across the Rocky Mountains, and they made things lively in the town, but no one dared to interfere in their movements, for each man carried a rifle, and knew how to use it, when occasion required." Some of them visited the ship in search of powder and lead, and laughed when told of the rumor that General Castro, the Mexican Comandante, intended to drive the foreigners out. Saying that they had no fear of Castro, as long as they had plenty of ammunition, the trappers gave the ship's crew a demonstration of their marksmanship. They wanted to borrow one of the ship's boats to go after sea otter, but Captain Peterson declined to give it to them. He did not

---

[29]Ibid., 252-257.
[30]Ibid., 180.

want to break Mexican law (at least, not obviously or in a case where little profit could come to the ship owners), and the men had no licences to
hunt for otter. Later at San Diego Thomes saw a number of sea otters in
the kelp, and learned from the hunters there the technique for taking
them, which again underscored the skill with firearms of these Americans. The otters, they told him, had to be killed instantly, with the first
shot. If only wounded, they would sink to the bottom and cling to the
kelp in death. Even when killed at once, there was just a brief amount of
time to collect them before they sank.[31]

Thomes considered San Diego to be one of the best and safest anchor-
ages on the coast. But the people there failed to impress him. He thought
the town was "the deadest, sleepiest hole in California, and the inhabitants had not enough energy to go in their houses, such as they were,
when it rained, or to crawl into the sunshine when it was pleasant." The
climate was wonderful, however, and there was an abundance of fruit—
when the locals mustered enough energy to plant. Disease, said Thomes
(with the exception of smallpox!) was almost unknown in San Diego.[32]

At San Diego too, Thomes saw something else floating in the kelp.
He and his shipmates watched as the body of an old Indian was slowly
borne out to the open ocean on the tide. They watched, but as Thomes
explained, " no one cared for it, and so it drifted to sea, and was eaten by
the sharks." This image could almost stand as a metaphor for the fate of
the California Indians generally, and Thomes' appraisal of them placed
him with the mainstream of his countrymen. The first Indians he saw
were from the Carmel Mission. They had come into Monterey with a
few beaver and deer skins which they traded for liquor. Then they got
drunk and yelled, he said, until some Californian rode out with a lasso
and broke up their party, roping one of them and dragging him through
the street till he was half dead. "Such cruelty was not rare," Thomes
commented, "but then the Indians did not amount to much in those
days." They went around the countryside naked—a custom that shocked
Thomes and his pal Lewey, but which they managed to get used to in
time. And just as Dana had marveled at the Indian ox-cart drivers who
would not help the sailors load the cargo into their carts, Thomes too

[31]Ibid., 258, 305.
[32]Ibid., 259.

alleged to have experienced a similar incident in which some Indian ox-cart drivers refused to help the sailors from the *Admittance* carry boxes and bales up from the beach.[33]

Thomes also had his acquaintances among the Sandwich Islanders on the coast, and he agreed with Dana about them. They were good-natured and gentle people, who had "a perfect horror of harsh words or blows from quick-tempered officers." Their work habits met with his approval too. When treated kindly, he thought, they made willing and faithful workers, honest and capable of considerable hard labor when it was necessary, "but they would not endure abuse." Perhaps this was what clearly separated them from the Indians he saw, who appeared to be both lazy and passive. A solid, middle-class American would never have admitted to either of such character defects.[34]

William Henry Thomes was such an American and he unquestioningly took American life as the normative foundation for his judgements about other cultures. In this he was doubtless typical of most nineteenth century Americans and Europeans, confident that their civilizations represented the pinnacle of human achievement, or at least the highest point reached so far.[35] People and practices that lay outside of the yardstick of their national cultures were often deemed inferior, and the greater the differences, the more negative the estimation. Thomes was not an intellectual. He did not, like Richard Henry Dana, see the absurdities in both the politics of California and the United States. He was, however, perceptive enough to identify several of the factors involved in the "revolutions" that were a hallmark of California life during his time there. He believed, nevertheless, that Mexicans simply had a penchant for comic-opera revolutions. He recorded that the soldiers were in a state of revolt most of the time because they were unable to obtain their wages, and thus were easily "tempted by revolutionary chieftains." On a shore leave at Monterey, in a typical practical joke of the sort that occurs throughout *On Land and Sea*, Thomes and his pal Lewey tossed some firecrackers in the midst of a group of Indians who were playing a game

---

[33]Ibid., 83-87, 181.

[34]Ibid., 185-186.

[35]For Americans, this was a conviction with its beginnings in the earliest English experiences in the New World. See James Axtell, *The Invasion Within*, 3-6, where he discusses the bases for this "unlimited confidence in the superiority of their way of life...."

with sticks. The Indians quickly scattered, believing, according to Thomes, that a new revolution had broken out and that the soldiers were impressing Indians into the army to do all the fighting, "as was customary in the country." And at a later date in Santa Barbara, when a salute was fired in honor of Don José de la Guerra, Thomes claimed that everyone fled the town except for

> forty of the principal men of the place [who] wrote proclamations, outside of the village, calling upon their friends to rally around them, and see that they were installed as treasurer, or secretary of State, or some other good paying office in the new government....[36]

Thomes had put his finger on at least some of the goals and means of the Californians in their revolutions, though he was not in a position, and probably lacked the motivation, to develop a greater understanding.[37] A common sailor, and a youthful one at that, had little occasion to discuss politics with the leading men of California, despite Thomes' claim to have known such men as Thomas Larkin and José de la Guerra. In fact, Thomes' status was most forcefully brought home to him in his relationships with California women. As ship's boys Thomes and his friend Lewey were given the job of rowing customers out to the *Admittance* for shopping. They were often called upon too for the pleasant task of carrying young women through the surf to and from the ship's boat. A major component of Thomes' romanticizing was to make these occasions into opportunities for the boys to be rewarded with kisses for their gallantry. How much of this was wish-fulfillment fantasy can never be known for certain. But Thomes revealed at least one time when he was definitely not kissed. This incident, whether it actually happened as Thomes told it or not, showed that Thomes was well aware of his position. Ordered to take a "bundle" to Mr. Alfred Robinson in Santa Barbara, Thomes did so, and commented on the kind treatment he received from Robinson.[38] Once again he disagreed with Richard

---

[36]Thomes, *On Land and Sea*, 113, 244.

[37]See George Tays, "Revolutionary California: The Political History of California During the Mexican Period, 1822-1846," iv-v, where he states that after Echeandia's rule, the desire for mission properties "soon engendered mistrust and avarice among those who were in a position to profit by the missions."

[38]It seems that Alfred Robinson was not even in California at this time. In December of 1842 he had returned to the United States overland through Mexico with gold discovered in the San Gabriel Mountains and entrusted to him by Abel Stearns. He deposited the gold—first to be discovered in California—at

Henry Dana and pointed out that Robinson "did not put on airs because he was a man of position, and I a common sailor." Then, accompanied by Robinson, the de la Guerras came down to the shore where Thomes was granted the privilege of carrying one of Don José's daughters—"the handsomest unmarried daughter in the town." In this instance, Thomes entertained no illusions that this act entitled him to any greater familiarity. It was made obvious that the young lady "cared no more for me than she did for one of her father's peons, for there was a vast difference in our stations in life, and a common sailor, in her estimation, was not an elevated specimen of humanity." Thomes turned the whole thing into humor at his own expense by having the young woman say in Spanish, assuming Thomes would not understand, that he had an honest face, but "*muy feo*" [very ugly].[39]

In his sequel, *Lewey and I,* Thomes was to let his fancy carry him away to such an extent that he had the wife of Don José Castro, the Comandante General of California at the beginning of the Mexican War (Thomes mistakenly called him "Don Juan Castro" in *On Land and Sea*)[40] reward him with kisses after he saved her life.[41] But in his first book he was more circumspect. Upper class California women at least were models of propriety, and Dana of course was incorrect about their propensity for infidelity. "I never heard," said Thomes, "of a single case of domestic unfaithfulness on the part of the rich señoras...." Yet he confirmed Dana when he pointed out that these ladies were too carefully watched over by their husbands, brothers or fathers to be at all flirtatious; the men would have mortally avenged any insult to their women "had one been offered by an unprincipled adventurer."[42]

But with the "Indian half-breed women" as Thomes called them, it was a different story. Speaking from his own experience, Thomes said that these women "were not patterns of goodness, but no one cared

the Philadelphia mint on July 8, 1843. He did not return again to California until after the conquest. So either Thomes was mistaken, after forty years, about the identity of the person to whom he was to deliver his bundle, or he simply used Robinson's name to add "historical authenticity." See Doyce B. Nunis, Jr., *A Commentary on Alfred Robinson,* 3-4, and Adele Ogden, "Alfred Robinson, New England Merchant in Mexican California," 201-202.

[39]Thomes, *On Land and Sea,* 235-243.
[40]Ibid., 267.
[41]Thomes, *Lewey and I,* 264-265.
[42]Thomes, *On Land and Sea,* 109.

whether they were or not." It was in fact these women who would provide Thomes and Lewey with the "romantic" element that Thomes exploited in both his works on California.[43]

In *On Land and Sea*, Thomes had the boys attend fandangos and make love to the "half-breed" girls, in spite of and in opposition to Captain Peterson's warnings and objections that such women were low and unacceptable. And Thomes did not try to conceal his amours; he displayed them. He just made certain that the context was clear. The reader was supposed to believe (on the surface) that the boys' flirtations were of the same order as their practical jokes and their petty thefts from the ship's galley—the naive or adolescent acts of innocents. Captain Peterson, whose ideas of propriety Thomes felt were too "rigid," was to be the first of a series of older, responsible representatives of American society who would try to warn the boys away from the "half-breed" women. But the boys did not listen (if they had, Thomes would most likely have been without one of the devices that contributed to the popularity of his novels). Instead, they just posted a lookout for the Captain when they went to the dances.[44]

It must have been common knowledge, even in Thomes' Victorian era, that sailors enjoyed themselves with women while in port, and that the ports of California were no exception to this rule. It was just not something that was made a theme for public discourse—at least not until the turn of the century. Thomes knew intuitively that Americans liked to believe in their own special virtue. He thus found a way around the prohibitions of his day by giving his callow alter ego the façade of innocence. The boys could then attend the fandangos and dance with girls who encouraged them to squeeze more tightly, and who sweated as they danced, so that Thomes could even describe the musky smell of his partner! At least in *On Land and Sea*, Thomes was still trying to be somewhat true to his actual experiences, so he directed his amorous interests toward the "half-breed" girls who would very likely have been the only ones open to his attentions. He spelled this out in his description of an entertainment that he and Lewey attended with Captain Peterson, at the Refugio Rancho north of Santa Barbara. There, they each danced once, clearly out of their hosts' "good nature and politeness to us...."

[43]Ibid., 109.
[44]Ibid., 27, 117-19.

Thomes admitted that the gracious Californians tried to make them feel "as though we had been gentlemen of high degree, and worth fifty thousand head of cattle," but he could see that his dance partner "was condescending, in her own estimation in dancing with me," which he said was "gall and wormwood to a boy of ambitious ideas."[45]

The boys soon had enough humiliation, and wandered away from the rancho hacienda. They heard music and came across another fandango in more modest surroundings, where they found some girls who

> were several grades lower in social position than the senoritas we had just left, but, to our eyes, they were nearly as beautiful, although their skins were not quite as fair, and their long, black hair a trifle coarser, but their eyes were as brilliant and flashing, and more inviting and free...and just the kind of females to attract a boy's fancy, and flatter their [sic] vanity by being noticed.

Thomes traded a pair of white stockings for a kiss from Anita, one of the young ladies there. Then, in a mixture of comedy and prurience, he professed his love to her, and she responded that he could not really love her, having only known her for an hour. Always conscious of racial and class differences, Thomes put into Anita's mouth another objection. His skin was light; hers was dark. "If I was like you," she told him, "perhaps you would love me when you become a man." They retired to a nearby grape arbor where the kissing continued. When Thomes was ready to leave, he presented Anita with several silver dollars, and the reader is left to draw his own conclusions![46]

Just as they were about to make their exits, Captain Peterson showed up and once again cautioned them to stay away from the kind of girls who "weren't nice." But what were young sailors to do? "Respectable" women in California were decidedly beyond their reach, yet they were being told to stay away from the lower class "half-breed" women. But these women were earthy and, as Thomes said, "free"; they were attractive and accessible, but they were not the kind of women that good, middle-class American (or French) boys were supposed to want to marry. Yet this was exactly what Thomes and Lewey were now professing to desire. For Thomes, part of the comic appeal of both his California books depended on the "absurd" aspirations of youth, the chief one

---

[45]Ibid., 117-18, 227-31.
[46]Ibid., 231-34.

being marriage to the two girls they met at Rancho Refugio—Anita, and
Lewey's lady, Engracia. As the *Admittance* was about to return to
Boston, the boys pledged to remain in California. One year from the day
they had first left Boston Harbor, they went once more to San Pedro.
There the boys discussed how to get discharged and paid "so that we
could buy a ranche [sic], and marry Anita and Engracia...." They talked
about the necessity for Thomes to become a Catholic. Lewey, being
French, had no need to convert, and told his friend that it was only a
minor obstacle, which prompted Thomes to say that Lewey's attitude
was "decidedly Californian." The foreign residents in California, he
thought, "changed their creeds at the dictation of love, or self-interest."[47]

On Land and Sea thus ends with the boys faking smallpox so that they
will be left behind in San Diego to pursue their plans for marriage and
for becoming California rancheros. This is a major thread in the sequel,
Lewey and I, where Thomes indulged in more racism toward Mexican
Californians, and where he achieved even greater excesses of name-
dropping. He claimed to have met almost every major figure involved in
the American conquest of California, on both sides, from José Castro to
John C. Fremont. He put himself and Lewey at the center of the action,
carrying messages between Castro and Fremont, and dispatches for
Consul Larkin.[48] It soon becomes clear that with *Lewey and I*, Thomes
had moved from the primarily autobiographical with romantic overtones, to the primarily romantic with autobiographical overtones. Readers might believe correctly that Thomes knew the country he was
writing about, even some (possibly most) of the people he mentioned.
But these were now being used as historical props for Thomes' crude
fantasy of "heroism" and "romance." And in the course of their continuous heroics—as was meant to be—the boys managed to evade their
socially unacceptable marriages. They actually in the course of their
adventures avoid marriage to a number of California women of the
"half-breed" sort, for which they were congratulated by their American
friends in California. It was these people, like Captain Peterson, who all
along had been discouraging them from marrying "beneath" them.

[47]Ibid., 234, 313, 325.

[48]This is clearly fictional. I could find no evidence to support Thomes' claims in either the *Larkin Papers* or in Donald Jackson and Mary Lee Spence, eds., *The Expeditions of John Charles Frémont*.

Thomes had Henry D. Fitch try to appeal to their sense of shame. "To think," he told them, "that boys who have been well brought up, and have a little education, should lower their record by taking half-caste girls for wives. I never heard of such greenness."[49] That Fitch had himself taken a California woman for a wife, albeit an upper class one, and that he had indeed eloped with her in opposition to the wishes of the Governor of California at the time, José María Echeandía—these were facts about his "friend" which Thomes appeared not to know.[50]

Lewey and I, narrowly considered, may not qualify as autobiography, in spite of the internal evidence showing that Thomes had very likely been actually present in California in 1846. Nevertheless Thomes continued to posit an explicit identity between himself and the central character of *Lewey and I*, and if too many of his exploits lack the resonance of real experience, the book is still of considerable interest for what it reveals of Thomes' attitudes and prejudices (perhaps increasingly colored by the new wave of immigrants then coming into the United States in the 1880s), and for his assessment of California and the American conquest, forty years later.

With their sham smallpox, the boys were left behind to stay at the hide house at San Diego, the one made famous by Dana, to whom Thomes may have owed more of a debt for his material than he was willing to acknowledge. There, under the care of a tough old sailor called Scotch Jack, they finalized their plans to marry and live a California life, which they professed to believe meant that they would only have to "pass our days in idleness, riding horseback over ranches, and rounding our cattle, in imagination, when we wanted a little pleasant excitement, aside from fandangos and cock-fighting." Obviously aware that this was a caricature of California life, Thomes presented it as further evidence of the ridiculous naivete of his youth, but one with an edge of sarcasm directed at the Californians and their life-style. Thomes also continued to have the older men look out for the boys, giving them advice and trying to discourage them from their marriage plans. Even an ignorant sailor like Scotch Jack asked them how their families would feel "if you married a bloody greaser?" And as if to emphasize what this might

---

[49]Thomes, *Lewey and I*, 27.

[50]For an entertaining account of this elopement, see Richard Batman, *The Outer Coast*, 221-22.

mean, Thomes had Scotch Jack pointedly stare at a "half-breed Indian woman" who was trying to attract the attention of some of the Kanakas, for the unstated though obvious purpose of selling her favors. But the boys failed to get the message about what kind of woman it was that they were considering for marriage. To be a "half-breed" was to be equated with a lack of morality, and only a kind of obtuse innocence, meant to be comic, prevented the boys from seeing that their marriage plans violated both their own culture's "cult of domesticity" whereby a woman was to be the virtuous keeper of the family's morals, and its ethnocentric taboo against miscegenation.[51]

Indeed, racism against the Mexican Californians was a major component of Thomes' second work, and only certain individuals were exempted. These were almost always members of the upper class. As we have seen in the case of Henry D. Fitch, even some of those warning Thomes about marrying "half-breeds," were themselves married to California women. Perhaps the difference was as much in their class position as in their race. Some Indian blood could be tolerated in a wealthy Californian, one with standing in the community. It was the lower class that was objectionable, and it may be that like many people who succumb to racism, at least on one level Thomes could only escape the sense of his own lowly status in California (rankling even from the distance of forty years and a successful career) by looking down on the lower class to which he once belonged. He could set himself apart from them by the clearest and most inescapable difference—as Anita had pointed out to him—skin color. More immediately likely, however, was that Thomes simply reflected the predominant American opinion about Mexicans, a carry-over from Elizabethan times of the so-called "Black Legend" that portrayed the Spanish in the New World as treacherous, cowardly and cruel, updated by the Mexican War and continued as Americans displaced the Spanish-speaking residents of the Southwest from their lands.[52] It was the males who would be the most dangerous in such a process, and it was almost exclu-

---

[51]Thomes, *Lewey and I,* 6-8. For discussions of the "cult of domesticity" in the nineteenth century, see Nancy F. Cott, ed., *Root of Bitterness,* 113-177.

[52]See Phillip Wayne Powell, T*ree of Hate: Propaganda and Prejudices Affecting United States Relations with the Hispanic World,* 79, "With pen and printing press, Elizabethan Englishmen parlayed defeat of the Armada, Bartolome de las Casas, and a large envy into a vast, hypocritical, and unqualified superiority complex over the baser, less efficient, and more cowardly Spaniard."

sively the lower class men whom Thomes labeled dirty, thieving, treacherous and villainous. He scarcely bothered to vary his phrases when he characterized them, but then he had the thinnest ability to create character. Even his friend Lewey was drawn as a comic-opera Frenchman who could never leave the girls alone. "A Frenchman nebber miss a chance to pay his respects to de softer sex," according to Lewey, whom Thomes rendered in a dialect which he used indiscriminately for anyone who spoke English with an accent. Thomes' one-dimensional caricatures of the men and women of California can be summed up by what he said when he looked in at one of the numerous fandangos that provided backdrops for the action: "There was a room full of dark-faced greasers, and brilliant-eyed women." Though the men were portrayed in negative terms, the women were almost always at least physically attractive. But as Thomes would have it, the lower orders were to blame for their own degradation and poverty. They were, he said, more interested in gambling at *monte* than paying their debts, an indictment that recurs in both his California books and his reminiscence for Bancroft. It was their apparent lack of concern for honest business practices—prompt repayment of debt—that seemed to have galled Thomes the most. He looked on it as a moral failing.[53]

Thomes personified his stereotypical ideas about the lower class Californian in the Sanchos brothers, who were set up early in *Lewey and I* as antagonists and foils for the boys. These brothers, according to Thomes, "would steal and murder all who were thrown in their way, unless the intended victim was well armed, and then they were too crafty to make an open attack." One of them, Antonio Sanchos, carried a grudge against the boys for an incident in San Francisco. Sanchos had rudely shouldered aside a woman to get into the ship's boat, which the boys were crewing, and Thomes chastised him with a boathook. He sought revenge, and threatened the boys throughout the course of the story, even forcing them at one point to join the Mexican forces. This of course was just a further opening for Thomes to exploit both sides of the conflict for his juvenile adventures.[54]

Thomes and Lewey set out from San Diego on their way to Rancho

---

[53]Thomes, *Lewey and I*, 81, 101.
[54]Ibid.,10, 65-68.

Refugio and marriage. They went through a tedious and repetitive series of situations in which they were attacked by Indians (Thomes claimed they were Apaches!), had numerous confrontations with their enemies the Sanchos brothers, and rescued endangered women who invariably rewarded them with kisses.[55] On their horseback journey, they passed through miles of uninhabited country. The countryside around Los Angeles in particular attracted Thomes' attention. He thought that "better land, or a finer location for a farm, could not have been found in the whole State [sic], as the grass was rich and luxuriant, and the water supply ample, at that season of the year."[56]

Here was the mature Thomes speaking through his adolescent persona, yet both of these voices united on the idea that the people who were being displaced in California (or had largely been displaced by the time Thomes got around to writing about his "experiences" there) deserved their fate. The one or two Californians whom Thomes tried to treat with some sympathy were shown engaging in practices that Thomes could invidiously compare with the "civilized" methods practiced by citizens of the United States. For example, the captain in command of the Mexican company into which the boys were forced at Santa Barbara was a gentleman—honorable, courageous and patriotic. In one of Thomes' characteristic scenes the boys saved his life when a drunken ranchero, also pressed into service, tried to kill him. This Captain Fernando, immediately and without a trial, hanged the ranchero to the nearest tree. "This may have been Mexican law," Thomes commented, "but if it was, some changes were needed...."[57]

Thomes and Lewey also rescued the wife of José Castro (Thomes got his name right in this book) in a scene that stretches the readers credulity even more than usual. When they delivered his wife to the General, they found that the Mexican Comandante was henpecked! Señora Castro berated her husband about his courage, telling him "if you could fight as hard as you talk, Fremont and his band of *ladrones* would all be dead long before this." In marked contrast to this image of the Mexican General was Thomes' depiction of Fremont's famous stand and retreat from

---

[55]Ibid.,139-147, 259-265.

[56]Ibid.,116.

[57]Ibid., 259-263. This seems more a projection of American vigilante justice onto the Californians, than an actual event. I could find no evidence of any such occurence.

Hawk's Peak. The boys were recruited to take a message from the nag-ridden Castro to the bold warrior Fremont. As Thomes explained it, Fremont was difficult to recognize at first. He did not put on the undemocratic airs of a fancy dress uniform, but wore garments that were indistinguishable from those of the rest of his followers. But he stood out from the rest for Thomes, because "his face and eyes were attractive, and showed power and endurance, and when he spoke there was something in his tones that denoted will and courage."[58]

Thomes also added his own twist to the legend of John C. Fremont. He said that the latter's stand and then departure from Hawk's Peak was a ruse designed to get Castro to mass his forces in front of Fremont, who was then enabled to slip away towards San Francisco and obtain more ammuntion, the lack of which was given out by Thomes as the sole factor that had saved José Castro and the Californians from a thrashing. And Thomes claimed that he and Lewey were the instruments in this. They had carried the message from Fremont to José Castro that said Fremont intended to proceed *south* to Santa Barbara, so that Castro would attempt to block his way.[59]

Thomes' "history" would appear to have been largely a prop for his self-serving fantasies.[60] He made himself and Lewey witnesses to a lot of the actions involved in the American conquest, and usually glorified the Americans. He may actually have been with the *Mexican* forces at the Battle of San Pedro, however, where from a safe vantage point he saw the drubbing taken by Captain William Mervine's sailors and marines. This

---

[58]Ibid., 299-310. I could find no evidence of Fremont's democratical mode of dressing, but he seems to have been loved and respected by his men. See Ferol Egan, *Fremont: Explorer for a Restless Nation*, 181, where he quotes Peter Burnett to the effect that Fremont's men "all loved him intensely," and 286, where Egan summarizes Fremont's relationship with his men as follows: "The captain asked nothing of them that he wasn't willing to do; he had the stamina and drive to keep moving against impossible odds; and he treated his men as equals. There was never a barrier of race, education, or family background. He gave respect to his men. In turn, they respected him."

[59]Ibid., 317-318.

[60]George Stewart, op. cit., 5, 25-27, maintains that in *Lewey and I* there was also a base of facts. Thomes had indeed jumped ship in 1845 and stayed in California. He may even have participated in some of the events of the conquest. Stewart believes that his description of Mervine's defeat at Dominguez Rancho in October of 1846—where Thomes claimed to have been with the Mexican forces—rings true. Stewart believes Thomes might also have been in San Diego when Kearny's forces came in after the Battle of San Pasqual. Unfortunately, Stewart cites no sources in support of his assertions. He says only that he has used Thomes' books and recollections for Bancroft, and "a miscellaneous lot of letters, etc., which I collected...."

was to be one of the very few places where he had anything positive to say about the Californians; he criticized the Americans for underestimating their fighting spirit:

> They seemed to think that the Mexicans were a set of vagabonds and destitute of courage and skill, and that an American could walk away with a dozen of them on foot or horseback, forgetting for the moment that the rancheros were as expert riders as could be found in the world, and not devoid of a certain amount of desperate pluck, when well led by men in whom they had confidence.[61]

Of course Thomes' opinion of the Mexicans throughout was precisely that they were a set of vagabonds, destitute of courage and skill, but he was never to be troubled by his own inconsistencies.

In the absurd final pages of *Lewey and I*, the boys at last meet up with Anita and Engracia, only to find that these two had already been married—to their old enemies the Sanchos brothers! These husbands came out and pulled knives on the boys, in a scene that epitomizes Thomes' contrivances. Anita and Engracia threw their bodies in front of Thomes and Lewey just as the husbands hurled their knives. The girls were killed and Captain Fernando had the murderous husbands executed, thus clearing the stage (California) for the onset of the new order, which Thomes had Thomas O. Larkin prophetically explain to them. Larkin told the boys that they should always remember July 7, 1846, the day Commodore Sloat raised the flag over Monterey, because

> if you live long enough you may see this great territory teeming with life and industry, with wealth and contentment, prosperity and happiness and so it will grow until people wonder at the enterprise and intelligence of its inhabitants, and from all parts of the world will commerce come to us, our harbors teem with life, and grain on every hill and in all the rich valleys.[62]

Thomes did live to see the fulfillment of at least one phase of the vision he placed in the mouth of Thomas O. Larkin. He published his California books in 1884 and 1885, several years before the beginning in California of the "boom of the eighties." His books had perhaps helped to swell this tide of "enterprising and intelligent" Americans, and strengthened them in their conviction of superiority over the Spanish-Mexican Californians.

---

[61]Thomes, *Lewey and I*, 383.
[62]Ibid., 354-362.

PART III
The Mountain Men

CHAPTER VI

James Ohio Pattie

For some years before the American conquest, Mexican California had became a topic of conversation among the fur trappers and mountain men of the Rockies. Beginning with Jedediah Smith's entry into southern California in the fall of 1826, American fur hunters drifted into the territory. They brought with them reputations for hard work, courage and self-reliance, the ability to endure incredible hardships, and a deadly skill with the rifle—an expertise which they were not averse to using ruthlessly when necessary, and sometimes without any apparent provocation at all. They formed an American "fifth column" in the sparsely populated province held so tenuously by the young and struggling new nation of Mexico. Jed Smith and his men were the first Americans to come overland. At the San Gabriel Mission where they were hospitably received, they marveled at the productions of its fertile gardens and its riches in cattle. Several of Smith's men were too weak to travel and so remained behind. For example, the free trapper Isaac Galbraith (the same man Alfred Robinson witnessed shooting the heads off little blackbirds), had apparently had enough of the mountains and just wanted to stay in the warm climate and pastoral surroundings of California.[1] Almost every subsequent expedition of trappers into California returned minus men who had chosen to make a life for themselves where there was pleasant weather and a high demand for anyone with mechanical skills. Even those who did not remain became publicists for California at the Rocky Mountain rendezvous, and many a story must have been told around the campfire in sub-zero weather, about the warmth and ease of this country at the end of the West. Several of these obscure trappers (and one not so obscure—Kit Carson) have left behind autobiographical accounts of their experiences and impressions of California.

---

[1]See Dale L. Morgan, *Jedediah Smith and the Opening of the West*, 193-215; 236-255.

They were intimately tied to California's early history because they showed the way even when they did not take up residence, marry local women and acquire land. They made their marks on California, and in a more enduring fashion on the popular imagination of the American people. They were shaped by the dangers and struggles of their lives as mountain men, and in turn brought their habits, personalities and prejudices to bear on events in California. Like the American merchants and sailors who were also settling in California at this time, the mountain men too carried with them a sense of the superiority of American culture, the inevitability of American expansion and a conviction of their own particular fitness to make the best use of the opportunities so evident to them in California.

The Mexican authorities at first found it hard to believe that Jedediah Smith and his companions could have arrived in their country on foot and from the east. They were soon to see that Smith's feat was only the beginning. A little over a year later, James Ohio Pattie arrived, accompanied by his father and six others. They had traveled from the settlements in New Mexico on a fur trapping expedition that eventually took them to California where they were imprisoned at San Diego by a suspicious Mexican governor. They began their journey in the fall of 1827 and James Pattie was to remain in California until 1830, when he returned to the United States. There in 1831, with the help of Timothy Flint, the well-known early chronicler of the frontier experience, young Pattie published his autobiographical account of his experiences, *The Personal Narrative of James O. Pattie*.[2] This was the first recounting of an overland trapping expedition into Mexican California.

Pattie's narrative was a mixture of fact and fancy which has only recently been given scholarly treatment in an effort to separate the actual experiences from the tall tales and stories the young man had heard and then appropriated as his own.[3] But even if there were no way to tell with any certainty what exploits Pattie had really gone through himself, as

---

[2] James O. Pattie, *The Personal Narrative of James O. Pattie* (1831; University of Nebraska Press, 1984).

[3] See Richard Batman, *American Ecclesiastes: The Stories of James Pattie*, for an excellent, interesting and thorough analysis of the *Personal Narrative* and of James Pattie's educational and family background. I have relied on this book throughout my treatment of the *Personal Narrative*.

opposed to adventures he had heard about from others, *The Personal Narrative* would still be an interesting and compelling inside view of the mentality and feelings of a young, literate, middle-class American of the late 1820s experiencing life as a trapper for the first time. James Pattie came from an educated family in Kentucky. His grandfather had been a school teacher. His father, who moved the family to Missouri and prospered, was chosen to write letters to the newspapers while serving in the Missouri militia during the War of 1812. After the war, Sylvester Pattie became a wealthy and leading citizen of Gasconade County, Missouri. His son James seemed to have been studying Greek and Latin in a preparatory school at a time when most other frontier youths had long since been out on their own. As a frontiersman then, he was inexperienced and atypical; as a writer, however, he may not have needed the help of Timothy Flint, even though Pattie was to incorporate into his own narrative echos of some of the situations he could only have found in Flint's novels.[4]

Perhaps James Pattie had absorbed the frontier Kentucky tradition of bragging. He made himself the hero of all his adventures whether real or fabricated. According to his biographer, many of his exploits were more about what he wished he had done than what he actually did. In contradiction to assertions of his own prominence, he made very little impression on his fellow trappers and mountain men who were in a position to witness his alleged heroics. He seems to have been an ordinary young man, dependent upon his father and with no particular leadership skills.[5] Yet if he was not the most conspicuous actor in the drama, he nonetheless lived through some genuinely dangerous and harrowing experiences.[6] When he told his story, however, he mixed in his self-aggrandizing fantasies, even though the things he had done and seen were sufficiently remarkable in themselves.[7] In his imagination, he could

---

[4]Ibid., pp. 10-11; 16; 37-39; 52-54; Batman says (16) that "the basic attitudes, thoughts, and stories, as well as the credit or blame and ultimately the responsibility for the narrative, rest solely with James Pattie."

[5]Ibid., pp. 17-18.

[6]Timothy Flint, in his preface to the 1831 edition of *The Personal Narrative*, said that he had excluded "circumstances of suffering...as too revolting to be recorded."

[7]For example, the Patties' trapping expedition along the Gila River in Arizona in the winter of 1825-26 may have been the first time any Americans had explored that region; they were also the first to travel down the Colorado to the Gulf of California. See David Weber, *The Taos Trappers*, 112, 137.

always show his courage, competence and good judgement. He could also demonstrate the superiority of American civilization by contrasting himself to the barbarism of the Indians, and the vice and cowardice of the Spanish-Mexicans. His *Personal Narrative* was thus both an individual wish-fulfillment fantasy and a cultural expression representative of an expansionist United States.

The phenomenal success of William Becknell, who opened trade with Santa Fe in 1821 and returned to Missouri with sacks full of silver dollars, must have made a profound impression on his friend Sylvester Pattie. When the elder Pattie's wife died several years later, he sold his holdings in Missouri and taking his oldest son James with him, set out in the spring of 1825 for New Mexico with a group led by Bernard Pratte.[8] Several hundred miles out on the Santa Fe Trail they encountered a Pawnee chief who had been to Washington D.C. There, as he informed the Patties in a statement that carried with it a prophecy of doom for the Indians' traditional way of life, he found that the whites were not at all a small tribe like his, but were "as numberless as the spires of grass on the prairies." The whites had huge guns with bullets as large as his head that astonished the old chief. Here James took his first opportunity to compare the civilized behavior of the Americans with the savagery of the Indians. The latter engaged in "an indiscriminate slaughter, of men, women and children," whereas his party purchased from the Pawnees a captured Indian child to save it from death. He also cast his first aspersions on the character of the Mexicans when he said that "partly through timidity and partly through indolence" they would not pursue Indians who had stolen their horses.[9]

Arriving in Taos, James expressed surprise at the marked difference between the local residents and the Americans. He apparently expected them to look, dress and act just like the people he knew back home. The citizens of Taos, though poor, nevertheless treated the Patties hospitably, inviting them into their homes and feeding them. But the visit was not to be without its troubles. According to James, his group was forced to

---

[8]Batman, op. cit., 40-44; James Pattie errs in his dating throughout the narrative. He said, for example that they began their trip to Santa Fe in 1824, whereas Batman shows (51) that they actually set out on June 20, 1825.

[9]*Personal Narrative*, 15-19.

whip some "Spaniards" who had stolen several of their mules—or so James said—and then had asked how much the Americans would pay to get them back. The whipping provoked the townspeople, but their sense of justice must have prevailed, because after the Americans explained what had happened, the offending "Spaniards" were put in the stocks.[10] Yet such an experience was not enough to shake the underlying prejudices James Pattie held about Mexicans. The fair and kind treatment meted out to the Americans by the citizens of Taos, and the respect James later professed to hold for the governor of New Mexico, Antonio Narbona, did little to soften his characterizations of "the Spaniard," which remained contemptuous throughout his narrative.

At Santa Fe James told his first heroic tale. He described how the Americans found the local people in an uproar over a Comanche raid. The women were hysterical, rushing up to the Patties and screaming that the Indians were in the town. James said, however, that "the women...got the story wrong, as most women do in a case of the kind...." The Patties immediately offered their assistance in recapturing those whom the Comanches had seized, and James' father was put in charge. They chased the Indians, caught up with them and James sprang forward to rescue one of the women, who turned out to be "a beautiful young lady, the daughter of the governor...." The women were all naked, herding sheep ahead of their Indian captors, and James gave this young lady his hunting shirt. Meanwhile, in James' account the local citizens, after firing off their weapons once, fled to a safe distance leaving the Patties to do all of the fighting. James claimed that they lost ten men and that his father was slightly wounded. He also maintained that the rescued women refused to go with their own craven countrymen, but preferred to remain under the protection of the Americans. He himself was singled out for a personal "thank you" by Governor Antonio Narbona's daughter Jacova. "I cannot describe," he said, "the gratitude and loveliness, that appeared in her countenance, as she looked on me, when I was pointed out to her." He professed to be embarrassed at this, feeling he was only doing his duty and that no special merit should be attached to his actions. After this, of course, the Patties were given the special privilege of a trapping license by the governor, and the rescued daughter

---

[10]Ibid., 38-39.

refused to return James' hunting shirt, insisting on keeping it "as long as she lived."[11]

James Pattie's biographer failed to find any supporting evidence to indicate that this daring rescue actually took place. What he did discover was a remarkably similar story in one of Timothy Flint's novels, *Francis Berrian*.[12] James' adventure was evidently a mix of borrowed materials. But his reading public doubtless took it seriously. It was very likely what they wanted and expected to hear about the exploits of an American frontiersman, and James Pattie was making his contribution to the construction of this particular American hero—modest, dutiful and courageous, chivalric and kind to helpless women. Such a type surely would be favored over the pusillanimous male inhabitants of the northern Mexican frontier territories that the United States was beginning to covet. Even the Mexican women showed their preference for the Americans.[13]

As a spokesman for the values of a "civilized" United States, James Pattie sometimes had to deal with the very uncivilized behavior of his fellow American trappers. On an expedition down the Rio Grande, the Patties were deserted—as James put it—by seven of their companions. These men were all cursed roundly and a horrific fate was wished on them, namely, to be massacred by Indians or eaten by bears. This wish came true when the seven were attacked by Indians and one of them was killed. But this would not do for James, who instead of rejoicing at the "poetic justice" done to the deserters, insisted that those who remained would all risk their lives to save the seven from death, "so ready are the hearts of mountain hunters to relent." And when four of the seven returned, "we received them as brothers." In their contacts with the Indi-

---

[11]Ibid., 40-46

[12]Batman, op. cit.,115-116. *Francis Berrian* also has a hero who remarks upon the lack of civilization on the frontier; James Pattie would try to portray himself as a civilized hero. See Henry Nash Smith, *Virgin Land*, 256.

[13] As late as the Twenties this idea was still a standard for some historians. In his biography of Kit Carson, *Kit Carson: The Happy Warrior of the Old West*, 82-88, Stanley Vestal described a fight at a fandango in Taos between mountain men and some Mexican men of the town which he claimed was caused by the local women's attentions to the former. David Weber, the editor of *Foreigners In Their Native Land: Historical Roots of the Mexican Americans*, 60, says that Americans of Patties time—almost all of them males—who went into the adjacent Mexican territories, combined "their inherited belief in the Black Legend with racism and their exposure to frontier Mexican culture, [and] came to the conclusion that Mexican people were inferior." But for obvious reasons, Mexican women were usually exempted from this condemnation.

ans too, James continuously juxtaposed Indian cruelty with the fair treatment the whites offered to the Indians, and with his own even and humane temperament. For example, they discovered the corpse of a white man who had been killed by Indians. It had, he said, been mutilated, cut into quarters and the head shot full of arrows. Such treatment of war captives was certainly calculated to inflame white sensibilities against the Indians. Yet shortly after this, James came upon some Indians who ran away at the sight of the whites, leaving behind a child. The Patties secured the child for its own safety and continued their hunt. The Indians returned, retrieved their child and left a present for the white trappers. This act, in James' words, was "proof, that the feelings of human nature are the same everywhere, and that the language of kindness is a universal one." But this did not mean that the Americans were soft or weak. At the Santa Rita copper mine which Sylvester Pattie had been granted a license to operate, James cautioned the Indians to remain peaceful. If they did not, the Americans would be after them, "and ... we could shoot a great deal better than either they or the Spaniards, and that we had no cowards among us, but true men, who had no fear and would keep their word." These "true men" could be provoked into their own savage conduct, however. After one particularly galling Indian attack, James said that the Americans went around and cut off the heads of the slain. Nor did civilized conduct necessarily mean equal treatment for the "Spaniards" he met.[14]

James O. Pattie would take his contempt for Spanish-Mexican culture into California, where he would sharply contrast the beauty and promise of the land with what he considered to be the indolence, incompetence, cruelty and oppression of the Mexican authorities and institutions. And he would prepare his readers to accept his judgements by showing in practice what happened when people did not listen to him. An Indian massacre provides a good illustration. Lured by the apparent friendliness of a tribe of Papago Indians, Pattie's group of trappers spent the night in their village along the Salt River near present-day Phoenix. But James was suspicious of the Indians' intentions from the beginning and tried to warn the "French Captain" (Michel Robidoux) not to remain overnight with them. Pattie and Robidoux argued, and Pattie left with an unnamed

[14]*Personal Narrative*, 51-55; 107.

friend to camp apart from the Indians. These two thus managed to escape the massacre which killed everyone except Robidoux who, though wounded, got away from the Papagos and rejoined Pattie. James' judgement had once again proved sound, superior even to that of an experienced leader like Robidoux. Robidoux apologized for not listening to his warning, but James was too civilized to rub it in: "I exercised too much humanity and forbearance to think of adverting to our quarrel of the preceding evening." James, Robidoux and the third survivor then joined a large party under the veteran trapper Ewing Young.[15]

Returning to Santa Fe, they found a new governor in charge, Manuel Armijo. He refused to honor their trapping licenses and confiscated their furs. James' father Sylvester was also deprived of his copper mine. So the Pattie's found themselves once again obliged to go trapping to recoup their loses. In the fall of 1827, under Sylvester's leadership, the Patties obtained passports, recruited men and entered into a compact in which the trappers agreed that anyone who deserted could be shot dead. Nevertheless, for whatever reasons, they did split up after reaching the Colorado River. Six men stayed behind with the Patties.[16] James, offering insight into the shaping of the trappers' characters by their wilderness experience, attributed the break-up to personality conflicts, differences in skill and ability, "[a] perception of their own comparative importance, a keen sense of self-interest, which sharpens in the desert, the mere love of roving in the wild forest, and a capacity to become hardened by these scenes to a perfect callousness to all fear and sense of danger...."[17]

The journey was indeed fraught with hardships: Indian attacks, floods on the Colorado, starvation and a crossing of "the Sahara of California" during which they were reduced at one point to drinking their own urine.[18] When they finally reached the Mission St. Catherine in the deserts of northern Baja California, weak and exhausted, they were treat-

[15]Ibid.,77-80; see also Weber, *The Taos Trappers*, 123-124; Batman, *American Ecclesiastes*, 168-171, states that Pattie was with Ewing Young from the start.

[16]The six men were Nathaniel M. Pryor, Richard Laughlin, Jesse Ferguson, William Pope, Isaac Slover and Edmund Russell. See Weber, *The Taos Trappers*,136-138, where he also cites evidence that would make the Patties the deserters from the majority of the party, with the apparent aim of selling their furs to American merchant captains on the Pacific Coast.

[17]*Personal Narrative*, 93; 119-123.

[18]Ibid.,127-130; 145-146.

ed with suspicion by the Mexican authorities and made prisoners. To
James it was just another illustration of "the Spanish character." "The
cowardly and worthless," he said, "are naturally cruel." They then proceeded under guard to San Diego to be dealt with by Mexican Governor
José María Echeandía who had his headquarters there. On the way to
San Diego James observed the "strange and charming" country. Along
the coast they saw seals, sea otters, whales and sharks. They passed
"splendid orchards and vineyards," and "plains literally covered with horses and cattle belonging to the mission. The wild oats and clover grow
spontaneously, and in great luxuriance, and were now knee high."[19]

At San Diego, the Patties were accused of being "spies for the old
Spaniards," in James' words, and were placed in separate cells. James'
melodramatic account of this incident included a message from his
dying father, written on a hat band in his own blood, asking James to
visit him on his death-bed. James claimed that this request was heart-
lessly refused by Echeandía, who was to play the cruel Spanish villain to
James' persecuted heroics. News of his father's death was greeted by
James with relief, and the disclaimer that he was "a hunter, and not a
person to analyze the feelings of poor human nature." Perhaps he was as
much relieved that his father could no longer exercise authority over
him as he was to see an end to his father's suffering. Prison was a horror
he said, for one who was used to roaming freely over the prairies, but he
had as a consolation the attentions of a beautiful and sympathetic
woman, the sister of the sergeant of the guard, who visited James in his
cell. (One would think that if Echeandía were as tyrannical as James
made him out to be, he would have forbidden such visits.) Finally, his
opportunity for at least temporary release came when the American
merchant-Captain John Bradshaw, in trouble with the authorities for
smuggling, needed a translator. James was paroled to serve in this
capacity, after Bradshaw posted bond for his good conduct. With his
characteristic false modesty James said: "Though I put forth no claims
on the score of scholarship, I perfectly comprehended the meaning of
the words in both languages."[20]

James believed that his new status as a translator would secure his

---

[19]Ibid.,152-56.
[20]Ibid.,158-170.

complete release. But when this did not take place, he refused to do any more translating, for which defiance he claimed that Echeandía struck him over the head with the flat of his sword. Yet Captain Bradshaw's difficulties still required James' services, so he was again summoned to resume his translating duties. This time Bradshaw took James on board his ship and offered to transport him to Boston; but once more playing the hero, James refused, saying that he could not desert his companions still in prison. Bradshaw decided not to wait around for a verdict that might have meant the confiscation of his cargo and made his exit, firing a broadside at the fort as he left. To James Pattie, Bradshaw's unpunished defiance was just more evidence of Mexican cowardice. In a statement that would find remarkably similar echos in the writings of later American visitors to California, he claimed to have "no faith in the courage of these people, except where they have greatly the advantage, or can kill in the dark, without danger to themselves." Echeandía, meanwhile, had decided to permit the retrieval of their furs which they had left cached on the Colorado. Only James was to remain behind as a hostage to ensure that the others returned. He indulged himself throughout his prison ordeal by entertaining thoughts of revenge against Echeandía. He even took pleasure in what he believed to be Echeandía's disappointment when his companions came back empty-handed. He thought that the governor only let them go because he coveted the furs, which had been ruined by a rise in the river.[21]

James Pattie's "eyewitness" account of their imprisonment and his father's death was not to go unchallenged. A member of his party, Nathaniel Pryor, remained behind in California when James returned to the United States to publish his narrative condemning his foul treatment at the hands of the wicked and cowardly Californians. Twenty years later Pryor told a different story. He said that Sylvester Pattie in his illness had been taken care of by the leading women of San Diego. Before he died, Sylvester Pattie became a Catholic, and Pryor has him say: "it must be a good religion that makes these women care for a poor old man like me...." Pryor also told how Sylvester was sponsored as a Catholic by Pío Pico and Doña Victoria Dominguez de Estudillo, two of the leading Californians in San Diego. The whole town marched in his funeral pro-

---

[21]Ibid.,172-185.

cession; his coffin was borne on the shoulders of four Californians; he was buried in consecrated ground, the first American to be interred in California soil. As to his son's narrative, Pryor maintained that most of it was "false, and has the same relation to the true narrative that Robinson Crusoe has to the journal of Alexander Selkirk."[22]

When he made his statement about their imprisonment and Sylvester Pattie's death, many years had passed and Nathaniel Pryor was thoroughly assimilated into California life. If he had felt mistreated by Governor Echeandía in 1828, any resentment had long since been buried. Echeandía has been described as a man of uncertain character, self-indulgent, whimsical and capable of surrendering to his impulses no matter what the consequences, but by no means a tyrant.[23] The Californians themselves would prove less than tolerant of oppressive Mexican governors. As a representative of a nation which had only recently and at great cost thrown off the yoke of Spanish colonial rule, Echeandía had his own obsessions. A second set of trappers coming into California so soon after Jedediah Smith, and telling a similar story of hardship and need, aroused the suspicion in Echeandía that the expedition had a military purpose. The governor had never heard of the fur trade and did not believe that anyone would cross the deserts just to hunt beaver. So the Patties and their friends were indeed incarcerated for a few days, but James' account of the harshness of their imprisonment, and his claim that he was denied access to his dying father, would seem to be some more of his exaggeration. He was soon set at liberty, though for his narrative he fabricated a smallpox epidemic as the reason he was released from prison.[24]

According to James, he made a bargain with Echeandía, agreeing in

---

[22]*Historical Society of Southern California: Publications*, I, pt. 3, 30-35, "A Sketch of Some of the Earliest Kentucky Pioneers of Los Angeles"; Pryor told his story to Stephen C. Foster who was "intimately acquainted with Pryor, from March 1847, until he died, May 1850..." (30).

[23]See Batman, op. cit., 225; Batman relies on H. H. Bancroft for his assessment of Echeandía. He also says (235) that Pattie's view of Echeandía as a tyrant was contradicted by all other views of him.

[24]Ibid., 227-28; Batman, op. cit., 235, states that James' story of being kept from his dying father went against James' own evidence of good treatment, and (240) that Sylvester's death seems to have relieved his son of insomnia and a loss of appetite. As to the smallpox epidemic, there is absolutely no evidence in the contemporary records of any epidemic. Batman (258-259) explains it this way: "Having committed himself to a tale of long imprisonment by an unreasonable tyrant, he now needed a dramatic event to explain the governor's decision to give him freedom to travel throughout California."

exchange for his liberty to travel through the settlements vaccinating people against smallpox.[25] He also convinced the governor to let his companions go, and they bribed the guard to return their guns. James was now free to proceed up the coast, as he said on his mission of mercy. It would be an occasion for recording his impressions. He was struck by the richness of Mission San Luis Rey, where he thought the Indians were "better dressed in general, than the Spaniards." He noticed too that the priests locked up the women whose husbands were absent, as well as all of the girls over the age of nine. Nevertheless, he said, the padres' precautions were "found insufficient." How he knew this he did not explain. Nor did he offer any evidence in support of his assertion that the Indians at the mission were brought there "against their own inclinations, and by compulsion, and then baptised; which act was as little voluntary on their part, as the former had been." At San Juan Capistrano he was quick to note that the padre there enjoyed his liquor, while what impressed him about San Gabriel were the enormous herds of cattle. He remembered the flat-roofed houses of Los Angeles were covered with "bituminous pitch," and could not pass up San Buenaventura without mentioning that "two priests had eloped [in an American vessel] … taking with them what gold and silver they could lay their hands upon." [26]

James claimed to have gone as far north as the Russian settlement at Fort Ross in the company of some Kodiak Indian sea otter hunters whose kayaks he admired.[27] Yet he gave no details for his travels above Santa Barbara, and he confused the order of the northern missions that he said he visited. His biographer believes he did not get further north than Santa Barbara, and left the country by sea.[28] But not before he had taken yet another opportunity for righteous posturing against the Californians. James expected payment for his services as a vaccinator, but when he was offered the only kind of payment that the specie-poor government of California could make available, he scorned it in the most

---

[25]James claimed to have vaccinated 18, 962 people whereas the entire mission population in California at the time was only 12, 851. See William H. Goetzman's introduction to the 1984 edition of *The Personal Narrative of James O. Pattie.*

[26]*Personal Narrative,*185-196; see also Batman, op. cit., 262, who states that stories of priests drinking and absconding with money were "common tales told by Americans, and only occasionally true."

[27]*Personal Narrative,*198.

[28]Batman, op. cit., 267-268.

disparaging phrases. As the self-conscious representative (at least in his narrative) of a "superior" culture, he would not, like some, "leave his conscience at Cape Horn" and succumb to the blandishments of Mexico's immigration policy. He was offered land and cattle on the basis of Mexican law, which required that foreigners become Catholics and citizens of Mexico, conditions that did not prove to be obstacles for many Americans who were to come to California. James had no intention of remaining in California, however, so such a payment was useless to him. Money was what he needed to pay for passage home. But the response he gave in his narrative was no doubt calculated to inspire his countrymen with respect for his patriotic principles. He said to one of the local padres

> that I would not change my present opinions for all the money his mission was worth; and moreover, that before I would consent to be adopted into the society and companionship of such a band of murderers and robbers, as I deemed were to be found along this coast, for the pitiful amount of one thousand head of cattle, I would suffer death.[29]

It does not seem likely that he could actually have made such a statement within ear-shot of any Californians. He had no personal basis for calling anyone in California a robber or murderer—not even his alleged ill-treatment by Echeandía warranted such exaggerated charges. Ironically, before he left California, he would participate in a "revolution" on the side of the very man for whom he professed so much hatred! While on board a hide and tallow ship which stopped at Monterey, James found out "that there was a revolution in the country," fomented by Joaquín Solis and promising liberty of trade along the coast to foreigners. James said he wanted to join it just for the chance of shooting Echeandía, but was dissuaded by some of his countrymen on the ship who advised him to take a wait-and-see attitude. Then he came under the influence of a Boston merchant and sea captain who had begun to establish himself in California. This man, John R. Cooper, convinced young Pattie that Joaquín Solis intended to expel all of the foreigners. Cooper, who James said "looked rather deeper into things than those around him," persuaded the young man to join a force of foreigners being mus-

---

[29] *Personal Narrative*, 200-202.

tered at Santa Barbara in support of James' old enemy Echeandía. Though the men were Scotch, Irish, English and Dutch as well as Americans, the latter were in a majority, so according to James the force was called American. Americans—including trappers like James Pattie and merchants such as John Cooper—were thus involved in California politics at a very early date. They routed Solis' forces at Santa Barbara in a comic-opera battle in which, according to James, "The cannon balls discharged from the fort upon the enemy were discharged with so little force, that persons arrested them in their course, without sustaining any injury by so doing...."[30]

The Solis revolt offered James the chance to be a hero one last time. He said he *commanded* the men who chased Solis, and *personally* received Solis' surrender . He was about to leave California for Mexico City (with a passport given him by Governor Echeandía),[31] where he would make an unsuccessful claim for damages against the Mexican government. With the exception of his short imprisonment and the death of his father, his stay in California had been a generally positive experience, though it did not profit him in the way that he desired or believed that he deserved. He would take back with him and present to the American public of his day his own particular view of a land rich and beautiful, controlled by a people unworthy to possess it. His final assessment should be quoted in full:

> The misery and suffering of various kinds, that I had endured in some por-
> tions of it [California] , had not been able to prevent me from feeling, and
> acknowledging, that this country is more calculated to charm the eye, than
> any one I have ever seen. Those, who traverse it, if they have any capability
> whatever of perceiving, and admiring the beautiful and sublime in scenery,
> must be constantly excited to wonder and praise. It is no less remarkable for
> uniting the advantages of healthfulness, a good soil, a temperate climate,
> and yet one of exceeding mildness, a happy mixture of level and elevated
> ground, and vicinity to the sea. Its inhabitants are equally calculated to
> excite dislike, and even the stronger feelings of disgust and hatred.[32]

---

[30]Ibid., 202-206.

[31]In a further contradictory twist to James Pattie's story here, Batman, op. cit., 261, states that James actually requested permission from Echeandía to *stay* in California, and that Echeandía's passport described Pattie as "not vicious...but of regular conduct."

[32]*Personal Narrative*, 216-217.

James Ohio Pattie was one of the first Americans to write about his experiences in Mexican California. He set a tone for public opinion in the United States concerning this distant but increasingly inviting territory. He gave to his ambitious fellow Americans further incentives for pushing their westward course to the Pacific. And in his portrayal of the Mexican Californians, he created biases (or reinforced existing prejudices with his own) that would continue to operate in the minds of his countrymen, conveniently rationalizing conquest by war and, generations later, institutionalized racial discrimination. Innumerable spin-offs of the righteous and heroic persona he created for his narrative would also descend through American popular culture.

CHAPTER VII

Kit Carson

There were many unsung "heroes" of the fur trade, men who pursued their calling with skill and fortitude and who would not have looked upon themselves as especially noteworthy or deserving. One such man was Kit Carson, whose life was intimately tied up with the early history of Americans in California. Kit Carson was an honest and uncomplicated man who disliked braggarts. He was not a leader of men like Joseph Walker or Thomas Fitzpatrick. He was just a free trapper who might have remained mainly of interest to historians and specialists if it had not been for his connection with one of the great self-publicists in United States history, John C. Fremont. Fremont, his wife Jessie Benton Fremont, and his father-in-law Senator Thomas Hart Benton of Missouri, all helped to bring Kit Carson before the public eye. Through a fortuitous meeting with Fremont, who was recruiting men for his second expedition, Kit Carson was to become the best known and enduring of the mountain men, an American archtype. He possessed certain qualities that when brought to the public's attention, would make him a popular hero. He was a model example of the frontiersman—honest, brave, resolute, dutiful and unpretentious. In 1856, when he was already famous, he was persuaded to tell his story. He needed money and his friends convinced him that he might realize a profit from his memoirs. His unassuming character would probably have prevented Kit from such an act of hubris as writing his autobiography. But Kit Carson was illiterate, so he just sat down, like he might have done hundreds of times before around a campfire in the mountains, and told everything he could remember about his life and adventures. The result can be instructively compared with the labors of James O. Pattie. Unlike Pattie, Kit Carson was not an educated man. He had to dictate his story to someone who was able to write. Whereas Pattie exaggerated his exploits (and his literary style), and affected a false modesty, Kit Carson characteristically understated his accomplishments. His story came right "off the top of his head" without the adornments necessary to a writer with literary pretensions. Pattie railed against the Mexicans, while Kit Carson's ethnocentrism was more ambiguous. He did not escape the typical prejudices of his day, yet he could at times recognize character and courage in people regardless of their race. He had had an Arapahoe "wife," and would later marry a New Mexican woman, Josefa Jaramillo. Both Kit Carson and James Pattie were in California around the same time. James O. Pattie left in 1830 never to return; Kit Carson made six trips into the territory and was an important participant in the American conquest of California. James O. Pattie's narrative was a calculated attempt by its author to create a meretricious image; Kit Carson's autobiography largely succeeded in presenting the man as he was. The few lapses of memory and omissions just showed that he was human and could sometimes (though rarely) give himself more credit than was his due and forget those few acts of which he was not particularly proud.[1]

Much has been written about Kit Carson—beginning with his first mention in the Reverend Samuel Parker's published journal in 1838, through Fremont's reports and memoirs, fictionalized "Kit Carsons" in dime novels, and dozens of biographies, the latest by Thelma Guild and Harvey Carter published in 1984. The focus here will be on his activities in California, his attitudes toward the natives (both Mexican and Indian), and on events useful to an examination of his personality as expressed in his autobiography (which he dictated to John Mostin, his secretary or interpreter from 1854 to 1859 when he was Indian agent in New Mexico).[2]

Kit Carson's childhood was like those of many contemporary frontiersmen. He was born in Kentucky on Christmas Eve, 1809, and in 1811 moved to Boone's Lick, Howard County, Missouri, where he said that because of the ever-present Indian danger, "we had to remain forted

---

[1] A review of much of the literature on Kit Carson is available in the preface to Harvey Lewis Carter's definitive edition of the Kit Carson memoirs, 'Dear Old Kit,' The Historical Christopher Carson. Carter reproduced "The Kit Carson Memoirs, 1809-1856" from the original manuscript with a minimum of editorial changes. Only paragraphing and punctuation have been added; the original spelling has been retained. See also Thelma S. Guild and Harvey L. Carter, Kit Carson: A Pattern for Heroes.

[2] See Carter (ed.), 'Dear Old Kit', xii ff.

and it was necessary to have men stationed at the extremities of the fields for the protection of those that were laboring." He thus learned at an early age to live and cope with an ever-present danger and threat to his existence, and he probably needed little more in the way of psychological preparation for his life as a mountain man. Neither his father's farm nor David Workman's saddle shop in Franklin, Missouri, where he was an apprentice, could contain his restless spirit. So in 1826, at age fifteen, he ran away. In his own words, "I concluded to join the first party for the Rocky Mts."[3]

Kit never learned how to read or write, but he was intelligent, and seemed to have a facility for languages. Over the years he would acquire a number of Indian languages. In Taos he quickly mastered Spanish, and acted as an interpreter for one "Col. Tramell." In August 1829, he joined a fur trapping expedition to California under Ewing Young, an experienced fur trader. Few men had preceded them. They had to cross a desert country that Kit described as "sandy, burned up, and not a drop of water." It would be many years before any Americans would (or could) write about the desert's spiritual qualities or its beauty. To the mountain men it was a nightmare landscape to be escaped as rapidly as possible. They made tanks for water out of three deer skins and posted guards over them at night to make sure no one took more than his share. Nevertheless, they used up this supply before finding any more and were on the desert for four days without water. In his typically laconic fashion, Kit said, "we suffered extremely on account of it." When they finally arrived at the Colorado River—which their mules had scented long before they were aware of its proximity—Kit maintained that their joy could be more easily imagined than described.[4]

Fortified at the Colorado River with water and with food obtained from the Mojave Indians, they continued over the arid country to the San Gabriel Mission. Here the California missions' tradition of hospitality to travelers was upheld. The trappers "received good treatment," and Kit was impressed with the mission's evident prosperity. He found San Gabriel staffed by one priest (Padre José Bernardo Sanchez), fifteen soldiers, and about a thousand Indians. "They had about eighty thousand

[3]Ibid., 38.
[4]Ibid., 42-46.

head of stock, fine fields and vineyards—in fact," Kit said in a comparison that would in later years become a booster's cliche, "it was a paradise on earth."[5]

The little group of Americans proceeded from San Gabriel north to the San Joaquin Valley, where they found few beaver but plenty of other game. They ran into a party of Hudson's Bay Company men under Peter Skene Ogden, a reminder that the British were still a presence in the west. They finally made there way to the Mission San Jose (Kit mistakenly called it "San Rafael") where the California authorities had just been defeated by Indians who were harboring runaways from the mission. The Californians had been unsuccessful, so the Americans, experienced Indian fighters, offered help. According to Kit, Ewing Young directed him and eleven others to join the Californians on a raid against the Indians. They attacked and "routed" the Indians, burned their village and secured the runaways. Then they managed to sell what beaver skins they had collected to a trading schooner at the mission, and bought horses from the Californians. But shortly after acquiring the horses, the animals were run off by Indians. Kit and twelve others were once again sent in pursuit. They caught up with the Indians, surprising them while they were feasting on several of the stolen horses. As Kit told it: "We charged their camp, killed eight Indians, took three children prisoners and recovered all our animals, with the exception of six that were eaten, and returned to our camp." He did not say what they did with the Indian children but it seems most likely that they turned them over to the mission.[6]

No doubt actions like these, in which the trappers demonstrated their courage and prowess against the Indians, contributed to the reputation the American mountain men were soon to have in California. But Kit attributed the Californians' alleged fear of them to an altogether different incident. On their way back to New Mexico the men passed through Los Angeles with their furs and their pack animals. Kit said that the authorities demanded their passports, which they did not possess. He also concluded that the Californians "wished to arrest us but fear deterred them." So to make it easier and safer, as Kit believed, the Californians plied them with liquor, hoping to get them drunk. But Young

[5]Ibid., 46.
[6]Ibid., 46-48.

saw through the scheme and ordered Kit to take three men and all the pack animals, and go in advance. Young would stay with the men, who refused to pass up an opportunity for a spree. He told Kit that if he and the others did not show up the next day, to push on home and "report the party killed, for he would not leave them." Kit did as he was ordered. Young and the rest, accompanied by some Californians, finally caught up with Kit at dark. Kit thought the Californians wanted to ride along with them to San Gabriel where with reinforcements they could have arrested the Americans. The only thing that prevented this was

> a man by the name of Jas. Higgins dismounting from his horse and deliber-ately shooting Jas. Lawrence. Such conduct frightened the Mexicans, and they departed in all haste, fearing that if men, without provocation, would shoot one another, it would require but little to cause them to murder them.[7]

This incident is given a slightly different interpretation by Ewing Young's biographer, Kenneth Holmes. Holmes does not consider it very likely that the Americans would have been in Los Angeles without their passports. Young had left them at San Jose when trapping, and Holmes believes he almost certainly picked them up. He does not think either, that the Californians deliberately wanted to get the Americans drunk. They were selling aguardiente; the trappers wanted it—that was enough. Young himself, in a letter to John R. Cooper, described the shooting this way: "an Irish man [John Higgins] and an English man [James Lawrence] in the rear had a falling out about some frivolous thing and one shot the other dead off his horse. I could not stop to do anything with him. Left him lying in the rode where he was kild [sic]." Perhaps Kit was wrong about the passports, and he might have jumped to the wrong conclusion about the liquor, but he was probably correct about the possibility of arrest, though the reason for it will never be clear. Holmes cites a report by José Antonio Pico from the "Departmental State Paper" in which the Californian noted the passing of Young's party (exaggerating their numbers), and said that he could not comply with the order to detain "Gefe Joaquin Jon" (the Spanish equivalent for Ewing Young) because he (Pico) had only three soldiers at his disposal. Pico also mentioned that one of the Americans had killed another and

---

[7]Ibid., 48-49.

the body was left unburied. It seems plausible that Young had to leave the body unburied in his haste to escape from the threat of arrest. It also appears that Kit was correct and the Californians were appalled and intimidated by this wanton killing, enough at least so that José Antonio Pico and his three soldiers did not wish to risk their lives in a futile effort to detain the remaining seventeen ruthless and obviously well-armed mountain men.[8]

It would be almost twelve years before Kit would again see California, as a scout for John C. Fremont on his second expedition. The intervening time was spent as a trapper in the Rockies, where he perfected the habits of mind and skills which would make him a useful guide and hunter on the surveying expeditions that helped call the nation's attention to the Mexican province of California. Kit was unconscious of himself as an instrument of Manifest Destiny, yet he personified the type of individual then on the cutting edge of westward expansion—the mountain man.

In numerous encounters with Indians, he learned early that the best way to deal with them was "to act in a fearless manner." And this Kit Carson was always prepared to do. His instinct was to charge the enemy head on, though occasionally such a tactic could backfire. Unlike James Pattie, Kit did not pretend that his judgement was faultless though neither did he dwell on his mistakes. On one probably not unusual hunt, Kit and his friends had a fight with some Crow Indians who had stolen their horses. Then two men of their company deserted, taking all the beaver skins which had been cached. Kit chased them, but never saw them again. He presumed they had been killed by the Indians who continued to lurk about, trying to run off the horses. "Such a fate," he said, revealing his own convictions, "they should receive for their dishonesty." Finally, on a tributary of the Arkansas River after much harrassment by smaller bands of Indians, Kit sighted four warriors whom he immediately proposed to charge. But when they got near these Indians, "we found we had caught a tartar." The mountain men had ridden into the midst of about sixty Indians. "They had surrounded us and our only chance to save our lives was by instant flight." The trappers had to "run the gauntlet for about two hundred yards" with the Indians firing at them from all

---

[8]Kenneth L. Holmes, *Ewing Young: Master Trapper*, 54-6.

sides. They made good their escape though one man was severely wounded.[9]

Kit seemed to lead a charmed life in the mountains. He was almost constantly in danger, barely escaping death many times. In one skirmish with the Blackfeet in the fall of 1835, the Indians set fire to the brush, trying to flush the trappers out into the open. The fire came right up to where Kit was concealed, but did not reach the brush under which he lay. He considered this to be "miraculous." "It was," he said, "the hand of Providence over us that was the cause."[10] A belief in Providence was a part of the mental make-up of most Americans of Kit's day, a legacy of the Puritan past.[11] Actually, another trapper had, unknown to Kit, set a backfire which prevented the flames from reaching them.[12] Regardless, a conviction that Divine Providence was protecting him was a useful outlook for a mountain man faced on an almost daily basis with the paralyzing prospect of death.

When Kit offered his praises for the Catholic missionary Father Pierre Jean de Smet, he said that the priest was "a man that wished to do good...He never feared danger when duty required his presence among the savages...." Father de Smet was the kind of person Kit Carson admired. Kit too tried never to let fear stop him from doing his duty. Through all of his conflicts with Indians or French bullies,[13] and during his service in California, he never once mentioned being afraid. Courage, of course, was a commodity highly prized by the mountain men. Those who displayed a lack of it lost caste and did not last long in the mountains. Yet Kit Carson was human and not immune under certain circumstances to feelings of terror. In his autobiography he confessed to one incident which badly frightened him. He had left camp on foot to kill something for supper. In about a mile he came across an elk which he shot. Immediately afterwards he heard a noise behind him and

---

[9] *'Dear Old Kit'*, 49; 54-57.

[10] Ibid., 76-77.

[11] See Lewis P. Saum, *The Popular Mood of Pre-Civil War America*, 25, "In popular thought of the pre-Civil War period, no theme was more pervasive or philosophically fundamental than the providential view."

[12] See Guild and Carter, *Kit Carson*, 71-2.

[13] See *'Dear Old Kit'*, 65, for Kit's famous duel with the Frenchman "Shunar" at the 1835 rendevous.

[14] Ibid., 61.

turned around to see "two very large grizzly bears making for me." His gun was unloaded and he had to run for it, saving his life by climbing a nearby tree. One of the bears quickly left, but the other one stayed around and made several attempts to get at Kit. Finally, this one too left and Kit could come down. In his autobiography he admitted to "never having been so scared in my life."[14]

In two separate reflections on his life, Kit Carson presented the essential horizons of the mountain man's existence. Returning to Taos after his first trip to California with Ewing Young, Kit characterized the carefree, spendthrift viewpoint of the typical mountain man:

> We passed the time gloriously, spending our money freely—never thinking that our lives were risked in gaining it...Trappers and sailors are similar in regard to the money that they earn so dearly, daily being in danger of losing their lives. But when the voyage has been made and they have received their pay, they think not of the hardships and dangers through which they have passed, but spend all they have and are then ready for another trip.[15]

Just before his chance encounter with Fremont which was to change his life and make him famous, Kit pondered his sixteen years in the mountains. It was an experience mixing self-reliance with great loneliness and a deprivation taken for granted:

> The greater part of that time passed far from the habitations of civilized man, and receiving no other food than that which I could procure with my rifle. Perhaps, once a year, I would have a meal consisting of bread, meat, sugar, and coffee; would consider it a luxury.[16]

Such were the boundaries of Kit's world. They were soon to be expanded when in 1842 Kit took a trip back to Missouri to see his family. He quickly tired of the settlements, as he said, and took a steamboat up the Missouri River. "As luck would have it," he met Fremont on board. The young officer was preparing to outfit his first expedition to map a route to the Pacific, and Kit told him that he "thought I could guide him to any point he would wish to go." Fremont later described the meeting—and Carson—in his memoirs:

> I was pleased with him and his manner of address at this first meeting. He was

---

[15]Ibid., 50.
[16]Ibid., 79.

a man of medium height, broad-shouldered and deep-chested, with a clear steady blue eye and a frank speech and address; quiet and unassuming.[17]

In January of 1844, after having searched in vain for the mythical Buenaventura River that was supposed to flow to the Pacific, Fremont and his men found themselves struggling to make a winter crossing of the Sierra Nevada. California may have been a paradise, but Americans who wanted to get there had either to cross the inferno of the desert or chance the possibility of being trapped in the frozen hell of the Sierra. Kit's description of their extreme hardships was remarkably restrained. The snow was so deep that in order to move forward at all, as Kit told it, they had to beat it down in front of them with mallets. The men were reduced to eating the flesh of mules which were themselves starved enough to chew on "one another's tails and the leather of the pack saddles...." When they reached Sutter's fort, two of the men were so traumatized by the experience that they became deranged. Kit attributed it to their first starving and then overeating.[18]

Coming out of the mountains Kit said he could see "in the distance the green valley of the Sacramento and the Coast Range. I knew the place well, had been there seventeen years before." At Sutter's Fort they were treated "in a princely manner" and soon recovered from the wear and tear of their journey. They stayed for about a month, and then began the homeward trek down the San Joaquin Valley, across the Tehachapis to the Mojave River and on to the old Spanish Trail. On their return they aided a party of Mexicans bound for New Mexico whose horses had been stolen by Indians. Fremont said anyone who wanted could volunteer to help them, so Kit and Alexis Godey stepped forward, thinking, as Kit said, "that some men of our party would join us. They did not." Nevertheless, Kit—like Father de Smet whom he respected—also "wished to do good" when he had the opportunity. Kit and Godey went after the

---

[17]Ibid., 81-84; Fremont's *Memoirs* quoted in a footnote on p. 84. See also Donald Jackson and Mary Lee Spence, eds., *The Expeditions of John Charles Frémont*, 3 vols. In vol. II, p. 170, of this work is Fremont's first mention of Kit Carson, in his Report to the Chief of the Corps of Topographical Engineers, Colonel John James Abert. Fremont listed the members of his expedition, and said that "Christopher Carson, more familiarly known, for his exploits in the mountains, as Kit Carson, was our guide." Later in the report (p. 180) he gave an admiring description of Kit: "Mounted on a fine horse, without a saddle, scouring over the prairie, Kit was one of the finest pictures of a horseman I have ever seen."

[18]*'Dear Old Kit'*, 90-91.

Indians anyway, engaged about thirty of them in a fight and recovered the horses. They found that the Indians had killed several of the Mexicans, men and women, "their bodies horribly mutilated." But Kit was used to Indian warfare and was not given to moralizing over Indian barbarism versus the "civilized" conduct of whites.[19]

Kit returned home and, for a time, tried to settle down on a ranch 45 miles east of Taos. But in 1845 he again received the call from Fremont. He said: "I had given my word to Fremont that, in case he should return for the purpose of making any more exploration, that I would willingly join him." It's doubtful that Kit was yet capable of leading the quiet life of a rancher. When word came from Fremont, he and his partner, Dick Owens, sold their land "for about half it was worth...." Fremont praised Carson as "prompt, self-sacrificing, and true."[20]

Kit Carson joined Fremont's fateful third expedition to California at Bent's Fort on the Arkansas River, unaware that he and his commander would soon be involved in war against the Californians, though how much Fremont knew about the impending conflict with Mexico and what his instructions were, are still matters of conjecture.[21] From Salt Lake Kit was sent ahead to reconnoiter the Great Basin; he said "Fremont was bound to cross. Nothing was impossible for him to perform if required in his explorations." Fremont's persistence was something Kit understood and appreciated. He had fully absorbed the work ethic. The crossing of a sixty mile stretch of desert was described matter-of-factly. Kit said simply that "no water or grass, not a particle of vegetation could be found" in a country "as level and bare as a barn floor...." The company had divided, with Theodore Talbot going south under the guidance of Joseph Walker, and Fremont with Kit crossing into California (via Donner Pass which had yet to receive its name from the grisly experiences of the trapped Donner Party), and arriving at Sutter's Fort on December 9, 1845.[22]

Kit recalled that "Captain Sutter was happy to see us and furnished us everything we wanted." But his memory must have failed him, because Sutter was not at his fort when Fremont and company arrived this

[19]Ibid., 91-93.

[20]Ibid., 95-96; Fremont quoted in fn., 98.

[21]See Ferol Egan, *Fremont: Explorer for a Restless Nation*, 310ff, for a discussion of Fremont in California.

[22]*'Dear Old Kit'*, 96-100.

time.[23] Instead the party was met by John Bidwell, Sutter's majordomo, who offended Fremont by pleading shortages when asked for supplies. Bidwell finally saw to it that Fremont received the horses and equipment he needed, but Sutter did not return until three days after Fremont and his men had left.[24] Kit said they went down the San Joaquin Valley to the headwaters of Kings River where they had a brush with some Indians and lost their animals. They then returned to the fort before going to San Jose. This time Sutter was there. In his narrative, Kit telescoped what had taken several weeks into the span of several days.[25]

Kit also omitted any mention of what was construed by the Californians as provocative behavior on the part of his fellow Americans when he next refered to "the very impertinent order from General Castro, ordering him [Fremont] to immediately leave the country and, if he did not, that he would drive him out."[26] Fremont had so far been treated courteously by the California authorities at Monterey, where he had been introduced by the United States Consul Thomas O. Larkin to both General José Castro, and former Governor Juan Bautista Alvarado. He had told them that his expedition was in the interests of science and commerce, and that his men were civilians, not soldiers. But José Castro may in the meantime have received orders from Mexico to expel Fremont. And Fremont's minor problems with several Californians just added fuel to the flames. Fremont contemptuously dismissed a complaint by the alcalde that a horse in his company had been stolen from a Californian. Fremont claimed the horse had been with them from the beginning, and that the man making the accusation was a "straggling vagabond" who should be horsewhipped. To make matters worse, some of his men had gotten drunk and one had insulted the daughter of Angel Castro, an uncle of General José Castro. This fellow's companions had quickly and forcefully escorted him from the premises, but Fremont's sending Castro ten dollars as a form of restitution must also have been seen as an insult.[27]

---

[23]Ibid., 100; in a footnote on pp. 80-81, Carter states that Carson made errors about dates, but not about his recollections concerning persons. Here is a case where Kit seemed to have erred, at least by omission.

[24]Ferol Egan, op. cit., 308-309.

[25]'Dear Old Kit', 100.

[26]Ibid., 100-101.

[27]See Ferol Egan, op. cit., 318; Neal Harlow, *California Conquered*, 66; Jackson and Spence, eds., *The Expeditions of John Charles Fremont*, Vol. II, 63-68, 70, 78, 80n, 85, 123n, 172.

Fremont had told the authorities that his men would winter in the San Joaquin Valley, away from the settlements. Yet in March he was still near Monterey. Both Castro and Fremont were aware that their two countries were on the verge of war. In retrospect, it is surprising that Castro did not immediately order Fremont out of the country. Fremont's raising of the American flag on Hawk Peak in defiance of Castro's order of expulsion was characteristically theatrical, but foolish in the light of the fact that he was outnumbered and had not been ordered to California to start a war. Kit Carson's comment on the situation displayed the sarcasm he would occasionally employ against people he felt lacked courage: "We remained in our position on the mountain for three days, had become tired of waiting for the attack of the valiant Mexican General."[28]

It was Fremont who retreated, however, not José Castro. The expedition went north on its way to Oregon. At Lassen's Ranch in northern California, American settlers requested aid against some Indians who they said threatened the settlements. Fremont and company, in a "preemptive strike," impetuously attacked the Indians in their encampment, killing a large number in what Kit Carson described as "a perfect butchery." This act may have been unnecessary and might also have been responsible for provoking the Klamath Indians to attack Fremont shortly thereafter.[29] Messengers had arrived with the news that a Lieutenant Archibald Gillespie was an hour's ride to the south with important messages for Fremont. Fremont turned back to meet Gillespie, and that night the Klamaths snuck into their camp and killed three men. Kit Carson's description of it revealed his admiration for bravery (even when displayed by an enemy), and his own military calculus of losses. He said that the Klamath Chief who led the attack was "the bravest Indian I ever saw. If his men had been as brave as himself, we surely would all have been killed." He went on to offer consolation for the deaths of his comrades by saying "that if we had not arrived, Gillespie and his four

---

[28]Egan, op. cit., 319-320; 'Dear Old Kit', 101. Kit could also be sarcastic at the expense of Americans when he felt they deserved contempt. He said (p. 130) of one army officer who had whipped a Cheyenne Chief: "I presume courage was oozing from the finger ends of the officer and, as the Indians were in his power, he wished to be relieved of such [a] commodity."

[29]'Dear Old Kit', 101. In Kit Carson: A Pattern For Heroes, 152, Guild and Carter state that "It is unlikely that the attack described by Carson was justified and Carson must take his share of the blame for it."

men would have been killed. We lost three, so two lives had been saved."[30]

Kit had no apologies to make for what may have been the unnecessary deaths of both Indians and whites. In fact, he made no apologies for any of his activities. He was a man of action who had no training and showed little inclination for reflecting on the moral or historical implications of deeds after they were done. On at least one occasion his memory distorted events in his favor, and he completely omitted another incident about which he could not have been too proud.

After Lt. Gillespie delivered his messages to Fremont, the party of Americans turned south for California again. Riding ahead of the rest, Kit and ten others had another skirmish with Indians. He claimed that they attacked the Indians and "chastised" them before Fremont and the rest of the party could come up, and that the latter "arrived too late for the sport." In fact Kit had gotten himself into trouble by leading the charge into a river to get at the Indians, and wetting his powder. They were extricated from their predicament by the arrival of Fremont and the others. But the way Kit remembered it he had "determined to attack them, charged on them, fought for some time, killed a number, and the balance fled." This was the usual way that Kit had successfully dealt with "hostiles" in numerous encounters, so his memory was only slightly less than completely accurate.[31]

The one really questionable act of his career in California, however, the killing of two unarmed Californians, José de los Berryesa and his twin nephews Ramon and Francisco de Haro, Kit omitted entirely from his autobiography. Hostilities had begun between the Americans and the Californians even though no official news of war with Mexico had yet reached the west coast. This did not stop Fremont, whom Kit credited with engineering the Bear Flag Revolt and dispatching the men who seized Sonoma. Kit also mentioned the killing of the Americans Cowie and Fowler by Californians under the command of Joaquin de la Torre,

---

[30]*Dear Old Kit*, 103-104; see Egan, op. cit., 328-331, for a detailed account of the attack.

[31]Ibid., 105. See also Thomas S. Martin, With Fremont To California and The Southwest, 1845-1849, 10-11. Martin made a revealing statement about the attitude of Fremont's party toward the Indians they met in California. He said (p. 8) on their way north up the Sacramento River valley, they killed game "and an occasional indian [sic]. Of the latter we made it a rule to spare none of the bucks."

who he said had been sent "to attack us and drive us from the country."[32] Revenge may have been a motivating factor in the murder of the Californians, though in 1853, when asked why they had been killed after they were already prisoners, Kit was reported to have shifted the responsibility to Fremont. The latter allegedly told Kit, "I want no prisoners, Mr. Carson, do your duty." Putting the matter in terms of duty was well calculated to elicit the desired response from Kit Carson, a man who took his assigned responsibilities seriously, even if uncertain of their moral boundaries.[33]

The war in California would further Kit's reputation for bravery, loyalty and devotion to duty. A question has been raised, however, as to how much Kit Carson himself may have contributed to American arrogance toward the Mexican Californians, an arrogance that helped to provoke the revolt in southern California, and that led to the disaster for American forces at the Battle of San Pasqual. Carson was accused of telling the officers under General Kearny that the Californians would not fight, that all the Americans had to do was charge down on them and they would run away.[34] From his autobiography it is clear that Kit's attitude toward Mexicans was at best ambivalent. He was acquainted with Mexicans whose bravery was unquestionable, and he credited them in his autobiography. In 1843, for example, while carrying dispatches from Santa Fe to traders on the Arkansas, Kit and an un-named Mexican ran into a large Ute war party:

> The Mexican advised me to mount my horse and make my escape, that the
> Indians had no animal that could catch him and, as for him, he thought the

---

[32] *'Dear Old Kit'*, 107-110; Thomas Martin, op. cit., 12, also said that Fremont told them he would make a campaign in the country and that they could disband and choose a leader. They chose Fremont, who then told them to elect an officer and go take Sonoma. Said Thomas: "This was fully a month before we heard of the war with Mexico."

[33] Guild and Carter, *Kit Carson: A Pattern For Heroes*, 154.

[34] Charles L. Camp, "Kit Carson In California," in *California Historical Society Quarterly*, vol. 1, (1922-23), 111-151; Camp cites a letter in the Bancroft Library written by one John M. Swan blaming Carson for mis-leading Kearny's forces about the Californians. Camp discounts this and cites (144) Lieutenant William Emory's report which said that Carson just brought the news that war in California was over and that "the country had surrendered without a blow...." Whether he actually said that the Californians would not fight may be disputed. I do not think that Kit Carson was entirely free from the generally held prejudices of his day, though I believe he had a greater tendency than many others who wrote or conveyed information about Mexicans to judge each case on its merits.

Indians would not injure him and they, in all probability, would kill me. I considered the advice very good and was about to mount my horse. I changed my mind and thought how cowardly it would be in me to desert this man that so willingly offered to sacrifice his life to have [save?] mine. I told him no, that I would die with him.

Together, the two men faced the Indians, who finally left after seeing that they could not attack without losing a few men themselves. Kit never seemed to have taken the trouble to learn his companion's name, or at least could not remember it thirteen years later.[35]

In the initial stages of the war, Fremont and his men were transported on board the USS *Cyane* from Monterey to San Diego. (Though he does not mention it in his autobiography, Kit was violently seasick.) From San Diego, they marched north against Los Angeles, where Kit maintained that the Californians, "hearing of our approach, though they were 700 strong, fled...." On the same page, Kit praised the bravery of Commodore Stockton and his sailors and marines. Kit did not need to resort to name-calling in order to make the contrast any more apparent. He now thought that the war was over, and from what he had seen the Californians were clearly no fighters.[36]

Kit was next ordered to carry dispatches to Washington, an opportunity for him to see his family in Taos and be lionized in the capital. It was to be, as Fremont put it, "a culminating point in Carson's life." Unfortunately, he ran into General Stephen Watts Kearny, on his way to California after having pacified New Mexico without firing a shot. General Kearny had other ideas for Kit. He was commanded to turn around and guide the General into California. Kit was not happy about this, but neither was he a man to disobey orders. He expressed no noticeable resentment in his autobiography about being deprived of this opportunity. He just made the terse statement that Kearny "ordered me to join him as a guide. I done so, and Fitzpatrick continued on with the dispatches."[37] It was left to others to explicate the full implications for Kit Carson of having been denied this opportunity. Captain Philip St. George Cooke, leading the Mormon Battalion to California, was present when Kit arrived in

---

[35] *'Dear Old Kit'*, 85-87.
[36] Ibid., 111.
[37] Ibid., 112. Fremont in footnote same page.

Kearny's camp. He recognized Kit's sacrifice and the measure of his commitment to duty, even when it was not to Kit's liking. He reported that

> Carson resisted very firmly, at first; he had pledged himself to deliver his mail in Washington.... Did the general [Kearny] stop to think what it was he demanded? A man had just ridden eight hundred miles over a desert—a wilderness — where he could meet no human being save a few savages likely to seek his destruction; (he rode ninety miles without halting, over a jornada of sand!) he had arrived at the verge of society, and *near the residence of his family!* He is required to turn right back, and for another year of absence! This was no common sacrifice to duty![38]

When Kearny's reduced forces reached California they learned that the war was not quite over. In spite of their exhaustion and the poor condition of their animals, the men were eager for a fight.[39] Kit described the Battle of San Pasqual in his usual matter- of-fact tone. Once again luck (or Providence) was with him, because he was thrown from his horse, broke his rifle and, in his own words "came very near being trodden to death. I being in advance, the whole company had to pass over me." Kit just grabbed a gun from a dead dragoon (there were to be many that day, most of them lanced to death by the skilled California horsemen) and "joined in the melee." Kit was not given to reflection. He did not call the battle an American defeat, nor did he make any comment on the bravery of the Californians. He just went on to tell of his own barefoot trek to San Diego for help, through the Californians' lines and "over a country covered with prickly pear and rocks." His final comment on the Californians—even after the Battle of San Pasqual had shown that they were quite capable of fighting—was that they "only stood a few rounds" from Stockton's artillery at the Battle of the San Gabriel River before running away. A few years later on the Santa Fe trail, when threatened by some Cheyenne, Kit would express in no uncertain terms his feelings about the reliability of the Mexicans who accompanied him: "I had [a] poor opinion of their bravery in case I was attacked."[40]

---

[38]Phillip St. George Cooke, *The Conquest of New Mexico and California: An Historical & Personal Narrative*, 44. Emphasis in original.

[39]See Harlow, *California Conquered*, 174-192 for a discussion of the Battle of San Pasqual. Harlow says (p.183) that "Carson and Gillespie had probably assured him [Kearny] that the Californians were cowardly and would not make a stand."

[40]*'Dear Old Kit'*, 113-116; 130.

Kit was to be a dispatch rider several more times before leaving California for his home in Taos. For a time in the winter of 1847-48 he was also posted on the Tejon Pass to guard against Indian raids. In 1853 he would return for the last time, driving a herd of sheep to Sacramento. While there he went over to have a final look at San Francisco which had grown so much that Kit said he would not have recognized the place if he had not been there so many times before. His years in the mountains had prepared him, and his experiences in California with Fremont had made him famous. He was not free from prejudice, but neither did he let it tinge every judgement, like some of his contemporaries. He was a compelling hero to large numbers of his countrymen because, like them, he too was a "common man" with qualities they could all respect, but which were by no means out of their reach. Every person who ever faced hardship and danger with fortitude, lived an honest life and tried to do what he or she thought right—without expectations of great reward or recognition—could identify with Kit Carson. He was a product of his times, with its particular strengths and weaknesses. On his last dispatch ride from California to Washington, D.C., he passed through Santa Fe where he learned that the United States Senate had failed to confirm his appointment as a Lieutenant in the U.S. Army. His friends there advised him not to continue on with the messages. This was his reply:

> ...I determined to fulfill the duty. That mattered not to me if, in the discharge of a duty of service beneficial to the public, whether I was of the rank of Lieutenant or holding the credit of an experienced mountaineer. Having gained much honor and credit in performance of all duties entrusted to my charge, I would on no account wish to forfeit the good opinion of a majority of my countrymen because the Senate of the United States did not deem it proper to confirm on me an appointment of an office that I never sought and one which, if confirmed, I would have to resign at the termination of the war.[41]

---

[41]Ibid., 116-121.

CHAPTER VIII

Zenas Leonard & George Nidever

In 1833 an expedition sent out by Captain B.L.E. Bonneville with the covert backing of the U.S. Government,[1] and led by the veteran mountain man Joseph R. Walker, made its way from the Great Salt Lake across the Great Basin and over the Sierra into California. These men were after furs, but they were also an advance party embodying the aspirations of American Manifest Destiny. Among this group were two men who would tell their stories and whose personalities were representative of these aspirations. They were the extraordinary "ordinary" men of the Jacksonian era who helped show their countrymen the way to California. One was Zenas Leonard, who returned to his native Pennsylvania and published his *Adventures of Zenas Leonard* in 1839. The other was George Nidever who settled down in California, living in Santa Barbara and ranging up and down the coast as a sea otter hunter.[2]

Like Kit Carson, both these men had the experience and survival skills that were typical of the westward ranging trappers who ended up in California. George Nidever was born into a large family on the east Tennessee frontier in 1802. His father was a farmer who had taken part in the wars against the Cherokees and Shawnees. The family moved to North Carolina when George was five, and then to Crawford County, Missouri, when he was almost fourteen. But the search for something better pushed him onward in a pattern repeated thousands of times during the settlement of the west, as it still drives Americans today. "When I was about 18 (in 1820 or thereabouts)," Nidever said, "a party of 7 families started through the wilderness for Arkansas, and my brother

---

[1]See Bil Gilbert, *Westering Man: the Life of Joseph Walker*, 97-100, for a discussion of evidence supporting this conclusion.

[2]Milo Milton Quaife, ed., *Narrative of the Adventures of Zenas Leonard*; William Henry Ellison, ed., *The Life and Adventures of George Nidever*.

Jacob and I accompanied them, with a few cattle we took to sell, for the purpose of seeing Arkansas and with the intention of going back for our family if we found the country good." They did, and the Nidevers moved to Fort Smith, Arkansas, where George lived with his family for a few more years before deciding that the life of a farmer was not for him.[3]

Neither was it attractive to Zenas Leonard, who informed his father in 1830 that he could survive very well without having to grub rocks from the soil of the family farm. His father showed him the door. Yet there must have been more than one moment when he wished he was back on the farm. Leonard survived some of the hardest times any mountain man had ever experienced, being in several instances close to death by freezing and from Indian arrows. He was also educated enough to keep a detailed journal of this part of his life which became the basis for his narrative. It is direct, thoughtful, and generally unembellished by exaggerations or tall tales.[4]

George Nidever too related his remarkable experiences without frills. But he was seventy five years old when he told his story and, like many of his fellow mountain men, he was illiterate. Nidever was a modest man and his adventures had to be coaxed out of him by Edward F. Murray, one of H. H. Bancroft's assistants. Murray was impressed with Nidever's understated, straightforward and unemotional recounting of the dangers, hardships, and feats of skill and courage that made up his life. His matter-of-fact telling had the ring of unvarnished truth and Murray could not doubt the basic integrity of the teller. Yet there was an obvious pride that the old trapper took in his reputation. When Nidever had finished his narrative, Murray read it back to the old man, who attested to its correctness by signing his name in a shaky hand.[5]

His hand may have been unsure when employed in the unfamiliar task of writing his name, but when it came to shooting, he was anything but unsteady. By the time that he was nine years old, George Nidever was familiar with firearms. In his own words, he was a "crack shot," impressing older men with his prowess and becoming "one of the most successful hunters in that portion of the country." He killed three times

---

[3] *Life and Adventures*, 1-3.

[4] For interesting information about Zenas Leonard, see Gilbert, op. cit., 123-124.

[5] *Life and Adventures*, xi; Nidever's signature is on facsimile of the final page of the dictation, 90.

as much game as any of the others. After he out-shot them using their own rifles, they stopped attributing his skill to his gun, and admitted he was the best.[6]

With this early success and recognition, being a farmer was not likely to satisfy him for long. There was a definite way to use such skills to make money, and George Nidever, like his Jacksonian contemporaries, looked for ways to turn a profit. First he went up the Canadian River with his friend Alexander Sinclair to cut cedar logs. The plan was to float them down the rivers to New Orleans and sell them. The partners worked for over a year getting their raft together, and even successfully evaded an attempt by the Cherokees to steal it; but nature intervened and the currents smashed the raft against the river bank, breaking it up and forcing them to abandon their project. In his own words: "This misfortune decided both Sinclair and myself to take to hunting and trapping...."[7]

On this expedition were a number of men who ended up in California, including the troublesome Isaac Graham who would be arrested and deported by the California government in 1840. Whatever he may have been to the Californians, to George Nidever Graham was a brave man and a friend. Caught in the open by some Arapahoes, Nidever and Graham made a run for the timber. Graham was much the faster runner but, as Nidever said, "it was not his character to desert a comrade in danger, so we kept together straining every nerve to reach the shelter of the woods." They had to run for nearly a mile. Exhausted and frightened, "although naturally a brave man," Graham was about to fire on the Indians when Nidever saw them throw down their guns. He prevented Graham from shooting, and they parleyed with the Indians. They succeeded in convincing the Arapahoes that they were traveling with some eighty other trappers who would certainly avenge their deaths. That night they were attacked by Pawnees, who ran off several horses and so thoroughly frightened the leader of the expedition, a Colonel Robert Bean, that he hid himself and forfeited the good opinion of his fellow trappers—and his leadership. After this display of cowardice, he "was totally disregarded and hardly treated civilly...." This incident displayed one of the essen-

[6]Ibid., 5.
[7]Ibid., 3-4

tial elements in the code of the mountain man: courage under attack and unwavering support for a comrade regardless of one's own personal danger. Colonel Bean was conveniently on hand as a contrast to Graham and Nidever. Bean soon left the mountains, never to return.[8]

The expedition was not to be without its casualties, however, one of whom was George Nidever's brother, Mark. Mark was killed by the same band of Arapahoes who had chased George and Graham. These Indians had simply feigned friendship, and waited for a chance to strike. From such a painful experience, George Nidever learned a valuable lesson, one which every mountain man needed for survival:

> In an Indian country one cannot take too many precautions, and I owe my life many times over to my habitual vigilance and caution in all my movements while in the mountains. Of the many trappers I have known that were killed in the mountains by Indians, a very large proportion of them were careless and imprudent in their habits.[9]

George's unfortunate brother, however, had been an experienced man and a good shot. In this case, it was not enough to save him!

Zenas Leonard too had his narrow escapes and saw his comrades perish. In an encounter with some Arikaras, Leonard said that the despair felt by the men when they were trapped inside a depression in the earth, surrounded by hostile Indians intent on killing them, and without any apparent possibility of escape, "may be imagined, but not described." As their only consolation, they vowed to sell their lives dearly. Still Leonard was oppressed by the thought that he was about to die. Without hope and without expectations, they waited for the end—when the Arikara chief arrived and called off his warriors. The chief's intervention, and his aid in helping them escape that night, were without any clear explanation except that the chief had not been consulted before his warriors took action. In this case, Indian protocol had saved the lives of all but one man who insisted on going after his strayed horses. In Leonard's words, "he never returned."[10]

Shortly after this incident, Leonard, alone and without his rifle, was

---

[8]Ibid., 10-14. See also David Weber, *The Taos Trappers*, 196-98, for a discussion of this incident and citations of several other sources confirming Bean's cowardice.

[9]*Life and Adventures*, 15-16.

[10]*Narrative...of Zenas Leonard*, 90-92.

caught out by a Blackfoot Indian who tried to induce him with signs of friendship to come out of the bushes where he had taken refuge, and to drop his knife which was his only weapon. But Leonard was not fooled; he knew the Indian meant to kill him, but he thought he might have a chance if he could drive the Indian off by throwing rocks. When he bent over to pick one up, however, he received an arrow in the side. Pulling it out, he ran back to camp with the Indian at his heels. The men in camp chased off the Blackfoot, and Leonard, after hovering on the brink of death with a high fever, recovered from the wound. Bur he was losing any illusions he had about the quick and easy fortune to be made from the fur trade:

> When we first embarked in this business it was with the expectation that to ensure a fortune in the fur trade only required a little perseverance and industry. We were not told that we were to be constantly annoyed by the Indians, but that it only required the observance of a peaceful disposition on our part, to secure their friendship and even support. Some Indians with whom we had intercourse, it is true, had been of great advantage to us in our trapping expeditions; but then it would be of short duration,—for, if they would not render themselves obnoxious by their own treachery, our friendship with them would be sure to meet with an interruption through some ingenious artifice of a neighboring jealous tribe. Such had been the life we had led, and such the reward.

Some men wanted to leave; others seemed to lose all concern for what might happen to them, and became, as Leonard saw it, like the savages they lived among. Most thought their luck would change.[11]

There were many ways to die in the mountains: Indians, grizzly bears, accidental wounds, blizzards—and other mountain men. The trappers were beyond any recourse to civilization and its laws, often precisely because they wanted to escape such laws. They were a law unto themselves, and a life led constantly on the edge of violence could sometimes spill over into murderous attacks on each other. George Nidever chronicled one such attack in which a man named James Anderson, a big man and evidently somewhat of a bully, was killed by another trapper named Cambridge Green. According to Nidever, who heard about it after it happened, Anderson kept tossing the smaller man's beaver traps into

---

[11]Ibid., 97-101.

the river and setting up his own in their place. Green warned Anderson that if he continued to do this, he, Green, would kill him. Others in the company (Ewing Young's party which went to California from Taos in 1830) also tried to warn Anderson that Green meant what he said, but Anderson brushed them aside. He kept removing Green's traps until one day, according to Nidever, Green "returned quietly to camp, walked up to him, and shot him through the heart."[12]

Zenas Leonard had his own experience with the "law of the strongest" when he and two of his companions were forced to give up their furs because their leader had made a deal with some other trappers. Without consulting Leonard and the others who had actually done the work, "Captain Stephens" agreed to give these men a share in the furs that Leonard and his friends had trapped, if they would go into the mountains and retrieve them from where they were cached. When finally informed of this arrangement Leonard protested, but was told by Stephens

> that he would not be accountable for any of the furs, and the only way to obtain any of it was to take it by force. Seeing the folly of further resistance— 18 against 3—we were obliged to surrender our earnings, which they took and divided equally among themselves.[13]

In general, Leonard was not pleased with the business ethics of the mountain men. In his first meeting with the veteran Thomas Fitzpatrick, Leonard was appalled at the latter's apparent selfishness. Here they were, wintering at Fort Laramie in a terrifying wilderness where they did not expect to meet any civilized beings, and they were surprised by a visit from Fitzpatrick and several other trappers. These men were also taken aback to see Leonard and his companions, but not happy about it. More men in the mountains meant more competition, fewer beaver and smaller profits. Leonard said that Fitzpatrick and his men were treated hospitably, yet they still "refused to give us any information whatever, and appeared disposed to treat us as intruders." It caused him to reflect on the disgraceful selfishness of human nature.[14]

[12]*Life and Adventures*, 20.
[13]*Narrative...of Zenas Leonard*, 45.
[14]Ibid., 11-13.

Neither man had yet soured on the life of a trapper in spite of its ethics and its perils. George Nidever brought his beaver skins into Taos, easily avoided the Mexican customs duties, and received around $10.00 per pelt. So he set out again in September of 1831, trapped the headwaters of the Arkansas, wintered in a valley of the Green River where "snow seldom fell and even then never remained," and made his way to the summer rendezvous of 1832 at Pierre's Hole on the western side of the Grand Tetons in what is today Idaho. He arrived just in time to participate along with Zenas Leonard in the famous "Battle of Pierre's Hole" between the gathered fur trappers and their perennial enemies the Blackfeet.[15]

This was the biggest battle ever fought between Indians and trappers, and both men left realistic accounts of it that reflected little glory on the mountain men. A large band of Gros Ventres (closely allied with the Blackfeet tribes) was discovered approaching the rendezvous. Ordinarily hostile, when they saw the large numbers of well-armed whites facing them, this band sought to parley rather than to fight. Their chief rode up carrying a white flag, but he was met by a man with a grudge, Antoine Godin, whose father had been killed by these Indians. Godin was accompanied by a chief of the Flathead tribe, traditional enemies of the Blackfeet. When Godin gave the signal, the Flathead chief fired and killed the Blackfoot chief—and the battle was on.[16] The Indians took shelter in some thick timber and constructed a fortification of logs while the mountain men, in George Nidver's version, held a council and elected as their leader William Sublette, an experienced trapper. Many of the men feared to attack the Indians in such heavy timber but, Nidever said, their objections "were overruled by Sublette and others, who said we would have to fight them anyway and now that we had them at a disadvantage, we must profit by it." Some liquor was apparently handed round at the beginning of the battle, and one man, half intoxicated, tried to display his bravado by climbing up the logs of the Indians' fort and peering over the top. Here was another lesson in avoiding foolhardy behavior. As Nidever put it: "He paid for his temerity with his life." Several of the

---

[15] *Life and Adventures*, 22-26.

[16] For a detailed account of the Battle of Pierre's Hole, see Hiram Martin Chittenden, *The American Fur Trade of the Far West*, vol. 2, 650-656.

mountain men, including William Sublette and Nidever's friend
Alexander Sinclair, were wounded in trying to get at the Indians. Sinclair later died of his wounds. The others kept up the fight until by sunset they had approached close enough to set the Indians' fort on fire. But
before doing this they decided to give the Indians a chance to surrender,
and sent "a renegade Blackfoot" to try to persuade them. The Indians
now displayed an uncomman courage, and the mountain men proved
they were human and, despite their reputations, quite capable of being
inspired with panic. The Indians refused to surrender. Instead, as Nidever remembered it, they sent back the message that "although they
would all be killed that day, the next day it would be our turn, as they had
sent word to a very large village of their nation, situated only a short distance from there, numbering 1500 lodges." This information was
enough to immediately scare off one contingent of trappers, who with-
drew and forced the others to follow suit.[17]

Zenas Leonard told a similar story which also revealed the importance the mountain men placed on their reputations for bravery. When
the battle began, he was primarily concerned with leaving the proper
impression of his courage. Any man who seemed to show undue caution
was treated as a coward by the others, and anyone who rushed boldly
into the fray enhanced his reputation among his fellow mountain men.
So Leonard and a companion named Smith charged into the Indians'
fort where the latter was almost immediately shot and wounded. Smith
asked Leonard to carry him out, much to Leonard's relief. As he
explained it, "I was glad to get out of this unpleasant situation under any
pretext—provided my reputation for courage would not be questioned."
Soon the Blackfeet stratagem worked so well in spooking the mountain
men and their Indian allies that in five minutes not one of them
remained within one hundred yards of the fort. Leonard had to admire
the Blackfeet for their cleverness and courage when he saw that each
trapper "thought only of his own security, and run for life without ever
looking round...." But since the panic seemed to infect everyone, no single reputation suffered.[18]

Leaving the vicinity of Pierre's Hole, where they feared more conflict

---

[17]*Life and Adventures*, 26-30.
[18]*Narrative...of Zenas Leonard*, 71-74.

with the Blackfeet, Nidever's group continued trapping around the Yellowstone River. As winter came on "the cold was very severe." The men also had a confrontation with some Crow Indians who had stolen horses from them. They went to the Crow village and tried to get the horses back, without success. Here George had a run-in with one of the Indians,

> a large powerful fellow [who] took a fancy to my powder horn. He made signs for me to give it to him, and upon being refused he took out his knife and was about to cut the string with which it was hung from my shoulder and take it. I had my hand on the handle of my knife and was determined to kill him the moment he cut the string; at the same time I called out to our men to look out for themselves. Our Capt. spoke some Crow tongue and warned the Indian, who immediately desisted from his design, all of our men having at that time laid hold of their rifles. The Indians saw that we meant to fight them if necessary and they wisely let us alone.[19]

Nidever thus proved himself an experienced mountain man, for this was the typical way that troublesome Indians were dealt with—a show of force and the use of it if necessary. It is easy to see that such habits would make the trappers respected and even feared by the relatively peaceful inhabitants of California.

That winter in the mountains was severe; it was enough to prompt George Nidever and several others "to seek a warmer climate, and having heard many wonderful stories of California, we settled upon coming here." He joined the expedition led by Joseph Walker which was going to California under the auspices of Captain Benjamin Bonneville. His motivation, like so many others after him, was to escape the harsh winter weather and he must have been impressed by the descriptions of California from several of the other mountain men who had been there.[20]

After the difficulties and disappointments he had experienced in the Rockies, Zenas Leonard too was ready to go to California when the

---

[19]*Life and Adventures*, 30-31.

[20]Ibid., 31-32. William H. Ellison, who edited Nidever's autobiography for publication, states in a footnote (p. 102) that this was the George Nidever of 1878 speaking about California, and that he could not have had these thoughts in 1833 when he knew nothing of California. But at the rendevous of 1833 was at least one man who had been to California with Ewing Young in 1831, and was to accompany Nidever on the 1833 trip to California led by Joseph Walker. That man was Powell (Pauline) Weaver. There were probably others, so that Nidever could easily have heard talk about the climate and hospitality to be found in California. See Bil Gilbert, op. cit., 124; David Weber, op. cit, 148.

opportunity arose. To him it was a chance to trap what he thought would be a rich and virgin territory abounding with beaver. So he hired on as Joseph Walker's clerk, a responsible position that showed he was several notches above his fellow trappers in education and probably in steadiness, reliability and organizational skills. He must also have been inspired with something of the westward-driving spirit of his times because he said he was "anxious to go to the coast of the Pacific" and offered no further reason.[21]

On their way down the Humboldt River, Walker's party had their famous (or infamous) encounter with the "Digger" Indians. These Indians stole some traps, and in retaliation Zenas Leonard said that some of Walker's men killed several of them in spite of Walker's orders not to molest or provoke them. According to Nidever, these Indians—actually Paiutes, a Shoshonean people—then began to harass and threaten them in ever increasing numbers. Zenas Leonard feared that "if they could succeed in getting any advantage over us, we had no expectation that they would give us any quarter." Certainly, the mountain men did not give the Indians any. In a confrontation with 400 or 500 Indians (Nidever's estimate), the trappers, Nidever included, charged the Indians' advance guard of 34 or 35 and killed almost all of them. "This," in Nidever's opinion, "appeared to completely disenhearten our enemies for they permitted us to pass without further opposition."[22]

The trappers doubtless lost little sleep over killing Indians who appeared to threaten them. George Nidever had further provocation in the death of his brother Mark. After the massacre of the Paiutes, as Walker's party entered the Sierra Nevada, Nidever went ahead with Walker and Zenas Leonard to look for a campsite with water. They had separated and George was alone when he saw two Indians coming up the trail. He immediately assumed they were following him and stepped back among the trees.

I saw that they had not seen me or discovered my tracks, as they passed within

---

[21]*Narrative...of Zenas Leonard*, 105.

[22]Ibid., 111-117; *Life and Adventures*, 32-33. Most later historians, including Bil Gilbert, defend the attack as necessary in an unknown country to discourage the Indians who so overwhelmingly outnumbered the whites, and as consistent with the mores of the times. Nevertheless, one wonders about the necessity of such a slaughter.

a few feet of me, jabbering as they went along. I at first had a notion to let them go but the death of my brother, so treacherously murdered by these red devils, was too fresh in my mind. The Indians were travelling in single file, and watching my chance, just before they would have to turn around a small point of rocks, I fired, shooting both of them dead at the first shot.

This may have bothered Nidever more at the time than he was to recall later, because as Zenas Leonard told it, Nidever was sorry when he discovered what he had done. These Indians, who had had nothing to do with the death of George Nidever's brother half a world away, suffered George's retribution for having been Indians. But this was the way of the frontier. The Indians too exacted their revenge indiscriminately against whatever whites were available.[23]

Walker and his men reached the Sierra and began their crossing in October of 1833. According to Zenas Leonard's account, they were introduced to these great California mountains by encountering snow one hundred feet deep in some places. The men were starving. Some of them were mutinous and wanted to turn back to the buffalo country. They would not listen to the majority opinion which Leonard said must always prevail in such circumstances. Finally, however, the mutineers were pacified when Walker ordered some of their exhausted horses killed for food. Struggling through the snow and living on the leanest of horsemeat, they passed along the heights overlooking Yosemite Valley. They were the first white men to see this stunningly beautiful region. Leonard was aware that they were in an area of unusual natural grandeur, but they had few sensibilities at the moment for anything other than their own immediate survival. As he put it: "Our situation was growing more distressing every hour, and all we now thought of, was to extricate ourselves from this inhospitable region; and, as we were perfectly aware, that to travel on foot was the only way of succeeding, we spent no time in idleness—scarcely stopping in our journey to view an occasional specimen of the wonders of nature's handywork."[24]

They wanted to get down to the valley floor, but could see no way to do it. They observed many streams falling through deep chasms more than a mile high, but no apparent route by which men could descend,

---

[23]*Life and Adventures*, 33; *Narrative...of Zenas Leonard*, 122.
[24]Ibid., 128-129.

much less horses. So they kept on, encountering "one hill of snow and one ledge of rocks after another." Their scouts returned bringing no news of a way out, though one of them had stumbled across an Indian. This fellow had come from the west, so they knew there must be a trail through. He had also dropped a basket of acorns in his fright at the unexpected encounter with a white man. This was welcomed as food and as a sign that they were approaching a country mild and fertile enough to produce acorns. Eventually they reached a point where they could see "a beautiful plain stretched out towards the west," but still no apparent way to get out of the seemingly endlesss mountains. Further scouting, however, finally revealed a way down. As they made their descent they came across another California marvel which they may also have been the first white men to see. Zenas Leonard remarked upon the size of some giant redwood trees, which were as much as sixteen to eighteen fathoms around the trunk at eye level.[25]

Coming out into the San Joaquin Valley after traversing the narrows of the Merced River, they reached a country abounding in game of every kind except buffalo. Zenas Leonard could now more easily reflect on the beauty of his surroundings, which he felt were "quite romantic." They knew that their needs would be taken care of, and they were eager to begin trapping since they had made no profits and lost a lot of horses on their journey. Despite these hardships, however, according to Leonard "every man expressed himself fully compensated for his labour, by the many natural curiosities which we had discovered."[26]

Zenas Leonard was an alert and thorough observer, though he filtered what he saw through the characteristic American mind-set of his times. He seemed to be interested in learning as much as he could about this new and appealing country, from the local resident "Spaniards" as he called them, to the California Indians whom he contrasted with those he had known in the Rockies. Walker and his men were treated hospitably by the wild tribes of California. They never seemed to be in fear for their lives from these Indians as was often the case with those in the fur country of the Rockies. They stayed in several Indian villages and Zenas Leonard had a chance to examine the Indians' appearance

[25]Ibid., 130-136.
[26]Ibid., 136-139.

and way of life. He was not impressed. They seemed physically inferior to the Indians he had known in the buffalo country, darker and smaller in stature. They wore almost no clothing, lived in huts made of dry poles and logs planted in the ground, and slept on beds of grass. They subsisted on a diet of acorns and horsemeat, a diet which Leonard felt contributed to their "delicate and feeble" appearance. They were in his opinion "more indolent and slothful" than any other Indians he had met. They also made him nervous. Though acting friendly enough, they did not really seem to care how they treated the white men. Yet, unknown to Leonard, there was sufficient reason for the Indians' lethargy and indifference. He was probably seeing tribes whose ranks had been thinned by a cholera epidemic which swept through northern California in 1833.[27]

Leonard believed that the local "Spaniards" had the Indians under complete control and could if they wished induce them to attack the trappers. So the trappers wanted to find the nearest California authorities and "cultivate their friendship." But the first non-Indians they ran into were Americans. When they reached the ocean below San Francisco Bay, they discovered and hailed a ship which turned out to be the Bryant & Sturgis Company hide trader *Lagoda,* with Captain John Bradshaw in command.[28] Here at this meeting of the two American forces that were beginning to make inroads into Mexican California, the mountain men were invited on board the ship to drink Cognac and trade their furs for supplies. The captain informed them that they were about seventy miles north of the capital at Monterey. He also told them about a settlement of Russians who had established a base for hunting sea otter some one hundred miles further north. Leonard noted the "great value" of the sea otter "on account of the quality of the fur," and this may have been where George Nidever learned about a lucrative enterprise exactly suited to his skills, and one that could be pursued if he remained in California.[29]

On their way to Monterey, they met their first Californians whom Leonard described as "fine, portly men." Leonard also had a chance to

[27]Ibid., 143-145. For the cholera epidemic, see Charles L. Camp, ed., *George Yount and his Chronicles of the West,* 94.

[28]In his narrative, Leonard called him "Baggshaw." For background on John Bradshaw, see Bil Gilbert, op. cit., 139ff.

[29]*Narrative...of Zenas Leonard,* 148-49; 151-153.

look over a California mission when they were given permission by the padres to camp at San Juan Bautista. Here Leonard remarked upon the differences between the dwellings of the Indians and those of the padres, which he felt "plainly show the superiority of the white man over the Indian...." At Monterey, they were also received hospitably and given permission to hunt and trap, but were warned not to trade with the Indians or trap on Indian lands. The Californians, according to Leonard, were friendly and protective toward those Indians under their jurisdiction, and "were constantly reminding us of the dangers of wronging the Indians." While at Monterey they had lots of visitors, Californians and Indians, who were curious about how they lived. Leonard said they lived just like the "Spaniards" except that the latter occupied "habitations built of wood, brick, mortar, &c. while we lived in huts made of skins of animals." Unlike his contrasting of the padres and Indians, however, Leonard nowhere expressed the idea that the difference in dwelling places meant that the mountain men were inferior to the Californians.[30]

Invidious comparisons between the relative merits of the Californians and Indians on the one hand, and the Americans on the other—typical of virtually all U.S. citizens who saw and wrote about California at this time—would involve Zenas Leonard in many an inconsistency. It did not occur to him that the trappers in their Indian-style skin tents may have appeared just as "primitive" to some of the sophisticated and highly educated Spanish padres as the California Indians in their stick huts did to him. Nor was he able to present a less conflicting view of the Californians. He was eager to see as much of the country and its people as he could, and was pleased when Walker proposed "a tramp through the settlements for the purpose of taking a view of the country, and the manners and customs of the inhabitants."[31]

The ease and facility with which the Californians handled their horses and cattle impressed Leonard as it did most other foreign observers. There were no fences, no barns and no stables. The cattle and horses ran wild and subsisted on the natural bounty of the land. The richer Califor-

---

[30]Ibid., 158-165.

[31]Ibid., 165-166. This is evidence that Walker was interested in more than just getting furs; it supports the idea that he was, through Bonneville, an agent of the U.S. Government sent to gather information about California.

nians made a good living from the hide and tallow trade. To Leonard these people were a definite aristocracy "surrounded with all the comforts of life...entirely independent and unconnected with the common people." The trade appeared to have been largely monopolized by American ships, and also "afforded an easy path to wealth for many of the American merchants." News of the arrival of a ship would "spread over the whole country like wildfire." Then (contradicting his assertion that the upper class existed in a kind of isolation from the lower) the California ranchos and missions had to enlist the aid of the poorer people. Indians did most of the labor, helping with the slaughter of the cattle and managing what little agriculture there was. In fact, the primitive methods elicited some scornful comments from the young man who had abandoned a farmer's life in Pennsylvania. Using just a log of wood with a branch sticking out as a plow, the Californians tilled the soil, usually plowing in wet weather. These methods were a clear indication to Leonard that the people of California were "ignorant," "indolent," and had "little or no ingenuity." Nowhere else but in the rich soil of California, thought Leonard, would such methods have succeeded.[32]

The customs of the Californians were also somewhat disturbing. Leonard believed that "vice of every description seems to be openly countenanced in some parts of the settlements, such as horse racing, card playing, and even stealing...." Horses were so abundant that when traveling through the country, people simply traded in their tired mounts for fresh ones. When one of their horses was thus taken, Walker reported the "theft" to the alcalde at Monterey who explained, as recorded by Leonard, that it was "not recognized as a crime, owing, probably, to the cheapness of these animals—as they can be bought at any time for from one to ten dollars." Furthermore, the Californians positively seemed to enjoy taking certain risks. All the men carried "dirks" which they used with great skill. They would catch bears from horseback with only a lasso. They liked to gamble, betting on horse races and on the outcome of bull and bear fights. They would even bet on whether a man could get in with a bull, touch it, and get out without being hurt. Leonard witnessed an example of this "sport" in which "an old time-worn Spaniard" was gored in the thigh. To him it was an indication that

---

[32]Ibid., 164; 166-172.

in their recreations the Californians seemed to care little about human life.[33]

In spite of being treated hospitably, the Americans (or at least Zenas Leonard) looked upon the Spanish-Mexican Californians as enemies even in 1833, indicating that the Americans had arrived in California with certain negative attitudes already in place. A time was coming when Americans would be contending with the Californians for control of the country, and would add the charge of cowardice to the "Black Legend" elements of Spanish cruelty and depravity (so clearly a part of Zenas Leonard's repertoire). Leonard may have thought they were vicious, but he would not have called the Californians cowards. Such an idea was in complete contradiction to his experience of them. The misunderstanding about their stolen horse and his assessment of "Spanish" character seem to have goaded Walker into preparing his men for a departure rather than a fight. As Leonard told it, Walker "thought it would be the best plan for us to pack up and leave the neighborhood, in order to avoid a difficulty with a people of a ferocious and wicked nature, at a time too, when we are not very well prepared to contend against such an enemy in their own country."[34]

It's hard to believe, after dealing with the Blackfeet and their fellow mountain men, that Walker or Zenas Leonard could have been particularly intimidated by the Californians, who had shown them only friendship. Certainly a "stolen" horse was not sufficient grounds for such apparent hostility and trepidation. In fact, they continued to cooperate with the Californians. When they left Monterey in January of 1834, they were asked to join with a group of Californians who were going after some renegade mission Indians. The Indians had stolen 300 horses from San Juan Bautista. The trappers agreed to aid the Californians in exchange for half of whatever horses were recovered. When they came upon the Indian village, most of the Indian men had gone. The disappointed Californians according to Leonard took revenge on the remaining old people, women and children, "massacreing, indiscriminately, those helpless creatures who were found in the wigwams...and cutting off their ears." Leonard did not point out that this act seemed to belie the

---

[33]Ibid., 183-185.
[34]Ibid., 185-186.

Californians' own reminder to the trappers about the dangers of wronging the Indians. To Leonard this was yet another indication of "the depravity of the Spanish character." Yet when one of the trappers' own horses was discovered among some wild ones rounded up by the Californians, "The Spaniards honorably gave him up after we proved our claim." Leonard never attempted to reconcile his conflicting images of the Californians. When Walker's party left California they took with them two "Spaniards"—deserters from the army—who proved to be very loyal and useful men, enduring without complaint all of the hardships of the return journey. They earned Leonard's praise for their skill with horses and for their unfailing good humor.[35]

When Walker and Zenas Leonard left California , six men stayed behind. Leonard said they were useful men, with skills like carpentry which—in a final dig at his California hosts—would "no doubt be profitable to themselves, and of great advantage to the indolent and stupid Spaniard." Leonard was one of the early prophets of Manifest Destiny and in his opinion California belonged by right to Americans, who could make the best use of her riches. In practical terms the Californians had proved fairly congenial, but they were nevertheless objectively the enemies of an American expansionist outlook that had gripped the minds of "ordinary" men like Zenas Leonard who were engaged in the historical process of making what they believed in a reality. When he looked at California, Leonard could almost visualize what it could be "if the proper spirit of enterprise prevailed among the inhabitants...:"

> What a theme to contemplate its settlement and civilization. Will the jurisdiction of the federal government ever succeed in civilizing the thousands of savages now roaming over these plains, and her hardy freeborn population here plant their homes, build their towns and cities, and say here shall the arts and sciences of civilization take root and flourish? yes, here, even in this remote part of the great west before many years will these hills and valleys be greeted with the enlivening sound of the workman's hammer, and the merry whistle of the plough-boy.

It only remained for the American government to assert her claim against the Spaniards, the Russians, even the British if necessary, "by taking possession of the whole territory as soon as possible—for we have

---

[35]Ibid., 186-91; 197; 217.

good reason to suppose that the territory west of the mountain will some day be equally as important to a nation as that on the east."[36]

One of the men left behind was George Nidever. He began his career as a sea otter hunter when he met George Yount in Monterey. Yount, an experienced mountain man and trapper who had been in California since 1831, invited Nidever to go with him on an otter and beaver hunt around the San Francisco Bay and up the San Joaquin River. Sea otter pelts brought $30.00 each at that time. While on this hunt Nidever discovered a little Indian girl of about three years old "among the Tulares" in some seemingly abandoned Indian huts. He went to find Yount, who advised him to wait before he helped the child, fearing that the Indians might return and take offense. Nidever's vengeful feelings towards the Indians clearly did not extend to their children. He was disturbed at leaving the baby there, and he expressed a pity and tenderness that showed a different, less publicized facet of the usual rough mountain-man image:

> All night it seemed as though I could hear the little one's cries. Early in the morning I went to the huts and found the little one so weak that she could not sit up. Upon bringing her out of the hut, we found her nothing but skin and bone. She had probably been without food for three or four days. We took her to camp and gave her a piece of boiled beaver, and it was pitiful to see the eagerness with which she caught it to her mouth and sucked at it voraciously. We feared to allow her to eat too much at first, and so took the meat from her...but so tightly did she have it pressed to her mouth that main force was necessary to take it from her. We made clothes for her and with a little care she soon recovered.

In fact, this little girl's parents were never coming back for her. The Indians of northern California had been decimated by an epidemic of Asiatic cholera. Yount and Nidever later met a group of Indians to whom they tried to give the child, but the Indians refused, even telling the trappers to kill her. Instead, Yount took the little girl and raised her as his own.[37]

George Nidever continued to hunt the sea otter, especially around the

---

[36]Ibid., 195; 174; 154-155, emphases in the original.

[37]*Life and Adventures*, 34-35; information on George Yount in Charles L. Camp, ed., op. cit., 94; 121-122.

Channel Islands off Santa Barbara, and the islands of Santa Catalina
and San Clemente. He related the story of the last of the Indians living
on San Nicholas Island. They were removed about 1837 at the instigation of someone in Los Angeles and for reasons that he could not
remember. All of them were taken off except one woman who went back
to fetch her child and was left when a storm forced the party to embark.
She remained, living on the island until 1853 when Nidever and
"Charley Brown" (Carl Dittmann, a Prussian sailor who came to California in 1841) took her to Santa Barbara where she died seven weeks
from the day of her arrival. But during her brief life in Santa Barbara, she
became an attraction. People came from miles around to see her, and
Nidever turned down an offer by a ship captain of a thousand dollars for
permisssion to take her to San Francisco and put her on display. Nidever's matter-of-fact report of the "lost woman of San Nicholas" concealed
a certain romantic appeal. The story has been embellished and retold
many times.[38]

The native population on the Channel Islands had been drastically
reduced a number of years before their final removal. Indians from the
Aleutian Islands, armed and employed as otter hunters by American and
British sea captains, had operated around the Channel Islands for years
and often killed the local Indians. George Nidever and his companions
clashed with these "Northwest Indians," who were determined to eliminate any competition. In January of 1836 on the Island of Santa Rosa,
Nidever, Isaac Sparks, a man known as "Black Steward" and about nine
others engaged in a running gun battle with these Indians and inflicted
on them a severe defeat. Nidever and Isaac Sparks were experienced
Indian fighters and doubtless the Northwest Indians had had few
encounters with their kind on the California coast before. Nidever
claimed that, prior to this fight, the Northwest Indians had been "the terror of the Coast." They chased other hunters off the islands, stole their
supplies and furs, and killed them if they tried to resist. Nidever with his
stolid style nevertheless gave a dramatic description of the battle. Just as
they were about a fourth of a mile from the beach in their own boats,
they saw the Northwest Indians coming out of the fog, "5 or 6 canoes

---

[38]Ibid., 37-38; 80-89. The "lost woman of San Nicholas Island" became the inspiration for the
novel, *Island of the Blue Dolphins*, by Scott O'Dell.

pulling with might and main to cut us off from the shore." But the American mountain men were more than a match for the Aleuts. They turned back and ran for cover "amidst a shower of buckshot," and were soon firing their own rifles with a telling effect. Three Indians were killed and four or five were wounded. "This was a reception they little expected...[T]hey sailed away and we never saw them again."[39]

George Nidever was one of the last men to hunt the sea otter in California. The Northwest Indians had been taking them for years before Nidever came on the scene. They were still plentiful in the early years of his career, but he was to see them hunted to the edge of extinction. In the meantime, however, a new source of income soon arose in the form of one of Mexican California's frequent family quarrels. In this case it was the struggle between two men, each claiming to be governor, and two sections, north and south, each claiming their "city" as capital. Juan Bautista Alvarado had come from Monterey to Santa Barbara on his way to confront his uncle, Carlos Antonio Carrillo, who was insisting on his legitimacy as governor and on Los Angeles as the capital of California. It is doubtful that George Nidever either knew or cared about the poltical dimensions of this struggle. He was approached by Alvarado and his old mountain companion Isaac Graham and offered two dollars a day and the right to take up land if he would join Alvarado's forces. He and Black Steward interrupted their otter hunting to march on San Fernando Mission with Graham's riflemen. There they formed up and prepared to charge Carlos Carrillo's men. The latter, however, broke and ran. Nidever attributed their hasty departure to the fact that "they did not care to face the foreigners, for whom they had a wholesome respect, especially the riflemen and hunters." Alvarado paid them off and Nidever resumed his career as an otter hunter, but soon decided to apply for the land that Alvarado had promised. He spent a year and about $500 in selecting a site around Santa Barbara, but when he saw Alvarado about the matter, the governor made excuses, finally telling him that a new

---

[39]Ibid.,40-45. Isaac Sparks was a trapper who came to California in 1832 with Ewing Young and immediately took up sea otter hunting (see ibid., 107, fn 96). "Black Steward" was a black man who may have deserted from Richard Henry Dana's ship *Pilgrim*. His real name was Allen Light, and he was a testimonial to the comparative lack of stigma or discrimination attaching to race in Mexican California. As an otter hunter, he was respected by men like Nidever and Isaac Sparks, and in 1839 he was appointed by the government to prevent illegal otter hunting (see ibid., 108, fn 104 for "Black Steward").

Mexican law made it illegal to grant land to foreigners unless they were married to Mexican citizens. It took him several more years to accomplish this prerequisite.[40]

In the meantime, Nidever put his hunting skills to a new use—killing grizzly bears! At this time (1837) they abounded in California, and George Nidever seems to have done his part to eliminate them from the landscape. He claimed to have killed 45 in 1837 alone, and at least 200 in his career as a bear hunter. He had a system for hunting them. He would ride up to them on horseback, upwind so they could not scent him, and then sneak up on them on foot, trying to get a shot from as close as forty or fifty yards, but no further away than one hundred. He never shot at the head, because the bullet would just glance off. He always looked around for a convenient tree to climb if necessary. He never followed a bear, wounded or otherwise, into a thicket. He had one really close call when a she-bear with cubs spooked his horse, which ran under an oak tree, knocking him to the ground. He lay there bruised and almost unconscious as the bears rushed by after the horse. Then he managed to struggle up the tree just before the bears returned, "discovered me and raised up on their hind legs, growling fiercely and scratching the bark off." Finally they left and Nidever was able to get down and make his way home. There was, as he said, no market for bear skins, and it is hard to see why he would continue in such a hazardous line of work, except perhaps for the challenge and risk in it. In fact he did set himself above his fellow hunters when he claimed "that very few even among hunters care to hunt the grizzly much. There are plenty who will talk about what they would do, but they *will* run when it comes to the point." Grizzly bear hunting simply added another facet to his already formidable reputation, a reputation in which he clearly took some pride, despite the generally modest tone of his narrative.[41]

Otter hunting carried less risk, and more profits, so he kept it up as long as he could. He said that around this time the otter hunters began to employ Mission Indians to help them, and the Indians eventually replaced the Hawaiians. In later years, some of the hunters began to

---

[40]Ibid., 45-49. For an informative and readable discussion of the north-south political struggles in California at this time, see Roy E. Whitehead, *Lugo: A Chronicle of California*, 190-195.

[41]Ibid., 49-53, emphasis in the original.

teach their Indian helpers how to shoot, and this , Nidever claimed, was a mistake. Teaching the Indians the use of firearms "soon spoiled them as, from being very docile and willing, those who learned to use the rifle became lazy and independent, even saucy." In other words, they were more like the white hunters, now able to go into business for themselves![42]

In 1840 George Nidever managed to slip through the net thrown by Governor Alvarado in his roundup of foreigners. He and his companions had as usual been out hunting sea otter. Landing at San Diego, they were warned by a local woman that Americans were being arrested and forced out of the country. Isaac Sparks refused to believe this until he was met by the *alcalde* who told him he had orders to seize Sparks and all of his American companions. Sparks told the *alcalde* that if he were arrested, his friends would just come and release him by force. They had all determined to resist any attempts to incarcerate or deport them. The Mexican official had no means at his disposal to cope with a dozen armed hunters, so he made no further moves against them. They reloaded their guns and posted a guard for the week or so that they were at San Diego. The ship *Alert* was there at the time, with Alfred Robinson on board as supercargo. He told them that many foreigners had been arrested, and that the government was trying to drive the Americans out of the country. A week later, they learned that the ship carrying the foreign prisoners to San Blas was on its way to San Diego, so they dropped down the coast in their own boats, made a fortified camp on shore, and were there watching as the prison ship sailed by. Nidever said that, "although they must have seen us, no attempt was made to take us."[43]

Nidever was apparently not harassed further by any California authorities. Later that year he bought property in Santa Barbara, and in February of 1841 he married Sinforosa Sanchez, a native of the town. He had almost nothing to say about his courtship or any personal details relating to his marriage. He simply mentioned the fact of his marriage in one sentence, and continued with the story of his life of action. He tried to stay out of California politics, refusing to join Micheltorena when the

---

[42]Ibid., 56.

[43]Ibid., 56-57. See below, Chapter 10, for a fuller discussion of the arrests of foreigners known as the "Graham Affair."

latter passed through Santa Barbara in November of 1845 on his way to the "Battle of Cahuenga" which would end Micheltorena's rule and make Pío Pico from Los Angeles the last Mexican governor of California.[44]

But when the war with Mexico began, it was almost impossible not to take sides. As an American citizen who had never bothered to become a naturalized Mexican like his friend Isaac Sparks, and in spite of his Californian wife, Nidever was treated by the Californians as an enemy. In March 1846, Nidever and several others embarked on an otter hunting expedition up the coast. On their way back down after a successful hunt, they passed through Monterey where they found that the Americans had already taken possession. There Nidever ran into Commodore Robert Stockton and John C. Fremont. Each of these leaders wanted Nidever, who knew the country, to join him. He told them he first had to return to Santa Barbara with his men, "but promised Fremont that I would join him at that place." In Monterey some of the naval officers and some of Fremont's men got up a target shoot. His companion Carl Dittmann (called Charley Brown in California; the same man who was with Nidever in 1853 when they rescued the woman from San Nicholas Island) gave an account of the contest, saying that "our Cap't. Geo. Nidever was asked to join them and he did better shooting than all of them." Nidever, shooting with a borrowed gun, put all three of his shots in the small paper target set up 70 or 80 yards away. No doubt it was after this display of his talent that Nidever was asked to join Fremont.[45]

First, however, he had to get home unmolested. At San Luis Obispo Nidever and his partners learned that a contingent of Californians under Totoi Pico were coming to capture them that night. According to Dittmann, they were asked by Nidever if they wanted to run all night "or stand and fight we said fight (sic)." Nidever simply stated that they "decided to make a fight and accordingly selected a place easily defended." But no one could sleep, so they elected to push on to Santa Barbara in their boats. Nidever learned later that the Californians had come for them in the night, shortly after they had left. He related how some of them "frankly admitted afterwards that they intended to kill all of us and

---

[44]Ibid., 58-60.

[45]Ibid., 60-63, 70-71; Carl Dittmann, "Narrative of a Seafaring Life on the Coast of California," 27.

take our skins...." Yet going out on the ocean did not put them out of danger either. A tremendous storm came up and their boats almost swamped before they rounded Point Concepcion and the sea became quite smooth. When they finally reached Santa Barbara and landed, after the harrowing experience at sea and having been without food or sleep for about three days, they were immediately arrested. The others were released because they were not Americans, but Nidever was disarmed and his house searched; he was further compelled to pay a two hundred dollar "duty" on his furs in spite of having a license, and finally told to go as a prisoner to Los Angeles. The Californians apparently trusted him to do this, which was their mistake. He obtained a rifle and ammunition which he had hidden, and headed for the hills, intending to kill the first Californian who happened along, take his horse and join Fremont.[46]

But one of the ironies of the conflict soon presented itself. Long-time American residents in California like George Nidever had established ties of friendship with many of the people who had now become enemies. The first Californian he happened to meet was Vicente Ortega, "one of the best Californians and men in those times, and I had not the heart to shoot him, although so mad was I at the treatment I had received that I would not have hesitated if any other man had come within range." And the California women, friends of Mrs. Nidever who knew of Nidever's whereabouts, never said anything to their menfolk but rather kept Nidever informed about the Californians' movements. The closest he actually came to shooting one of his wife's countrymen was when one of them spotted him in his position on top of a nearby hill and came riding up, yelling for Nidever to come down. Nidever did not respond, but waited to see how near the man would get to him. The fellow stopped about thirty or forty paces away, then turned around and left. "Had he approached a few steps further," Nidever asserted, "he would have been a dead man."[47]

This distance was clearly within range for a man of Nidever's skill with a rifle, and it would seem that had he really wished to take such a murderous revenge on a Californian, this was the perfect opportunity.

[46]Ibid., 64-66, 70; Dittmann, "Narrative....", 27.
[47]Ibid., 66-67.

Instead his retaliation was much less sanguinary. His own house (with him successfully hidden in it) had been searched at the instigation of Captain Francisco de la Guerra, so when Fremont's forces came to Santa Barbara, Nidever took pleasure in reciprocating. Nidever along with one of Fremont's lieutenants and several other men conducted a search of the de la Guerra household, much to the abasement and chagrin of the family. "The de la Guerra's never forgave me for thus humiliating them," Nidever claimed,"and would undoubtedly [have] had me put out of the way afterwards had they not feared me, for long after the Americans came they continued to control if not rule the native population." It was probably fortunate that Nidever had not indulged his desire for vengeance by shedding any Californian blood. After all, he had chosen to live among them in Santa Barbara, where he was to reside for almost another forty years. If he had killed a Californian, especially one connected with the proud de la Guerras, they might indeed have made his life difficult—or ended it altogether.[48]

George Nidever rode with Fremont to Los Angeles. No major engagements were fought, and Fremont received the surrender of the Californian forces at Cahuenga, ending the war in California. Nidever continued his career as a hunter, even during the gold rush, when he claimed to have done better selling the deer he shot than he ever did finding gold.[49] Like his contemporaries who made their livelihood by hunting and trapping, he was essentially a man of action, accustomed to living with danger, virtually taking his courage and prowess for granted. The highlights of his life, the recollections he chose to relate, almost all had to do with violent exploits which often placed his life in danger. A certain pride was evident when he talked about how some of the Californians feared him. He was obviously concerned to maintain such a reputation, which indeed the Nidevers had in Santa Barbara for years afterwards.[50] About

---

[48]Ibid., 64-69.

[49]Ibid., 70-72; 76.

[50]William A. Streeter in his "Recollections of Historical Events in California, 1843-1878," reprinted in the California Historical Society Quarterly, vol. 18 ((1939), 261, told the story of a Mexican bandit hanged for stealing cattle in 1859, apparently by the nephew and namesake of George Nidever. The Nidevers and several other Americans were arrested, but released for lack of evidence, though there continued to be hostility between them and certain Californians. But the latter, Streeter maintained, "knew full well the men they had to deal with and wisely refrained from exasperating them."

his family affairs, however, he told almost nothing; such was no doubt a private matter and not to be discussed with strangers. It also seems more than likely that the interviewer was not interested in hearing about those kinds of details, any more than George Nidever wanted to mention them. Nidever was not an introspective man, yet he clearly did possess a softer side which showed itself in his concern for the orphaned Indian baby. But his most prominent traits were those that would have made him a model for the hero of the dime novels beginning to appear in the 1860s, just as they were to do for his much better known contemporary, Kit Carson.[51] And California would provide the backdrop for the action, as it continues to do for our modern television and movie heroes who originated in such real-life sources.

---

[51]See Henry Nash Smith, *Virgin Land: The American West as Myth and Symbol*, 99ff.

CHAPTER IX

Benjamin Davis Wilson

Benjamin Davis Wilson never achieved the national fame of a Kit Carson. He did not reach a wide public with his autobiography like Zenas Leonard or James Ohio Pattie. Yet his is one of the more interesting stories in the life of Mexican California. Wilson, like George Nidever, made his home in California. Wilson came to know the Indians and native Californians well, and they knew him as "Don Benito." He was one of the most respected pioneers of the San Gabriel Valley, giving his name to the highest peak in the San Gabriel Mountains and naming the Big Bear region of the San Bernardino Mountains. Wilson was also the grandfather of one of the United States' most famous World War II generals, George S. Patton. He was connected to upper class California society through his marriage to Ramona Yorba, the daughter of Don Bernardo Yorba who owned Rancho Santa Ana in what is today Orange County. He was intimately involved with the politics of California before, during and after the Mexican War. As Indian agent for southern California, Wilson wrote an influential report sympathetic to the plight of the Indians. He was the first clerk of the County of Los Angeles, the second Mayor of Los Angeles, and the founder of the city of Alhambra. Wilson made his mark on southern California in numerous ways.[1]

Benjamin Davis Wilson was another pioneer whose life story we owe to the efforts of Hubert Howe Bancroft and his researchers. In November of 1877, from his Lake Vineyard estate in what is today San Marino, Wilson dictated to Thomas Savage an account of his life . Like those of Kit Carson and George Nidever, his is an "oral history," without literary

---

[1]*American Biography: A New Cyclopedia*, vol. 40, 144-145. I also wish to thank Doyce B. Nunis, Jr., who kindly commented on this chapter and saved me from several errors. Professor Nunis is now at work on what will undoubtedly be the definitive biography of Benjamin Davis Wilson.

BENJAMIN DAVIS WILSON, WIFE MARGARET HEREFORD,
HER SON EDWARD AND HER NEPHEW TOM
Courtesy, California Historical Society

pretensions, but with a lively sense of immediacy and sincerity. He retained a copy for himself and his family which, with some minor additions, was later published.[2] Both of these versions convey an image of Wilson as an American who, for his time, was unusually just and sympathetic in his judgements of the peoples—Indian and Mexican—with whom he was to live and work.

As a young man, Wilson operated a trading post in Yazoo, Mississippi. But the climate there was so unhealthy that Wilson was advised by several doctors that he "must either leave or die." So he joined a company of fur trappers and headed into the Southwest, reaching Santa Fe in the fall of 1833. He spent the next several years trapping in the Apache country of New Mexico, without the permission of the Mexican Govern-

---

[2]Benjamin Davis Wilson, "Observations on Early Days in California and New Mexico," *Benjamin Davis Wilson, 1811-1878.* For convenience of citation, the first version will be referred to as "Wilson I," and the second as "Wilson II." Wilson was an old man when interviewed, and his recollections of details were not always strictly accurate. His sympathies and sentiments, however, are evident throughout his narrative, and a noteworthy contrast to the prejudices of so many of his contemporaries.

ment. He claimed that he owed his success as a trapper to the friendship of an Apache Indian chief, Juan José. Juan José was chief of the Gila Apaches whom Wilson said had been Mission Indians under the Spanish.[3] The chief's father, according to Wilson, had been killed by New Mexicans, and Juan José was therefore hostile to the Spanish-speaking residents of the country. He did attempt, however, to maintain a friendship with the few Americans who trapped in his territory. In an unusually candid statement, Wilson explained the importance of Juan José's good will: "We were there as interlopers and smugglers, and would have fared badly had we fallen into the hands of their [Mexican] forces. Juan José's friendship was in every way valuable to us."[4]

As Wilson explained it, the Gila Apaches' amity with Americans was to be terminated by an act of treachery. The Mexican Government bribed an American trapper, John Johnson (Wilson called him "James"), to kill the Apache chief. Johnson was trusted by Juan José. Even when the chief was informed of the plot against his life, he refused to believe it. Johnson invited Juan José to his camp where, with the help of a man remembered by Wilson as Gleason, he killed him. The Indians—men, women and children—had crowded around a sack of pinole given by Johnson as a present. Johnson fired a blunderbuss "loaded with balls, chains etc." into the crowd while Gleason simultaneously shot Juan José. The shot did not kill the Apache chief, who called on his supposed friend Johnson to help him; instead, Johnson also shot him.[5]

The result of this murderous act was that the Indians turned against the Americans. Wilson and his party were made captives, and Wilson himself would probably have been killed if the Apache chief Mangas Colorado had not arranged for him to escape. He witnessed the further

---

[3]Frank C. Lockwood, *The Apache Indians*, 71, says "Juan José was fairly well educated; had, indeed, been partly prepared for the priesthood in the Catholic Church...." But James L. Haley, *Apaches: A History and Culture Portrait*, 41-50, says that the missionaries had been singularly unsuccessful with the Apaches, especially the western Apache tribes of which Juan José's was one. But William B. Griffen, "The Compas: A Chiricahua Apache Family of theLate 18th and Early 19th Centuries." *American Indian Quarterly* VII:2 (Spring, 1983), 37, states that Juan Jose had been "granted the privilege of attending the presidio school operated for the sons of the military at Janos."

[4]Wilson I, 2-6; Wilson II, 1-2.

[5]Wilson I, 5-10; Wilson II, 2-4.

results of Johnson's actions when he was called upon to bury the Keykendall party, massacred by the outraged Indians.[6]

New Mexico was becoming an unhealthy place for Americans. Apache hostility kept the trappers away from the Gila River country, and in 1837 an uprising led by José Gonzales of Taos killed Governor Alvino Perez and threatened the lives of Americans in Santa Fe. Wilson believed that only his friendship with the Pueblo Indian chief Pedro Leon had saved his life when a mob besieged the building he was in. "That time," Wilson said, "I did really expect that our (sic) life was not worth the purchase." But the Indian chief told the mob that Wilson was not there and he remained in hiding for six days until the uprising had subsided. Not long after this, in response to rumors of a Texan invasion, Americans were once again threatened. Finally, in September of 1841, Wilson and several other Americans left for California with a herd of sheep. They arrived in Los Angeles the next month, driving the first American wagon train to enter that southern California pueblo.[7]

Wilson did not intend to stay in California. He planned, he said, to sail to China and from there return home to the United States. But after repeated efforts to get a ship, "I arrived at the conclusion that there would be no chance for carrying out my original intention, and so I finally purchased a ranch in 1843—called the Jurupa, and stocked it with cattle." Other Americans were being given land grants by the California government, but Wilson never received one "as I would not apply for Mexican citizenship." Wilson's decision to remain a citizen of the United

[6]Wilson I, 12-16; Wilson II, 5-7. Wilson's memory, forty years after the fact, can be checked against a scholarly reconstruction of the Johnson massacre. See Rex W. Strickland, "The Birth and Death of a Legend: The Johnson 'Massacre' of 1837." *Arizona and the West* 18:3 (August, 1976) 257-286. Strickland states (p. 264) that "Wilson heard the story in the winter of 1837 at Santa Fe from Charles Ames, a participant in the battle, who spent some months there enroute to Missouri." He also notes (p. 264, fn. 10) that Wilson confused John Johnson, Juan Jose's killer, with James Johnson, an Englishman who had emigrated to California in 1833. Strickland calls Wilson's account (p. 265) "an *apologia* for Juan Jose which may contain some kernels of truth." Strickland's own anti-Indian bias seems clear, however, in the rhetoric he uses to describe Apache raiding and his failure to adduce any provocation for it. For a sophisticated account of the causes of Apache raiding, see Thomas D. Hall, *Social Change in the Southwest, 1350-1880*, 75-164.

[7]Wilson I, 19-22; Wilson II, 8-10. Wilson confused the year of the uprising, claiming it happened in 1836. For an account of the uprising, see Hall, *Social Change in the Southwest*, 190-191. See also Midge Sherwood, *Days of Vintage, Years of Vision*, 66.

States did not mean that he was contemptuous of the Californians. Unlike James Pattie's scornful portrayal of them as thieves and murderers, Wilson found the Californians to be a kind and upright people. His assessment contradicted so many contemporary Americans who commented on the Californians that it merits quoting in full:

> After many unsuccessful efforts to leave California, and receiving so much kindness from the native Californians, I arrived at the conclusion that there was no place in the world where I could enjoy more true happiness, and true friendship, than among them. There were no courts, no juries, no lawyers , nor any need for them. The people were honest and hospitable, and their word was as good as their bond; indeed, bonds and notes of hand were unknown among the natives.[8]

Benjamin Davis Wilson was perhaps the one American resident of Mexican California who was least infected with racial prejudice—against either the Californians or the Indians. His life among the native Californians taught him to respect them, just as his early friendships with Apaches in New Mexico showed him the humanity of people like Juan José and Mangas. Even when he led punitive expeditions against certain of the California Indians—like other mountain men, he could be harsh on those who attacked white settlements—he never spoke of them disparagingly, and for years he maintained close ties with certain individual Indians. In the summer of 1845, Governor Pío Pico asked Wilson to lead eighty men against some Mojave Indians who had been raiding the outlying ranchos, including his own at Jurupa. In the desert Wilson and his party caught up with three of the raiders. Wilson ended up shooting the leader when he sent an arrow into Wilson's shoulder. His admiration for their bravery was clear, however, when he said of them: "Those three men actually fought eighty men in open plain, till they were put to death." Wilson knew their leader as "the famous marauder Joaquin who had been raised as a page of the Church in San Gabriel Mission, and for his depredations & outlawing bore on his person the mark of the Mission—that is, one of his ears cropped off, and the iron brand on his hip." In this incident Wilson gave credit for saving his life to "a civilized Comanche Indian, a trusty man who had accompanied me from New

[8]Wilson I, 23-24; Wilson II, 11-12.

Mexico to California." The man removed the arrow from Wilson's shoulder and sucked the poison out. Badly wounded, Wilson was forced to give up this campaign when his men were unable to dislodge the main body of Indians from their rocky fortifications.[9]

Shortly after this Wilson was again called upon to go after "two renegade San Gabriel neophytes who had taken up their residence amongst the Cahuillas and corrupted many of the young men of that tribe, with whom they carried on a constant depredation on the ranchmen of this district." But this time instead of running down the Indians himself, he managed to persuade the Cahuilla chief, Cabezon, to deal with the problem. While the chief went after the "renegades," Wilson waited in the desert heat, which he described as "so hot that we could not sit down, but had to stand up & fan ourselves with our hats—the ground would burn us when we attempted to sit." After two days of waiting, Wilson said, Cabezon returned and threw the heads of the offending Indians at his feet.[10]

In a final campaign against the Mojaves, Wilson and some American trappers surrounded a village and called on the Indians to surrender. When they refused and shot one of Wilson's friends, Evan Callaghan, Wilson told how he and the other Americans kept firing "until every Indian man was slain." The women and children were taken prisoner and turned over to the San Gabriel Mission. This was, he said, the last time any expeditions against marauding Indians were needed (at least in his area) until after California came into American hands. He noted in passing that many of these Indians had once been on the missions.[11]

When Benjamin Davis Wilson made his autobiographical statement for Bancroft, he specifically requested that he be remembered as a friend of the Indians and given credit for urging their settlement on reservations containing substantial amounts of land. In his 1852 report as Indian agent, Wilson tried to explain the plight of the former mission

---

[9]Wilson I, 28-34; the first version adds that the branding was not actually done at the Mission but at El Chino, one of its ranches. Wilson II, 13-14; this second version says that Joaquin was branded on the lip. Wilson's use of the adjective "civilized" to describe his Comanche companion shows him deploying the same implicit comparison between civilization and its "opposite" (savagery? backwardness?) used by his contemporaries in their descriptions of Californians and, especially, Indians.

[10]Wilson I, 35-39; Wilson II, 15-16.

[11]Wilson I, 40-42; Wilson II, 17.

Indians. He blamed secularization of the missions for contributing to their decline. Once, they had done all of the work for the missions. They were, he pointed out, "masons, carpenters, plasterers, soap-makers, tanners, shoemakers, blacksmiths, millers, bakers, cooks, brick-makers, carters and cart-makers, weavers and spinners, saddlers, shepherds, agriculturalists, horticulturalists, vineros, vaqueros—in a word, filled all the laborious occupations known to civilized society." Secularization enriched a few whose "private cupidity and political ambition...too often...wielded the destinies of the poor aborigines...." Wilson saw the small number of Indians who had managed to retain some private lands gradually forced off of them. They had little recourse, since no Indian could testify in court against a white man. The remainder were treated as little better than slaves, often receiving no pay for their labor other than liquor; then when they drank, they were arrested and hired out to rancheros who paid their bail. In Los Angeles, he noted, every other house was a grog-shop for Indians. "What marvel that eighteen years of neglect, misrule, oppression, slavery, and injustice, and every opportunity and temptation to gratify their natural vices withal, should have given them a fatal tendency downward to the very lowest degradation." But Wilson's sympathetic voice largely went unheard; the Indians were too valuable a source of cheap labor.[12]

As a landowner and settled resident of the country, Wilson was quickly drawn into California politics. In addition to his campaigns against raiding Indians, in 1845 he took a leading role in events which were to lead to the expulsion of California's last Governor sent from Mexico. Governor Manuel Micheltorena's poorly paid and clothed troops, recruited from Mexico's prisons, had in Wilson's opinion "made themselves obnoxious by their thefts, and other outrages of a most hideous nature." So when summoned by the Prefect of the District of

---

[12]John Walton Caughey, ed., *The Indians of Southern California in 1852: The B. D. Wilson Report and a Selection of Contemporary Comment*, xi, 3-30. Wilson was certainly sympathetic to the Indians in comparison to most of his contemporaries, but he could not escape all the biases of his age, as is clearly displayed in his assessment of the Indians' "natural vices." Wilson's characterization of the plight of the Indians in California is reinforced by Navy Lieutenant Joseph Warren Revere, who came to California in 1846 on board the *Cyane*. In his *Naval Duty In California*, 242, Revere stated that slavery was unnecessary in California because of "the vast number of Indians whose labor is so much cheaper than slave-labor can possibly be...."

Los Angeles (Wilson thought it was Abel Stearns),[13] he readily joined with others—he said almost everyone he knew—in a concerted effort to keep Micheltorena out of Los Angeles. The Mexican Governor was, in the words of Pío Pico, "coming in anger, determined to make himself respected." He had antagonised the natives of both northern and southern California, so sectional rivalries were momentarily put aside as José Castro and the Picos (Pío and his brother Andrés) rallied the Angelinos for a stand against Micheltorena, whose Security Battalion of cholo troops was reinforced by a contingent of Americans under John Sutter. The Americans had been promised land grants.[14]

The Los Angeles residents and the northerners who had come down with José Castro marched out to the Cahuenga valley, where they determined according to Wilson "to give the enemy a regular mountaineer reception." Some canons were fired on both sides, but no one was hurt (Wilson said a horse had its head shot off). Wilson and several others managed to contact the Americans who were with Micheltorena and persuaded them not to fight. He convinced them that Micheltorena was just using them. He appealed to their desire to get ahead, saying that "If the Micheltorena rabble hold their own in this country, they will contribute an element hostile to all enterprise, and most particularly American enterprise." He also informed them on word from Pío Pico that Micheltorena's grants were no good because none of them were citizens of Mexico. Pío gave them assurances that as the new governor he would issue them proper titles when they became citizens. This apparently satisfied them. They agreed not to fire against the southerners and asked only that they not be expected to turn against Micheltorena and the people they had marched with. After some more maneuvering on both sides, Micheltorena surrendered and, with his men, was placed on board a ship at San Pedro and sent back to Mexico. Americans, including Benjamin Davis Wilson, had played a prominent role in his departure.[15]

---

[13]Wilson's memory was by no means perfect. Professor Doyce Nunis has pointed out to me in a letter that Abel Stearns was not Prefect of Los Angeles in 1845. At that time, there was a sub-Prefect, José L. Sepulveda.

[14]Wilson I, 48; Wilson II, 18; *Don Pío Pico's Historical Narrative*, 105. For a clear, succinct discussion of events leading up to the clash at Los Angeles between Micheltorena and the Californians, see Roy E. Whitehead, *Lugo*, 241-253.

[15]Wilson I, 49-55; Wilson II, 18-20.

The Mexican War was to find Benjamin Davis Wilson torn between dual loyalties. He had retained his American citizenship, but he had also plunged into the political and social life of his adopted California. Though not a native Californian, he was obviously accepted and respected by them, and he returned their feelings. He had been made *alcalde* of his district, and when hostilities began he was asked by the Californians to help raise forces to repel his invading countrymen. He declined, pleading that he was neither a Mexican citizen nor a military man, though the latter statement was somewhat disingenuous in the light of his campaigns against the Indians and his role in expelling Micheltorena. When threatened with arrest, he took some dozen fellow Americans and other foreigners, and retreated to the San Bernardino Mountains. From there he sent a message to Governor Pío Pico not to pursue him, "for I would resist—but if he would consider that I was not a Mexican citizen, nor a man disposed to do military duty, and allow me to remain quietly in my ranch, I would pledge my word to be peaceable and do no act hostile to the country." This was apparently satisfactory, because when Commodore Robert Stockton arrived at San Pedro, Wilson received a note from Pico offering to grant him a tract of land while the Californian still functioned as governor. Wilson declined, again pleading the citizenship problem, and Pico soon departed for Sonora.[16]

Things were peaceful in Los Angeles when Stockton arrived, on a fine saddle horse that Wilson said was given to him by one of the Dominguez family. Wilson was confident that Stockton could enter the pueblo unmolested. "We rode into town together," he said, "and had a pleasant time.... The natives had dispersed and retired to their usual vocations." Wilson remained in Los Angeles helping Stockton until the latter gave him a commission and instructions to go to the mountains near his ranch and watch for any signs that Pico or José Castro might be returning with reinforcements. Wilson agreed to the assignment on condition that he would not be required to leave Jurupa; he called upon some of his Indian friends to be on the alert for troop movements on the frontier, and to report any to him.[17]

---

[16]Wilson I, 60-62.
[17]Ibid., 63-66.

As Wilson remembered it, he was in the mountains hunting (convinced that neither Pico nor José Castro would return from Mexico)
when he received a message from David W. Alexander and John Rowland that they were at his ranch, having fled from Los Angeles in the
wake of a revolt by the native Californians against the American occupation. Wilson was not surprised at this news, especially when he learned
from Alexander and Rowland

> that Gillespie's course toward the people had been so despotic and in every
> way unjustifiable that the people had risen to a man against him.... He had
> established very obnoxious regulations to annoy the people, and upon frivo-
> lous pretexts had the most respectable men in the community arrested and
> brought before him for no other purpose than to humiliate them as they
> thought. Of the truth of this I had no doubt then and have none now. The
> people had given no just cause for the conduct he pursued, which seemed to
> be altogether the effect of vanity & want of judgement.[18]

Wilson's sympathy for the Californians—or at least his effort to credit
them with some genuine grievances—was not generally characteristic of
the Americans on the scene. Wilson was soon to be attacked by a troop
of Californians, and made a prisoner. Yet even a long-time resident like
George Nidever harbored more resentment against his Californian
neighbors than Wilson did.

Lieutenant Archibald Gillespie had sent word to Wilson, asking him
to come to the beleaguered Marine's aid in Los Angeles. Wilson advised
the Americans who were with him (most of them new to the country) to
make their way to Los Angeles along the edges of the mountains so that
they could easily retreat if necessary. But these men held the usual opinion about the courage and fighting ability of the Californians, and they
refused to listen to Wilson. He said they believed "that a few shots would
suffice to scare away any number of them," and he tried to point out to
them that this idea was "erroneous." They all rode from Wilson's Jurupa
Rancho to the Chino Rancho of another American, Isaac Williams.
There they were eventually besieged by a small force of Californians, at
first led by José del Carmen Lugo, whose sister was Williams' wife.
Again, Wilson tried to persuade his men to make their escape at night,

---

[18]Wilson I, 67; Wilson II, 22-23.

but they still maintained they could "whip all they [the Californians] can bring against us." The Californians finally set fire to the roof of the house, and as Wilson told it, Cerbulo Varela assured them that if they surrendered, they would be treated fairly. In his own memoir of the event, José del Carmen Lugo reflected that the Americans in the house had lost their chance. Had the Americans charged out to fight before Varela and Ramón Carrillo arrived with reinforcements, "they would have finished us since we had no more than four of five guns and few pistols —plus one or two lances and a few Indian arrows."[19]

A Californian, Carlos Ballesteros, had been killed in charging the house, and there were some threatening gestures made toward the prisoners, but Wilson said that Varela restrained his men. The Americans, several of whom had been wounded, were taken to a small adobe room in the Boyle Heights area of Los Angeles. They were soon visited by a priest, who gave them all a fright since they assumed it was a prelude to their execution, but the priest reassured them. Wilson was then asked by the Mexican commander in charge of the Californians at Los Angeles, José María Flores, to write a message to Gillespie. As Wilson told it, Flores expressed the desire to avoid unnecessary bloodshed, and offered to let Gillespie and his men march out of Los Angeles unmolested and board ships at San Pedro. Flores stated further that his men were very anxious to attack and that one charge from them would destroy Gillespie and all of his soldiers. Wilson felt that Flores was correct in saying this, "for many of the old Californians who had been ill-treated by Gillespie felt revengeful."[20]

While they were prisoners, they were well treated by the Californians, particularly "an old Spaniard named Don Eulogio Celis," who brought them blankets and food. Wilson seemed to display some bitterness against his own countrymen when he said: "It is a satisfaction to me to state these facts of one who tho [sic] not of our nationality had the courage as well as humanity to stand for us and supply our wants whilst several of our countrymen, who were close around us did not even come

[19]Wilson I, 67-73; José del Carmen Lugo, "Life of a Rancher," in *The Historical Society of Southern California Quarterly*, XXXII No. 3 (Sept., 1950), 202.

[20]Wilson I, 77-80; Wilson II, 24-27.

to see us." Wilson and his fellow prisoners were even offered parole if they would agree on their honor not to take up arms or use their influence against Mexico, but Wilson set an unacceptably short time limit to this, so they remained prisoners. Yet they continued to owe their well-being to the help of Californians, who were instrumental in foiling a plot to send the prisoners to Mexico. Wilson credited William Workman with persuading key Californians, especially Ignacio Palomares, that they would all be held responsible by the United States Government if they permitted commander Flores to send the Americans to Mexico. Amazingly enough, in the midst of the struggle against the Americans, the Californians dealt with the problem in their usual fashion. They organized a revolution against Flores (who was not a native Californian), attacked his headquarters and put him in irons until he agreed not to send away the Chino prisoners. The prisoners themselves had been moved for their safety to the San Gabriel Mission. After giving his promise, Flores was put back in command again! [21]

Wilson continued to act as a kind of middle-man between his own countrymen and the Californians, trying to maintain both loyalty to his country and friendship for the natives of his new home. It is a testimonial to his integrity that he was trusted by both sides. The Californians had already chased off an American attempt to land at San Pedro, led by the impetuous Captain William Mervine. Now according to Wilson, José Antonio Carrillo, in immediate command around Los Angeles, called on him to deliver a message to Commodore Stockton who had arrived at San Pedro. Wilson reported that the Californians wanted no more bloodshed and would protect American interests. He quoted Carrillo's request that Stockton should not march his forces through the country "as this would cause the spilling of blood and engender bad feelings between two people who in all probability will have to live together." Wilson claimed to have been with the force of Californians sent to prevent Stockton's landing, and he corrected the historical record by asserting "from personal observation that Stockton did not land, but that four of his boats came to the water's edge, and returned to the frigate without having effected a landing at all." He had been reading a history of the

---

[21]Wilson I, 80-85; Wilson II, 27-29.

war which had Stockton engaging the Californians at San Pedro and killing a number of them, only abandoning the campaign because he thought it unwise to advance without cavalry. Wilson said of this history: "The whole thing is a fabrication."[22]

Wilson witnessed the final defeat of the Californians at the Battle of the San Gabriel River, where, he said, " the Californians rather gave way." He did not praise this as a great victory for American arms, however. Rather, he speculated that if all of the Californians had charged at once on that day, the Americans would have been routed and the end might have been very different. As ever, Wilson continued to work for a reconciliation between the Americans and Californians by accompanying Andrés Pico to see Stockton after Pico had surrendered to Fremont. Wilson observed that the Commodore was exceedingly angry at Fremont's conduct, and Wilson himself was not much of a Fremont partisan. "It was generally known," he thought, "that Fremont had designedly delayed on his way from Santa Barbara by taking circuitous route on the mountains, so as to keep himself out of danger from the Californians." This was what the Californians themselves undoubtedly believed. And here as in many other cases, Benjamin Davis Wilson was one of them. The war was over, at least in California. Americans and Californians had now, indeed, to try to live with one another. Wilson was and continued all of his life to be a living example of how this could be done. Perhaps more than any other American in Mexican California, he represented the American ideal of fairness to all. His statement at the constitutional convention a few years later, made in opposition to slavery, is still a timely sentiment and a fitting close to his autobiography: "We had enough of a vanity of races...."[23]

---

[22]Wilson I, 88-90; Wilson II, 30. Neal Harlow, *California Conquered*, 166-173, attributes to Wilson the information that the Californian force sent to meet Stockton was not a large one; the Californians fooled Stockton by marching their horses—mounted and riderless—around and around a hill, raising a large cloud of dust and giving the impression of a much larger force.

[23]Wilson I, 95-106, 113-114; Wilson II, 35-38.

PART IV
Exponents of Empire

CHAPTER X

Thomas Jefferson Farnham

After a harrowing journey across the continent from Peoria, Illinois, to the Willamette Valley in Oregon, Thomas Jefferson Farnham arrived in California just in time to involve himself in the controversial "Graham Affair." In 1840 the California authorities arrested about a hundred foreigners, including the mountain man Isaac Graham and a large number of other Americans. The men arrested were accused of plotting a Texas-style revolution. Also, they had never bothered to obtain passports and were therefore in the country illegally.[1] Thomas Jefferson Farnham is perhaps best known in California history for his "eye-witness" account of this affair. His discussion of the arrests made up a large part of his second book, *Travels in California and Scenes in the Pacific Ocean*, which came out in 1844, several years before the Mexican War.[2]

Earlier, he had published *Travels in the Great Western Prairies, the Anhuac and the Rocky Mountains*, memorializing his trip to Oregon, and both books piqued the interest of an American public eager for any information about opportunities and adventures in the western regions. Farnham's writings reflected the restless, optimistic climate of Jacksonian America. They also added their own stimulus to the forces that were impelling Americans across the continent, and well in advance of the influx that was to sweep into California, Farnham condemned the people who were to be conquered or eliminated. Historians from Hubert Howe Bancroft to David Lavender have drawn on Farnham's books in writing their histories of California, but no one has analyzed these auto-

---

[1]For detailed histories of the "Graham Affair," see Hubert Howe Bancroft, *Works*, (39 vols., San Francisco, 1886), XXI, 1-41; Doyce B. Nunis, Jr., *The Trials of Isaac Graham* (Los Angeles, 1967); Dorothy Allen Hertzog, "Isaac Graham, California Pioneer," (M. A. thesis, University of California, Berkeley, 1942).

[2]Thomas Jefferson Farnham, *Travels in California and Scenes in the Pacific Ocean*, (New York, 1844).

biographical writings as cultural artifacts useful in revealing the mentality of an individual whose outlook both mirrored and shaped the characteristic expansionist rhetoric of his time. The United States was soon to extend its control from the Atlantic to the Pacific, and Thomas Jefferson Farnham's experiences in Oregon and California were made to serve this cause.[3]

Thomas Jefferson Farnham was born in New England (either in Vermont or Maine), but like many others had moved west, and was practicing law in Peoria when he heard a lecture on the Oregon country given by Methodist missionary Jason Lee, who had gone there in 1834.[4] This inspirational talk aroused Farnham's desire to see the country about which, as he explained in the preface to his first book, he had heard glowing reports. The western prairies, the Rockies, Oregon, and California, all beckoned to his imagination. He also believed that the journey west would help to restore his health, broken by a long term of "sedentary labors." A further motivation for undertaking such an arduous trek was surely patriotic, though tinged with an element of megalomania. He thought he was the man to lead an expedition that would drive the British out of Oregon. To this end, he recruited eighteen other young men for the adventure, none of whom had had any experience with wilderness travel. But Farnham was an articulate and persuasive speaker, so much so that in spite of his avowed intentions toward the British, several of the men who accompanied him from Peoria were English.[5]

Carrying their flag, designed by Farnham's wife Eliza, and emblazoned with the slogan "Oregon Or The Grave," the self-styled dragoons,

[3]Farnham, *Travels in the Great Western Prairies, the Anhuac and the Rocky Mountains* (Poughkeepsie, N.Y., 1841); see also Reuben Gold Thwaites, ed., *Early Western Travels, 1748-1846* (32 vols., 1906; New York, 1966), XXVIII 14; S.A. Clarke, *Pioneer Days of Oregon History* (Portland, 1905), 446-448. Bancroft, *Works*, XXI, 26, writes of Farnham: "He was apparently an intelligent man, and was certainly in some repects a brilliant writer," but "his remarks on [the Graham Affair] are so evidently and absurdly false as to throw more than a doubt upon all that he says." David Lavender, *California: Land of New Beginnings* (New York, 1972), 119, states that while Farnham was in California, he wrote "jingoist letter to the American press. Later he would use the effusions as the basis of a popular book extolling California's resources while decrying the shiftlessness, immorality, and treacherousness of the Californios."

[4]Farnham, *Travels in the Prairies*, 6; for a description of Jason Lee and his mission, see Bernard DeVoto, *Across the Wide Missouri* (Boston, 1947), 179-181.

[5]Farnham, *Travels in the Prairies*, 6; Leroy R. and Ann W. Hafen, eds., *The Far West and the Rockies Historical Series*, 1820-1875, vol. 3: *To the Rockies and Oregon, 1839-1842* (Glendale, Calif., 1955), 97.

apparently wholly unaware of the comical element in their theatrical departure, set out in 1839 by a circuitous route that took them to Santa Fe. Only nine men out of the original nineteen finally made it to Oregon; the others turned back. And of the nine who did reach their destination, only three remained with Farnham. There was dissension on the trail, and a majority of the nine parted company with Farnham and his contingent at Bent's Fort on the Arkansas River. The ensuing altercation between him and those who left provides an important insight into the personality of Thomas Jefferson Farnham. Regardless of who was "right" in the dispute, Farnham was beginning to reveal himself as the kind of person who could not abide opposition. Anyone who disagreed with him was immediately branded a villain. His strongly biased writings on California and the Californians would be widely read, helping to publicize the country and its people to his fellow Americans. Farnham was not a tolerant or forgiving man. Once he had made up his mind to oppose some person or group, for offenses real or imagined, he was implacable in his hostility, and violent in his rhetoric. The five men who repudiated his leadership on the trail to Oregon—especially Robert Shortess who seemed to have had his own aspirations to leadership— earned Farnham's undying hatred.[6]

As the self-appointed captain of the expedition Farnham exhibited judgement and competence that were suspect from the beginning. Shortess questioned Farnham about his announced intention to drive out the British. Did he think that nineteen men would be enough for the job? Farnham thought so, but since some of the men were themselves English, would they fight their own countrymen? According to Shortess, Farnham replied: "they will not turn traitors; if they do, by God, we'll shoot

---

[6]See the Hafens' *To the Rockies and Oregon*, which reproduces the diaries and letters of the participants, and Farnham's *Travels in the Prairies*. It is infomative to compare Farnham's attitude, when faced with opposition, to that of Andrew Jackson. Michael Paul Rogin has shown how those who opposed Jackson's assumption of authority met with his violent rage and condemnation. The optimistic exterior of the Jacksonian era concealed much anxiety, and men were especially vulnerable to the vicissitudes of the market. "Widespread mobility denied men stable expectations about the positions and motives of their fellows....The search for conspiracies was the search in the outer world for negative feelings hidden within the self." Rogin, *Fathers and Children: Andrew Jackson and the Subjugation of the American Indian* (New York, 1975), 258. In several instances, Farnham's self-righteous stance clearly involved the attribution of some of his own characteristics to others.

them." To Shortess, this response gave "a pretty good idea of Captain Farnham's character, morally and intellectually." Shortess claimed that Farnham's authority had been repudiated even before reaching the crossing of the Arkansas,"in consequence of [his] intemperance and neglect of duty...and every one did that which was right in his eyes." Farnham was accused of being incompetent and wasting the funds that had been placed in his hands, accusations which, as we will see, he was himself to make against the Mexican regime in California. While on the trail, Farnham "saw fit to resign" as leader, said Shortess, "and narrowly escaped expulsion along with two other, who had become obnoxious to the party." At Bent's Fort, Farnham and the two others were "voted out."[7]

Farnham, of course, gave his own version, in which Robert Shortess, though not mentioned by name, was portrayed in the blackest terms. One of the men, Sidney Smith, had accidentally shot himself with his own gun on the way up the Arkansas River, and was in serious condition. In *Travels in the Great Western Prairies*, Farnham accused "certain individuals of my company" of wanting to leave Smith behind to die. Smith was apparently an obnoxious and argumentative sort, and none too popular with the travelers, but Farnham, who admitted that he "had abjured all command, and had no control over the company," also claimed to have prevailed on a majority to see that Smith remained with the party and was cared for. Smith was patched up and put on a mule where, as Farnham told it, he was forced by Shortess to keep up with the rest. Farnham's description of Shortess (whom he never named, but whose identity was clear to those of Farnham's contemporaries familiar with the history of the Peoria party) was characteristic of the kind of vitriolic rhetoric, mixing character with anatomy, that he typically employed against those he did not like:

> One of the principal mutineers, a hard faced villain of no honest memory among the traders upon the Platte, assumed to guide and command. His malice toward Smith was of the bitterest character [Farnham gave no reason why this should be so] , and he had an opportunity now of making it felt. With a grin upon his long and withered physiognomy, that shadowed out the

---

[7]Hafen and Hafen, eds., *To the Rockies*, 97-103.

fiendish delight of a heart long incapable of better emotions, he drove off at a
rate which none but a well man could have long endured.

Farnham continued to describe Shortess as a man of "foul character" and
"blackness of heart," and alleged that Smith's suffering "was delight to
the self-consitituted leader [Shortess]." He offered no evidence in support of his insistence that Shortess was incapable of any better feelings,
and this was typical of Farnham's style of polemics and ad hominem
attacks.[8]

Perhaps it was the leadership issue that most rankled Thomas Jefferson Farnham after a majority of the company repudiated him as their
captain and chose Robert Shortess in his stead. In a letter signed by this
majority and published in the *Peoria Register and North-Western
Gazetteer* on June 25, 1841, these men insisted that Farnham had an
"utter want of qualification for command." He would have been
deprived of his leadership even earlier "if Mr. Shortess would have
accepted it." At the crossing of the Arkansas, Shortess was chosen leader
and, "having reduced matters to something like order, the company proceeded more harmoniously than they had hitherto done, to the extreme
mortification of Farnham, and one or two others." Any suggestion that
Smith had been neglected, or that any proposal had been made to abandon him, was repudiated as "a base calumny." The splitting of the company at Bent's Fort was blamed on "the low intriguing disposition of
Farnham" and several others, "and resulted in their expulsion from the
company."[9]

Once in Oregon, far from driving out the British, Farnham was
forced of necessity to accept the hospitality of the Hudson's Bay Company which replaced his worn out and ragged clothing. Yet he did employ
his skills as a lawyer to help the cause of the American settlers in Oregon, drawing up a petition signed by seventy people and asking the United States for protection. Furthermore, he put his literary talents to good
use by writing about his experiences. Both of his books were very influential during his lifetime, ran through several editions (with varying
titles), and were widely read in the East and Midwest. Farnham's mani-

---

[8]Farnham, *Travels in the Prairies*, 31-36.
[9]Letter quoted in Hafen and Hafen, eds., *To the Rockies*, 296-297.

festly intolerant temperament was instrumental in forming the image of Mexican California for the American public opinion of his day.[10] His facility for language was used to portray the beauties and attractions of Oregon and California in terms that would appeal both to those interested in new opportunities for fertile farm lands and those with more intellectual or transcendentalist impulses. He also turned his eloquence to the service of American empire by his characterization of the people who already claimed California. They were inferior, degraded, and entirely unworthy of any civilized right to such a country, a land to which only the "Anglo-Saxon race" could do justice. As a propagandist for American expansion, he gave one of the clearest and most unabashed expressions to the vaunted American sense of superiority over the Spanish-Mexican-Indian peoples who were soon to be dispossessed. Today, the racism of a Thomas Jefferson Farnham is viewed with justifiable distaste, but at the time he was merely reflecting the common assumptions of his age, even in scientific circles.[11] Indeed, he tried to be systematic and scientific in his discussion of California, its people and resources. As a "philosophical" foundation for his views, Farnham subscribed to a "theory" of the hierarchical nature of humanity which was held by many (perhaps most) educated Americans of the time:

> From the New Hollander, who is connected to our kind by a physical form but little superior to that of the ape, and by the instinct and capacity to build a fire to warm his frame when beset with cold—to the Negro—the Hottentot—the Indian—the Asiatic and European species, there is a gradual development of beauty and capacity of body and mind....[12]

After recuperating at the expense of the Hudson's Bay Company,

---

[10]Robert Glass Cleland, *A History of California: The American Period* (New York, 1922), 98. Cleland states that Farnham's "accounts of western scenes and experiences ran through many editions," and that his readers "liked the exaggerated, the highly colored in literature as in everything else, and accordingly found Farnham's *Life and Adventures in California* [sic] a book decidedly after their own tastes. From it they learned to despise the Californians...." See also David Weber, "Scarce more than Apes: Historical Roots of Anglo American Stereotypes of Mexicans in the Border Regions," in *New Spain's Far Northern Frontier* (Albuquerque, 1979), 295-304, where he cites Thomas Jefferson Farnham as a primary example of an early Anglo-American writer responsible for the spread of racist opinions about Mexicans.

[11]See Stephen Jay Gould, *The Mismeasure of Man* (New York, 1981), 30-72, for a discussion of scientific racism in antebellum America.

[12]Farnham's *Travels in California*, 282-283.

Farnham sailed from Oregon in December 1839, for the Sandwich Islands and then California. His amusing and mostly sympathetic descriptions of his fellow passengers on board the *Vancouver* bound for Hawaii, and his warm portraits of the Hawaiians, lead the reader to expect a more objective and balanced assessment of things in California. He enjoyed the company of his fellow passengers and thought the British captain to be a straightforward fellow, generous to his friends but implacable to his enemies. He especially liked one passenger, an energetic and well-informed young Scotsman whom Farnham knew only as Simpson, in spite of the latter's tendency to be,"like most British subjects abroad, troubled with an irrepressible anxiety at the growing power of the States," a power which obviously pleased Farnham. He even drew amusement from the cabin boy, Tom. The only one of his cabin mates who bothered him was an itinerant singing master whom he called "such an animal as one would wish to find if he were making up a human menagerie, so positive was he of step, so lofty in the neck, and dignified in the absurd blunders wherewith he perpetually correct-ed the opinions and assertions of others." No doubt this was what both-ered Farnham most about the gentleman—his self-righteous attitude towards his own opinions—a character trait Farnham himself possessed in the extreme.[13]

During his three months stay in the Sandwich Islands, the natives impressed him with their kindness, affection and generosity, and he had nothing but praise for the missionaries who brought them civilization and Christianity and had ended the their practice of human sacrifice. The Hawaiians were "a talented people and anxious for new ideas," much more advanced (Farnham knew without yet having been to Mexi-co or California) than the citizens of the Mexican Republic. This was clearly due to the alacrity with which they accepted the moral leadership of Americans! Farnham could spare some sympathy for the Hawaiians; they were not immediate rivals for possession of lands that were coveted by the United States.[14]

Farnham got firsthand information about California from a person

[13]Ibid., 8-9.
[14]Ibid., 35-45.

who had lived there and was now on his way home. This man was a southerner who had worked as a carpenter in California and who had left because his California sweetheart had jilted him. The young woman apparently refused to marry the American and then found another man and got pregnant. Farnham referred to her new lover disparagingly as "a California Cavaliero, that is, a pair of mustachios on horseback." The southerner could not remain where the memories were so painful, but he had only praise for California as a place to live, telling Farnham that the climate was so balmy "that people went about half naked to enjoy it. The plains and mountains were covered with cattle, horses and wild game. The fried beans too, the mussels of the shores, and the fleas even, were all objects of pleasure, utility or industry, of which he entertained a vivid recollection."[15]

Farnham thus foreshadowed the attitude he would take toward the country he was about to visit: it was attractive, but there were doubts about the character of its inhabitants. He also adumbrated the eventual American priority over the British in that area—one of his favorite themes, as we have seen with his trip to Oregon. From the Hawaiian Islands Farnham sailed to California on the *Don Quixote,* captained by John Paty of New England whom Farnham called "a little man, with a quiet spirit, and a generous heart...." On the passage, he had a chance to observe the differences between some British and American sailors, naturally to the credit of the latter. The British sailors knew what to do on deck, but they did not know the entire operation of the ship or how the vessel was constructed as the Americans did. They were "specialists," whereas the Americans understood the whole process. The latter, concluded Farnham, could outsail and outmanage the British, and therefore "must succeed to the paternal power over the seas," a prophetic boast, and one that also showed Farnham's understanding of an important reason for the ultimate U. S. control over the region: Americans were generalists and able to see the many possibilities offered by the country.[16]

---

[15]Ibid., 24-25.

[16]Ibid., 46-47; see also William H. Goetzmann, *Exploration and Empire* (New York, 1966), 149-50, 155 ff., for a discussion of the role played by a flexible, multipurpose view of the West's possibilities in the American approach to exploration.

In his preface to *Travels In California*, Farnham sought to inspire his readers with scenes of the awesomeness and sublimity of nature. This was to be one of the more positive apects of his writing. He had an appreciation for the landscape and believed that "we may learn much from the pulseless solitudes...if we will allow its [sic] lessons of awe to reach the mind, and impress it with the fresh and holy images which they were made to inspire." He also tried to convey some useful knowledge about the country, relating not only what he himself had observed, but also what he was able to learn of "authentic information from every known source."[17] Though Farnham was occasionally given incorrect information by others, some of it can stand up to historical scrutiny and is not entirely the "worthless trash" that Hubert Howe Bancroft labeled it.[18] But Farnham blatantly selected his information to fit his presuppositions, and, more importantly, through this process further revealed his personality, his priorities, and those of his age. He saw what he wanted and needed to see, sometimes quite transparently so.

A good example is a letter from Farnham to William E. P. Hartnell, a prominent English resident who had lived in California since 1822 and married into the De la Guerra family. Hartnell had been appointed by Governor Juan Bautista Alvarado to inspect the missions and report on the progress of secularization as well as to oversee the administrators who had been given charge of the process at each mission. It was a thankless job and one which made for Hartnell not a few enemies.[19] Farnham correctly assumed that Hartnell could supply him with a great deal of information about the missions, and to get this he showed himself to be a man capable of flattery that bordered on the obsequious, perhaps the necessary compliment to his wrathful disposition. He wrote to Hartnell, whom he did not know personally (and whose British origins clearly did not trouble Farnham), requesting information about the California missions and padres. Regreting that he was unable to meet with Hartnell on his short stay in California, he asked permission

to express to you the sorrow I feel at this disappointment. The society of an

---

[17]Farnham, *Travels in California*, iii-iv.
[18]Bancroft, *Works*, XX 735.
[19]See Susanna Bryant Dakin, *The Lives of William Hartnell* (Stanford, 1949), esp. 214-240.

enlightened gentleman on these distant seas, where Literature and refinement has as yet scarcely shed a benignant ray—would, I assure you sir, have
been pleasure highly prized.

It was clear that Farnham had already made up his mind about the missions and padres when he asked Hartnell for a "true history of the California Missions—a view of the self denying zeal and holy patience of the
venerable Padres who founded them, and the benefits that the gentile
Indians derived from them." He was convinced that Hartnell, with his
"intimate knowledge—high attainments and unprejudiced judgement,"
could confirm his opinions. Two reasons prompted Farnham to solicit
information from Hartnell: "a great desire to be personally informed
...and a wish that certain false—I believe *false*—statements in regard to
the character of the Padres may be met and refuted by one—pardon
me—as able and as [illegible] as you yourself are."[20]

This revealing letter shows Farnham ingratiating himself—in the
guise of soliciting expert opinion—with one whom he believed could
provide support for the views he had already formed. It is another
glimpse into the personality of the man who would become the primary
source of "information" about the so-called "Graham Affair" in California, and who would convey to the American reading public perhaps the
most unremittingly negative stereotypes of the native Californians to
appear in print before the Mexican War. It was Farnham's obvious prejudice against the Californians whom he met in 1840, when Governor
Alvarado arrested many of the foreign residents there, which prompted
Hubert Howe Bancroft to call Farnham's account of the arrests "a tissue
of falsehoods."[21] Though Farnham professed to believe that "the regulating principle of human culture, is to sympathize with every form of
creation within our knowledge," he made no effort whatever to syp-
mathize with any Californians. His nefarious portrayal of them contrasted sharply with his descriptions of Isaac Graham, who he made out
to be the quintessence of nobility and generosity. Thus Farnham arrived
in California predisposed to see the part-Indian people he found there as

---

[20]Thomas Jefferson Farnham to W. E. P. Hartnell, April 28, 1840, in Mariano G. Vallejo, "Documentos para la historia de California, " XXXIII, no. 66, file C-B 33, Bancroft Library, University of
California, Berkeley.
[21]Bancroft, *Works*, XX, 735.

inferiors. To this he added elements of the anti-Spanish "Black Legend" ideology, by which even upper-class Californians of almost entirely European descent were looked upon with contempt.[22]

Sailing into Monterey Bay on April 18, 1840, Farnham may have been one of the first Americans to compare California to the Mediterranean: "A morning of the blooming spring poured down from Heaven on this Italy of America!" At first the California authorities would not let the passengers on the *Don Quixote* disembark because, as Farnham believed, there was a revolution in progress. But after a delay of several hours, and with an escort of government officers, they were allowed to go to the house of the influential merchant and future United States Consul Thomas O. Larkin from whom they learned, in Farnham's phrase, that "one hundred and fifty odd Americans and Britons were thirsting and starving in the prisons of the town, and destined to be sacrificed to Spanish malignity!" Without a moment's hesitation or any apparent efforts to get the facts of the case, Farnham assumed that the prisoners were innocent victims and resolved immediately to try to act in their behalf. He did this in spite of his professed belief that it would put his own life in danger from the California authorities.[23]

But before he could aid the prisoners, he had to obtain a passport from these very authorities to permit him to remain in California. Bancroft claimed that this inconvenience was at the bottom of Farnham's subsequent hostility to the Californians, though it seems clear from the evidence adduced here that he had already made up his mind about them well before his arrival. Bancroft (whose history gives the most detailed discussion of the arrests) recognized Farnham's talent as a writer and felt that his statements in the case would have been entitled to some weight "on account of his opportunities for knowing the truth," had it not been for what Bancroft saw as the completely one-sided efforts to vilify the Californians and exonerate (indeed glorify) the foreign settlers.[24]

---

[22]Farnam, *Travels in California*, 282-283. For the black legend, see Phillip Wayne Powell, *Tree of Hate: Propaganda and Prejudices Affecting United States Relations with the Hispanic World* (New York, 1971), 7, 10-11, 117-118.

[23]Farnham, *Travels in California*, 51-53; for a biography of Larkin, see Harlan Hague and David J. Langum, *Thomas O. Larkin: A Life of Patriotism and Profit in Old California* (Norman, 1990).

[24]Bancroft, *Works*, XXI, 25.

Farnham's first encounter with Governor Juan Bautista Alvarado was also his first opportunity in print to excoriate the Californian for his alleged treachery. During this brief meeting Alvarado did nothing more than refer Farnham to the alcalde of Monterey for his passport. Nevertheless, Farnham convinced himself of the governor's perfidy by reading a double meaning into Alvarado's politeness. As if he could decipher the Californian's character from his physiognomy, he called Alvarado "a well-formed, full-blooded California Spaniard" with the "clearly marked mien of a pompous coward, clad in the broadcloth and whiskers of a gentleman." Alvarado, he said, "received us with the characteristic urbanity of a Spanish body without a soul," and "smiled graciously at us with one corner of his mouth, while he cursed us with the other...."[25]

Farnham also took advantage of the occasion to inspect the Governor's guards and gave a description which was clearly intended to show that the troops of California were no threat to any Americans who might conceivably have to fight them. They were merely some half-breed Indians

> and what passed for a white corporal, lounging about the door in the manner of grog-shop savans. Their outer man is worth a description. They wore raw bull's hide sandals on their feet, leathern breeches, blankets about their shoulders, and anything and everything upon their heads. Of arms, they had nothing which deserved the name. One made pretensions with an old musket without a lock; and his four comrades were equally heroic with kindred pieces, so deeply rusted, that the absence of locks would have been an unimportant item in estimating their value.[26]

This was to be Farnham's pejorative tone toward the inhabitants throughout his stay in California. He continued to revile Governor Alvarado who, he claimed, took the customs duties charged to foreign ships in order to settle his own debts. Yet according to Farnham (who held the same opinion as William H. Thomes), a California Spaniard would never pay his debts as long as he could obtain what he wanted on credit. Furthermore, he would plunder, defraud and even murder to get what he wanted if he considered it safe to do so. The Californians in Farnham's opinion, were little better than beasts, living, not in houses

---

[25]Farnham, *Travels in California*, 54.
[26]Ibid., 54.

but in "adobie dens," and he exercised his sarcasm on what he called "Castilian industry..., lounging, grinning, sleeping, and smoking rolls of paper tinctured with 'the weed'." All of this was by way of a preface before he launched into his own "history" of the arrest and exile of Isaac Graham and 49 other foreigners, for no other crime as Farnham saw it than "their Anglo-Saxon blood."[27]

Some one hundred men were rounded up; fifty were shipped to Mexico for trial. There is no "definitive" explanation as to why this was done, but it is clear that the California authorities feared many of these men, especially Isaac Graham, and hoped to rid themselves of potential or actual troublemakers. Four basic elements have been cited. Isaac Graham was considered to be the ringleader in a plot to overthrow the California government and establish a Texas-style republic. It has also been alleged (by William Heath Davis) that Alvarado had secret orders from Mexico to round up all foreigners. José Castro, the military commander, has been blamed for initiating the incident as a move in his struggle with Mariano Vallejo for power. And finally there is Farnham's explanation: Alvarado feared the foreigners, especially Graham and his followers, to whom he had made promises he did not intend to keep. In 1836 Graham had helped Alvarado expel a general sent from Mexico to govern the Californians.[28]

Farnham, however, began his history in error, stating that Alvarado had overthrown a Mexican General named "Echuandra" [José María Echeandía] whose second term as governor had actually come to an end on January 14, 1833. Between Echeandía and Alvarado, there were eight intervening governors of California. Nor did Farnham mention Nicholas Gutierrez, the Mexican governor actually ousted by Alvarado's California forces in 1836.[29] Instead, Farnham attacked the secularization policies of the California government, accusing "Echuandra" of robbing the missions and the people and taking for himself the customs revenues.

---

[27]Ibid., 54-57, 113.

[28]Hertzog, "Isaac Graham, California Pioneer," 34-38.

[29]See Irving Berdine Richman, *California under Spain and Mexico, 1535-1857* (New York, 1965), 228-291; George Tays, "Revolutionary California: The Political History of California during the Mexican Period, 1822-1846" (Ph. D. dissertation, University of California, Berkeley, 1932), 387-475. A list of governors of Mexican California can be found in Andrew Rolle, *California History* (4th ed., Arlington Heights, Ill., 1987), 536-537.

Farnham's ostensible respect for the Padres and the missions became another club with which to beat the Californians, whose policies Farnham blamed for the decline of an institution he professed to admire. (Here we see the use he wished to make of the information he had hoped to obtain from Hartnell). According to Farnham, Alvarado had only conducted his revolution in order to do exactly the same as his predecessor. And in achieving power, Alvarado had used the services of foreign riflemen led by the American trapper Isaac Graham. Yet Farnham did not hold Isaac Graham responsible for despoiling the missions, even though he acknowledged that without the help of Graham and his "rifleros" Alvarado would not have been successful. If Alvarado and the Californians were the villains of Farnham's melodrama, Isaac Graham was its hero. In studied contrast to his image of Alvarado, Farnham pictured Graham as

> a stout, sturdy backwoodsman, of a stamp which exists only on the frontiers of the American States—men with the blood of the ancient Normans and Saxons in their veins—with hearts as large as their bodies can hold, beating nothing but kindness till injustice shows its fangs, and then, lion-like, striking for vengeance.[30]

Farnham continued his romantic portrait of Graham as a child of nature—brave, loving the wilderness and in contrast to his California jailors, epitomizing the man of free spirit who has no base motives. Many of his contemporaries, Americans as well as Californians, viewed Graham differently. They described him as the most turbulent of the foreigners in the country, quarrelsome, boastful and prejudiced against the Spanish-speaking Californians. Benjamin Davis Wilson, for example, called him "a bummer, a blowhard, and a notorious liar without a shred of honesty in his composition." He said that Graham was a drunkard who had to leave Tennesee, abandoning a wife and children there, "for some offence that he committed," and that Farnham and others who had praised Graham in print had "done an injustice to the public."[31]

In his discussion of the "Graham Affair," Bancroft cited a document

---

[30]Farnham, *Travels in California*, 66.

[31]Benjamin Davis Wilson, "Some Facts about Isaac Graham and John A. Sutter by a Pioneer of 1841," file C-E 102, Bancroft Library.

signed by some twenty citizens of California, nineteen of them naturalized foreigners, denouncing Isaac Graham as an assassin, duelist, adul-
terer and corrupter of morals.[32] Graham, a mountain man with the usual
reputation for pugnacity and bravery, had established a still at Natividad
where other trappers and deserters from the ships on the coast congre-
gated under his leadership.[33]

None of these strictures on Isaac Graham's character was to enter
Farnham's chronicle. According to Farnham, the issue that provoked
Alvarado to arrest Graham and the others was more immediately personal. Isaac Graham and some two hundred men, obviously well armed
with American rifles and experienced in Indian warfare, had assisted
Alvarado in his revolutionary maneuvers of 1836 on the promise that, if
he were successful, Alvarado would declare California independent of
Mexico and, most importantly, abrogate "the law which incapacitated
foreigners from holding real estate." As Farnham had it, Graham and his
men took all of the risks in the revolution of 1836 while Alvarado kept
himself out of harm's way.[34]

In Farnham's account, a major reason for Alvarado's actions against
Graham and his followers was suspicion that Graham would depose
Alvarado just as he had helped to remove the latter's predecessor. To
Farnham, Alvarado was indebted to Graham and his men, yet he
refused to deliver on his promise. He neither declared California independent, nor abrogated the law on foreign landholding. Alvarado owed
his position as Governor to Graham, without whom either Carlos Carrillo from southern California, or "Guadalupe Viejo" [Mariano
Guadalupe Vallejo] from Sonoma "would have torn him from his ill-got-
ten elevation." Farnham suggested that two additional considerations
contributed to the arrest of the foreigners. Graham had a winning racehorse, and many Californians, including the Governor, owed him money
lost in betting against the horse.[35] There was also resentment against the

---

[32]Bancroft, Works, XXI, 7-8.

[33]Hertzog, "Isaac Graham, California Pioneer," 34.

[34]Farnham, *Travels in California*, 62-64.

[35]See Alfred Robinson, *Life in California* (New York, 1846), 178-181, where Robinson states that
an agreement setting the terms for a horse race between animals belonging to Graham and some Californians was construed by Alvarado as a plan to overthrow the government.

foreigners because the California women preferred them as husbands over California men. Conveniently forgotten in adding this last cause was the contrary evidence given by the jilted southerner whom Farnham had met on the *Vancouver*.[36]

According to Bancroft, it was impossible to give an accurate version of the incident in all of its particulars because there had been false testimony on both sides. Isaac Graham and his men were hardly the innocents that Farnham made them out to be, but neither did Alvarado have any hard evidence of a plot against his government. There was, however, a Mexican law stipulating that residents of California should have passports issued by the government, and most of the people arrested by Alvarado were in fact in the country illegally, having come over the mountains or deserted from ships on the coast. Given the recent troubles for Mexico in Texas, Alvarado's fears were perhaps justified, and he was certainly within his legal rights in arresting those without valid passports (exactly what happens to undocumented immigrants from Mexico in California today). He exempted men married to California women, though some of these seem to have been rounded up anyway. Yet there was enough substance to Farnham's account (which clearly and maliciously exaggerated the treachery and cruelty of the Californians) to give it credence. Graham *had* assisted Alvarado in his bid for the governorship in 1836 and afterward; Graham *did* own a successful racehorse; and there were, no doubt, expectations on both sides which were never made clear and explicit. This context allowed Farnham to step in with his version, painting the Californians in the blackest colors, making the Americans the noble victims, and further feeding a public opinion already becoming receptive to the idea that California belonged by right to the United States.[37]

Farnham's portrayal of the prisoners was calculated to elicit pity for their plight. On his first evening in Monterey, he claimed that he was unable to sleep because of their cries for water and air. Fifty or sixty prisoners were crowded into a room 18 or 20 feet square. "[S]ome of them were frantic; others in a stupor of exhaustion; one appeared to be dying!" There were no beds; the ground in the cell was wet; the prisoners were

---

[36]Farnham, *Travels in California*, 65-66.
[37]Bancroft, *Works*, XXI, 2-6.

emaciated and sickly, with several of them barely able to walk to the single grated window in the cell for air; one was not able to stand at all and his fellow prisoners had to hold him up to breathe. There is no record of anyone succumbing, but one of the prisoners, who had no love for Isaac Graham, recalled that they were so crowded in the cell that only a few could lie down at a time.[38]

To further bolster his portrayal, Farnham presented the testimony of Isaac Graham and others about the circumstances of their arrest. He claimed to have taken down the statements of 41 of the prisoners, but he included only three in his narrative, starting with that of Isaac Graham himself. Graham apparently escaped death at the hands of his captors, not once, but four times! First they tried to shoot him with pistols, but missed. Then he was stabbed at with a knife which again missed the mark. Then more shooting, but this time "a faithful Indian in my service" (in Graham's words as reported by Farnham) covered Graham with his body. Finally, he was lassoed and was about to be dragged to death when the rope broke. If Graham (or Farnham) is to be believed here, this mountain man, horse racer, whiskey distiller and rowdy obviously led a charmed life. He went on to claim that his attackers robbed his house and threatened him with death (again) to get him to reveal where his money was hidden.[39]

Throughout his account, Farnham implied or stated explicitly that the California authorities wanted to kill the prisoners but were stopped by their own cowardly fear of the consequences: retribution by the United States government. Farnham introduced into his narrative a charac-

---

[38]Farnham, *Travels in California*, 58-59, 81; Charles Brown, "Statement of Recollections of Early Events in California," 15, file C-D 53, Bancroft Library.

[39]Farnham, *Travels in California*, 70-73. See also George P. Hammond, ed., *The Larkin Papers* (10 vols., Berkeley and Los Angeles, 1951-1965), II, 100-101. In April 1844, Thomas O. Larkin forwarded a copy of a letter written by Isaac Graham asking the U. S. government to pursue his claim against Mexico for false imprisonment. Graham wanted $1,500 per month "for my lost time" and $50,000 for having been attacked and wounded. This letter was much calmer than Graham was made to appear in Farnham's account. Graham's letter reads: "...in the month of April, 1840, I was forcibly attacked in my house in the vicinity of this town [Monterey] by armed officer and soldier of Mexico, wounded both by sword and pistols. Tied and brought to prison in this town in company of other Americans. Here kept in irons several days. Then put on board a vessel ironed and carried to San Blas. Thence taken into the interior and again imprisoned and returned to this town after an imprisonment and absence of fifteen months." Larkin sent this on with a covering letter in which he said: "I am of the opinion that Calafornia [sic] had no just cause for arresting and shipping these men."

ter whom he refered to only as "the American," though the reader is led
to believe that it was actually Farnham himself. "The American,"
according to Farnham, effectively intimidated the Californians by making them think he was a U. S. official or naval officer with the power to
summon a warship. Only this, Farnham claimed, prevented a worse fate
for the prisoners.[40]

In May 1840, forty-six of the prisoners were put on board a ship and
sent to San Blas in Mexico for trial. The rest were released. Farnham
believed these forty-six were not included in the pardon because they
had "acted a conspicuous part in Alvarado's revolution" and were feared
as likely to demand rewards and the promised rulings on land ownership. Farnham and "the American" followed these men to Mexico.[41]

The trip to Mexico was the occasion for more portraits of the prisoners calculated to arouse sympathy for the Americans and rage against the
Californians. Farnham described Isaac Graham weighted down with so
many chains that he couldn't walk but had to be carried by four Indians!
The wives of the prisoners were driven back by blows: "They were beat-
en with swords, but would not go. They led their children and helped
bear the chains that were galling the bleeding limbs of those whom they
loved." Farnham had "the American" shake Graham's hand and assure
him that he would be safe once he reached San Blas where "the American" would meet him. Isaac Graham did not appear to have been chas-
tened by this experience, however. He continued to denounce the
Californians: "Irons on the legs of a man who fought for them, who
made the cowards what they are! With my fifty rifles about me, I could
drive the devils from the whole coast or lay them to rot."[42]

Though this statement and others by Isaac Graham, as reported by
Farnham, lend credibility to Alvarado's fears that Graham and his followers posed a threat to his regime, Farnham was never concerned about
keeping his narrative free from contradiction. He had, for example, pro-

---

[40]Farnham , *Travels in California*, 81. Bancroft, *Works*, XXI, 26, states: "From the narrative I should
suppose this American to have been Farnham himself; but Morris [Albert F. Morris, one of Isaac Graham's riflemen] says there was another whose name he forgets. It may have been Chamberlain, an agent
of American missions at the Sandwich Islands...."

[41]Farnham, *Travels in California*, 92.

[42]Ibid., 92.

posed to drive the British from Oregon with the help of British citizens, and proclaimed a meretricious sympathy for every form of creation. Nevertheless, he was primarily interested in indicting the Mexican people and Mexican rule in California. In his characteristic style, he launched into a depiction of the physiognomies of the Californians. As we have seen with Robert Shortess, anyone who offended him was destined to have his physical features portrayed in the most repulsive terms. Corporal Rafael Pinto was given a narrow head, a sharp nose, small eyes like a snake's, a sharp chin "with a villainous tuft of bristles on the under lip, a dark complexion and the grin of an idiotic hyena." José Castro, the military commander, was "a thoroughbred ourang-outang" with "a very contemptible face, wrinkled and drawn into a broad concentrated scowl of unsatisfied selfishness." Alvarado, Farnham alleged, was angry because he had not shot Graham, to whom he owed $2, 235.[43]

The prisoners did not go straight from Monterey to Mexico, but made a stop first at Santa Barbara where they were kept locked up at the Mission for several weeks. There Farnham claimed that "the American" applied to see them, but was refused by José Castro. The mission itself was of interest to Farnham who gave a detailed description of it and the town. Because of their verisimilitude, such passages doubtless helped to lend credibility to the rest of his narrative. Writing about the mission was also a further opportunity for Farnham to attack the Californians, whose policies he believed had led to the ruination and decline of what were once such beautiful and productive establishments. At Santa Barbara, he reported another statement by Graham to the effect that two hundred good Tennesee riflemen could easily seize all of California. It was a pity said Graham that "it should be held by a set of vagabonds who don't regard the honor of God or the rights of man."[44]

From when the ship carrying the prisoners to Mexico left Santa Barbara, until its arrival at San Blas (where Farnham found them all alive but having "suffered greatly from thirst and hunger"), he digressed from his narrative of the "Graham Affair" to a general discussion of California, leaving out almost nothing that could be grist for the mill of American

[43]Ibid., 87-93.
[44]Ibid., 108-115.

Manifest Destiny. He first pointed out that California was an "incomparable wilderness," and that the study of nature brought man closer to God. Then he compared California to another wilderness, New England at the time of the Puritans. There could be no doubt that the same people who had settled and civilized the eastern seaboard would soon repeat the process in California. In fact, already at Yerba Buena Farnham had observed the results of Yankee enterprise, evidence to him that "almost the entire habitable parts of this great continent are feeling and enjoying the impulses to human Freedom which the American Saxons sent out to the race on the Fourth of July, 1776. These Yankees at Yerba Buena employ themselves in their characteristic business of doing everything."[45]

Farnham was intent on giving his fellow Americans as complete a picture of California as he could manage. He would promote the westward movement of Americans to the Pacific coast by showing the allure of California, beginning with its history from the first European exploration down to the time of his own visit. As a very general survey, it was reasonably accurate through the Spanish period, though Farnham committed such errors as having Portolá march north to San Diego, but arrive first at "a place now called Nuestra Senora de los Angeles."[46] Inevitably, his history too became an occasion for Farnham to demonstrate the degeneration of the present rulers of California when compared to the valiant Franciscan missionaries. They were men of heroic proportions who "entered this wilderness clad in their grey habits with sandals on their feet and the cross in their hands...whose equals in mental power, in physical courage and moral intrepidity [?], we shall seek in vain in these days...."[47] Their treatment of the Indians was exemplary in Farnham's mind because the Indians were "an ignorant, stupid species of the human kind," who could not be trusted to be free in a civilized society until their backwardness and ignorance were sufficiently corrected as to make them useful—or at least not harmful—citizens. The implications were clear: the present Mexican Government was incompetent and unfit to govern the country. The policy of secularizing the missions and removing the Indians from the paternal care of the Padres proved it.

---

[45]Ibid., 413, 117, 355.

[46]Ibid., 264.

[47]Ibid., 279.

Farnham once again took to task his favorite whipping boy, "Echuan-dra," who he claimed not only refused to uphold the Padres when they sought to chastise recalcitrant Indians, but even went so far as to assure the Indians who attacked the Padres that they had done "an act worthy of a citizen of the Mexican Republic." Administrators of the missions were "the hungry leeches of the California Government." The primary result of the Mexican Government's secularization policy was to decrease the herds of cattle and

> paralyze the industry, deteriorate the morals of the whole community, and introduce in the place of the mild and paternal government of the Padres, the oppressive anarchy of a weak and cruel military despotism...where liberty and equality was the theory, and slavery and robbery the practice of the governing class.

Here was indubitable evidence that the current regime did not deserve to exercise power.[48]

Farnham climaxed his indictment of Mexican rule with an attack on the character of the Mexican people. In a passage reaching new depths of racist invective—even for him—he stated that nowhere on the continent was there "anything Spanish, whether negro, Indian, mulatto, or mestizo," with any qualities other than "volatility, ignorance, stupidity and pride, coupled with the basest and most cowardly cruelty." In the latter part of his narrative he devoted a few pages to a "description" of the people of California. Those of mixed Indian and white blood were dull, lazy, filthy and brutish, "using freedom as a mere means of animal enjoyment." These people supplied the soldiers and were the herdsmen of the country; as soldiers they were treacherous and cowardly, never risking an attack unless the enemy was helpless. The descendants of the free settlers from Mexico were only "by courtesy" called white. These people were actually not white at all, but a "light bronze" in color, which Farnham called "a lazy color." Their habits were of the most slothful: they arose around noon, ate breakfast, smoked, then took a nap again until dinner time. They merely gave the appearance of being civilized. Only on horseback did they show some skill. And lest the reader be mistaken about Farnham's intentions in presenting such an unremittingly

---

[48]Ibid., 283-286.

negative picture of the Californians, he left no doubt about the implications he wished drawn: "In a word," he said, "the Californians are an imbecile, pusillanimous, race of men and unfit to control the destinies of that beautiful country." Farnham's animosity toward the Californians was in fact a component of his conviction that the land in all its richness was inevitably slated to belong to the Anglo-Saxon Americans: " No one acquainted with the indolent, mixed race of California, will ever believe that they will populate, much less...govern the country....The old Saxon blood must stride the continent...." [49]

California as a subject called forth all of Farnham's prolixity, and he became encyclopedic in his treatment of things Californian. He discussed the Indian tribes of the country—in his usual pseudo-scientific manner, with heavy reliance on physiognomy to prove their inferiority. "Their heads are small and badly formed, the mass of brain lying back of the eyes." They lived in squalid villages and clustered around rude huts made of reeds. They had no idea of industry and no rational or inventive thought, only an "incessant love of amusements of the most useless and brutal character." Dire necessity alone forced them to hunt or gather acorns. They were "a spectacle of the extreme filth and wretchedness of the most pitiable savage condition." Yet he did find something to admire in the Indians: "their faithful and ardent attachment to each other, and their admiration of true courage." This was more praise than he could ever bring himself to bestow upon the Californians.[50]

Farnham continued his compendium of California attractions by listing the animals to be found there, including the wolverine, polar bear, bison and moose! Birds, fish, flowers, minerals, all were illustrations of California's abundance. The climate was healthy in the extreme, and California's possibilities for agricultural wealth were boundless. The soil was so rich that whatever crops were planted would continue to yield year after year without further plowing, harrowing or planting. He was informed by Dr. John Marsh, an American pioneer of the Sacramento Valley, that a planting of ten bushels of wheat would return a harvest of over three thousand bushels. California was destined to become the granary of Western America, when "an intellectual and industrious race

---

[49]Ibid., 288, 363, 413.
[50]Ibid., 364-369.

shall plough that soil...." Farnham was so enthusiastic about California that he began to speculate in print about its development, proposing a canal which he believed could "easily be cut" from the head of steamboat navigation on the San Joaquin River all the way to the Gulf of California! A railroad could connect the Mississippi Valley with California, and in the meantime "an excellent natural road" ran from the Great Salt Lake to California, an expanse, he believed, of "not more than three hundred and fifty miles, with plenty of wood, water and grass the whole distance." And in a final excess of his imagination, he suggested that the Sierra could be crossed in six hours, through a "low gap." But he was not far off with his prophecy that California would one day be "a country capable of sustaining thirty five millions of people...."[51]

Thomas Jefferson Farnham the expansionist had no room in his psychology for any doubts about himself, his opinions, or his sense of the superiority of the United States and its inevitable predominance on the West Coast. As a publicist, his absolute conviction as to the certainty of such a future may indeed have helped to bring it about. Like his trip to Oregon to expel the British, the "Graham Affair" was another occasion for Farnham to demonstrate his patriotism. He would champion the cause of the American prisoners and call for vengeance against the "California Spaniards." His admiration for the ascribed character traits of his countrymen (and by implication his own) contrasted sharply with his contempt and ethnocentric hostility towards the native Californians who controlled the country in 1840. Farnham believed that the intelligence, courage and enterprise of his fellow Americans made them the predestined inheritors of a land whose riches and opportunities he did his best to portray for them. They were following in the footsteps of ancestors who had believed in their own divine election to the task of taming and developing a wilderness. Tolerance was as anathema to many of them as it was to Farnham. On the basis of a brief visit, he could percieve nothing of value in the people of Mexican California, yet he was equally blind to any of the faults or weaknesses in his own countrymen. An Alvarado was without redeeming virtues, and an Isaac Graham was conversely free from any venality.[52]

---

[51]Ibid., 381-384, 342-343, 411-413.
[52]Ibid., 413-414.

Thomas Jefferson Farnham's choleric and exaggerated rhetoric was taken seriously by his contemporaries. His books were popular and his hyperbolic mode fit easily into a boastful frontier tradition of buckskin heroes and "alligator-horses."[53] Moreover, on a deeper level, he represented a certain characteristically American way of thinking that has not entirely disappeared. It couples an incurable optimism with a self-righteous lack of objectivity or empathy. It fosters a belief in the unmitigated evil of our putative enemies, while clinging to a faith in the morality of our own (or our government's) actions, sometimes in spite of much evidence to the contrary. Thomas Jefferson Farnham exhibited this mentality in the clearest way. Yet he was a patriotic spokesman for his country and a defender of the rights of his countrymen, at some perceptible risk to himself. For this he was admired at the time. He also had a feel for the beauty and splendor of nature that remains a positive strain in the American character. He was unavoidably taken with the majesty and wild charm of the California landscape and included this sensibility in his compendium of the country. The spell of California affected him then as it still does emigrants today, with origins in the harsher climes of the East and Midwest. "No one," he said, "born and dwelling in the rugged changing seasons of the North can know, without experiencing, the delights of a climate like that of California." In Monterey he went on a picnic to a secluded and picturesque spot on the Bay. We will leave Thomas Jefferson Farnham with his reactions to the beauty of his surroundings:

> It was among the trees, a short distance southwest of the anchorage; a wild, rude spot. The old trees, which had thrown their branches over the savage before the white man had touched the shores, were rotting on the ground and formed the fuel of our fire! The ancient rocks stood around, covered with the moss of ages! The winds sang in the trees! The ringing cadences of the towering pines, the deep bass of the strong spreading oak, the mellow alto of the flowering shrubs, the low, soft voice of the grasses, nature's great Aeolian lyre, breathed sweet music! The old wilderness was there, unshorn, and holy, responding to the songs of birds in the morn of the opening year.[54]

---

[53]See Arthur K. Moore, *The Frontier Mind* (New York, 1963), 107-135.
[54]Farnham, *Travels in California*, 96.

CHAPTER XI

Henry Augustus Wise

By 1846, the United States was about to realize the dreams and expectations of people like Alfred Robinson and Thomas Jefferson Farnham. As a nation, the U.S. was completing its drive to become a continental power and establish the foundations for an empire on the Pacific. United States Navy Lieutenant Henry Augustus Wise was a participant in this process, as a naval officer on board the United States Ship *Independence* during the Mexican War and as a spokesman for the values and assumptions that propelled and rationalized American expansionism. He was an unabashed apologist for an aggressive "civilization," yet not blind to the destructive impact that this civilizing mission had on native peoples. But for him as for many of his contemporaries, these peoples were expendable, and the benefits to be derived from the expanding influence of the "advanced" countries far outweighed the costs. The march of the Western nations into the Pacific (as elsewhere) appeared inevitable.

Henry Wise was only fourteen when he began to travel. He was the son of an American naval officer, George Stuart Wise, and a descendant of an old English Royalist family taken prisoners after the Penruddock Rebellion and sent to Virginia in 1665. His cousin was Henry Alexander Wise, the last anti-bellum governor of Virginia, whose final act as governor had been the execution of John Brown. Wise's cousin secured for the young man an appointment as a mid-shipman, and he sailed first under Captain John Percival. He served in the U.S. squadron off the coast of Florida during the Seminole War and, after promotion to lieutenant, went on board the *Independence*. He sailed along the coast of California, Baja California, Mexico, and in the Pacific from 1846 to 1848. It was this cruise that formed the basis of his narrative in *Los Gringos*.[1] He also wrote several other books all of which detailed his exploits

---

[1]Henry A. Wise, *Los Gringos or, an Inside View of Mexico and California, with Wanderings in Peru, Chili, and Polynesia* (New York, C. Scribner, 1857).

as a career Navy man. Unlike his cousin the governor, Henry Wise (born in Brooklyn, New York, May 12, 1819) remained loyal to the Union during the Civil War. He made commodore in 1862, and was assistant to the Chief of the Bureau of Ordnance and Hydrography. Wise died in Naples, Italy, in 1869, having reached the rank of Captain.[2]

Wise was perhaps one of the more subtle and skillful exponents of American expansion, because he was more interested in drama than didacticism. His book is generally light in tone, and he called upon his readers to have charity in overlooking the careless style, since his intention was not to deal with statistics "or any abstract reflections, but merely to compile a pleasant narrative." His own conservative, royalist and Catholic heritage might have helped to put some distance between himself and the self-righteous moral accents displayed by his contemporaries of a more puritanical background. Throughout his cruise he appeared more interested in having a good time, enjoying the food, the outings and hunting excursions, and the various women he encountered, than in drawing weighty generalizations about the things and people he saw. He devoted a considerable amount of the book to descriptions of his many pleasure trips ashore, where the sport, the food and the ladies were the primary focus of his interests. He enjoyed his pleasures, and he did not pose as a heavy-handed critic of the various cultures he observed. Compared to a Richard Henry Dana, or a William Dane Phelps, his philosophy seemed to embody a kind of non-judgemental cultural relativism, or at least appraisals tempered with an understanding for the inherent "foibles and follies" of human nature. But when examined more closely, his professed policy of looking "with leniency upon the peculiarities of man kind"—he said he made it "a rule to respect the absurdities of others"— concealed an implicit stance of superiority. Others' behaviors and character traits might appear "absurd," but never his own. In fact, far from any real recognition of the relativity of judgements about different cultures, Wise's inferences concerning the people he saw on his voyage contained a tacit hierarchy which, if not as blatantly ethnocentric as that of Thomas Jefferson Farnham, was still clearly based on an unquestioned confidence in the superiority of his own society and nation. The Indians ranked low-

---

[2]Francis S. Drake, "Henry Augustus Wise," in *Dictionary of American Biography* (Boston, Houghton, Osgood and Company, The Riverside Press, Cambridge, 1879), 998-999.

est in his standing. Polynesians rated somewhat higher. The Hispanic cultures were given a more complex ranking, most often in terms of class, with the lower orders (many of whom were part Indian) accorded the least respect, while some of the "Creole" women were spoken of in a sentimental and chivalric vein. Overall, Wise established the (by now familiar) comparison throughout his narrative between the enterprising and civilizing activities of the nations of western Europe and the United States, and the backward and "indolent" Hispanic and native societies.[3]

Wise gave a first illustration of what his attitude would be when the *Independence* crew had a shore leave at Valparaiso. Here he attended a party. There were women and dancing, and he met an attractive young lady who immediately charmed him, thus establishing a pattern repeated in California, Mexico and throughout the course of his voyage, but always described with sufficiently genteel discretion concerning the content of his relationships. In this case he explicitly informed his readers that the young woman managed to preserve her virtue, leaving it unstated that perhaps there were several in the course of his adventures who did not. At Valparaiso, Wise enjoyed the dancing, even though he said it was suggestive and would have offended and shocked people of more refinement. For himself, however, he pleaded a fondness for the spicier side of life, or as he put it, "a notion of cayenne to existence...."[4]

The men he met in Valparaiso, again in a familiar motif, did not meet with quite the same approval as the women. They were almost always considered inferior to the ladies. In his estimation they were "an indolent, hairy, cigar-puffing race of bipeds." They seemed to exemplify the character of their governments, which exercised a "cramped policy, actuated by religious intolerance, and [once again] an indolence unknown elsewhere." This policy allowed foreigners (many of them Americans) to "dominate their commerce and to grow rich on their resources." Exactly this was happening in California, and Wise felt that the only way to encourage industry and commerce in Chile was simply to open the country up to emigration and permit the foreigners to develop the mining and agricultural wealth as only they could do.[5]

---

[3]Wise, *Los Gringos*, 14.
[4]Ibid., 33.
[5]Ibid., 36.

Wise felt that it was "melancholy" to see the lack of progress in a country like Chile when "the whole universe is subscribing to more liberal
notions...." But this was as far as he would go in his preaching. He
claimed philosophically that he had

> long since given over all philanthropic researches for that which does not
> affect my heart or digestion.... I care not for the foibles or follies of mankind,
> so long as people do not pick my pockets or tread on my toes.... I am an
> indifferent worldly person, I make the merit of my necessities, in striving to
> live the space allotted me in the world, and not for it.[6]

It may be that Wise favored a disinterested stance over a sermonizing
one because he had absorbed some of the current ideas reflected in the
fiction of his time about what the nature of a true American gentleman
should be. He must be well-mannered, disinterested, self-sufficient,
self-controlled and hard working.[7] While choosing not to preach, he
obviously favored the energy and enterprise he felt were the characteristic qualities of a society like that of the United States, over the seeming
lethargy and lack of progress he saw in the Hispanic and Polynesian
countries he visited. When he arrived in California, he could witness the
changes being wrought by the recent U.S. take-over. At San Francisco
Bay, the little village of Yerba Buena was thriving

> under the indomitable energy of our countrymen. Tenements, large and
> small, were running up, like card-built houses, in all directions. The popula-
> tion was composed of Mormons, backwoodsmen, and a very few respectable
> traders from the eastern cities of the United States. Very rare was it to see a
> native: our brethren had played the porcupine so sharply as to oblige them to
> seek their homes among more congenial kindred.

Here we glimpse the commencement of the fate of the Californians at
the hands of the acquisitive and ethnocentric Yankees, in a kind of ironic
reversal of the traditional Californian hospitality.[8]

Wise was also an early witness to a trend in the history of American
California—squatting. At the Mission of San Jose he attended Mass one

---

[6]Ibid., 36-37.

[7]See William R. Taylor, *Cavalier And Yankee: The Old South and American National Character*,
(1957, New York, Anchor Books, 1963), 199.

[8]Wise, *Los Gringos*, 70-71.

Sunday and was afterwards introduced to some American immigrants, several of whom were apparently Mormons. These people had just moved into some of the buildings at the mission, brushing aside any question of ownership. As Wise explained it (showing that he could apply the standards of the work-ethic to his own countrymen as well as Hispanics) these Americans were "not only averse to request permission to remain for a season, but were hugely indignant at the military Governor of California, Colonel Mason, for having issued a decree, requiring these lazy gentlemen to leave the lands of the Church." A few weeks later they had to be forced out by bayonets, but many thousands of squatters who soon followed them would eventually find their political concerns given the force of law in the Land Act of 1851; the native Californians would be dispossessed legally in a paradoxical but peculiarly American combination of litigation and lawlessness.[9]

If these Mormon squatters were "lazy," the same could not be said for those newly arrived Mormons Wise observed at Monterey. They had cleaned the streets of that town and were introducing vehicles "of a civilized build." The New York Volunteer Regiment was also at Monterey, so the town's businesses and especially the grog shops were thriving. The American alcalde, Walter Colton,[10] had established a school; stone buildings were being constructed amidst the adobes; a newspaper run by Colton and Robert Semple was in operation. To Wise, Yankee drive was clearly working to transform Monterey from a backward Mexican California village into a seat of energy and enterprise that could serve as a model for what could be done when the right people were in charge.[11]

Wise was also on hand to see the start of a continuous boom in real estate that was to be a hallmark of California history from his time to our

---

[9]Ibid., 115. On squatters, see W.W. Robinson, *Land In California*, (1948; Berkeley/Los Angeles, University of California Press, 1979), 91-132.

[10]See Walter Colton, *Three Years In California*, (Stanford, Stanford University Press, 1949), 19, for an interesting description of Monterey at that time and the people who were arriving there. According to Colton:"Almost every nation has, in some emigrant, a representative here—a representative of its peculiar habits, virtues and vices. Here is the reckless Californian, the half-wild Indian, the roving trapper of the West, the lawless Mexican, the licentious Spaniard, the scolding Englishman, the absconding Frenchman, the luckless Irishman, the plodding German, the adventurous Russian, and the discontented Mormon. All have come here with the expectation of finding but little work and less law."

[11]Wise, *Los Gringos*, 82-83.

own. He noted, even a year before the discovery of gold, that "a mania was raging in California about lands, and lots," and he reflected that if he had only known about the impending gold rush, he too would have made an effort to acquire land. He ventured to predict an almost unlimited positive future for California. But his earlier observations made around the San Jose area implied very definite limits to California's potential for growth. He questioned whether California could support a very large population because it was too arid:

> Under no contingency does the natural face of Upper California appear susceptible of supporting a very large population; the country is hilly and mountainous; great dryness prevails during the summers, and occasionally excessive droughts parch the soil for periods of twelve or eighteen monthes. Only in the plains and valleys where streams are to be found, and even those will have to be watered by artificial irrigation, does there seem the hope of being sufficient tillable land to repay the husbandman and afford subsistence to the inhabitants. Sheep and cattle may be raised to any extent; as the gentle slopes, clothed in rich wild grases, afford excellent districts for grazing.[12]

Wise early identified one of the long-term and continuing problems of California's growth, the need for water. He was also correct in his assessment that California was an excellent country for grazing livestock, as the Spanish-Mexican Californians had done for eighty years; it was the source of their wealth. Finally, though, land was the key to prosperity in California as elsewhere, and Wise could see the promise despite the need for water. It was land that was attracting pioneer settlers to California.

These people came despite tremendous hardships and sacrifices and none endured greater than the ill-fated Donner party. Wise was on hand when news of their terrible ordeal reached Monterey. Their "shocking inhuman cannibalisms and sufferings" appalled and fascinated him. Yet he was almost unable to convey the horror of these events. He told how the Donners were trapped in the Sierra "through a culpable combination of ignorance and folly," while winter set in and the trail became impassable. As he related what he first learned of the tragedy, he said that parents ate their own children and children were found eating the livers and hearts of the dead; one man ate the body of a nine year old girl in a single night of horror. The women, according to Wise's information, held on

---

[12]Ibid., 112-113.

to life with a greater force and tenacity than did the men. But at this point Wise's style breaks down, and he apparently became involuntarily comic (at least to a modern reader; I do not believe he was aware of the gallows humor here) when he tried to describe how one of the women survived. She had, he said, "feasted on her good papa, but on making soup of her lover's head, she confessed to some inward qualms of conscience."[13]

To Wise, all of this was "truly dreadful," especially the fact that the people who had gone through the horror of it seemed to feel it was nothing out of the ordinary. He thought their ordeal must have made them deranged, but beyond this terrible experience lay the courage and determination of the American pioneers to whom Wise paid tribute. These people were even then struggling across unknown deserts and over uncharted mountains to get to California, where they knew not what awaited them. They too entered into Wise's comparative calculus as testimonials to the American spirit.[14]

Wise missed the major events of the war in California, but he formed an opinion of them nonetheless. He believed that the people of California might well have attached themselves to the United States peacefully if it had not been for certain actions by lawless settlers. He was apparently referring to the Bear Flaggers; he called them "a few lawless vagabonds" who "committed excesses without the slightest recognized authority, but purely, it appears, from love of a little independent fighting and thieving on their own account." Their actions caused the Californians to be fearful and uncertain about the intentions of the United States towards them. He also implicated Commodore Thomas ap Catesby Jones' seizure and then relinquishment of Monterey. This he felt exhibited a vacillating policy vis-a-vis California which contributed to uncertainty among the Californians at the time of the conquest about whether the U.S. meant to hold the place permanently.[15]

Unlike William Dane Phelps and other contemporary observers, Wise did not romanticize the United States' role in prosecuting the war in California. Later, after some skirmishes with them on the coast of

---

[13]Ibid., 74.
[14]Ibid., 74-75.
[15]Ibid., 42-47.

Mexico, he praised the rank-and-file Mexican troops for their courage and endurance, and blamed their defeats on the poor quality of both their political and military leaders.[16] Nor did he apologize for or try to excuse American defeats. He pointed out for example that Captain William Mervine, in his attempt to re-take Los Angeles with three hundred men, had been beaten back by a much smaller force. His only aim in recounting the war appears to have been to absolve the regular forces of any responsibility for the excesses which he believed had caused the Californians to take up arms. This led him into some difficulties. He blamed the revolt in southern California on the depredations of

> a few mongrel bodies of volunteers, who enhanced their otherwise agreeable society by pillaging the natives of horses, cattle, saddles, household utensils and the like, in quite a marauding, buccaneering, independent way; all of course under the apparent legal sanction of the United States government, and not a doubt but demanded by the imperative necessity of the patriotic plunderers themselves.

Wise seemed to have mixed up his facts here, confusing events in the north with those in the south. He did not mention Lieutenant Archibald Gillespie, the regular Marine officer whose harsh and arbitrary restrictions helped to provoke the southerners. Nor did he credit the sources for the "information" he gave about the war in his narrative. Wise may have been expressing the career military man's contempt for volunteers and irregular forces that lacked discipline and military skill, but he was also interested in clearing the regular forces of responsibilty for provoking a revolt, especially after the country appeared to have been pacified with so little cost. Gillespie's men, he believed, were too few and presumably too disciplined to have been responsible for the depredations Wise described.[17]

Yet when he actually met some of Fremont's volunteers, he called them men with "an air of indomitable courage hovering over them...." Wise and the mountain men had a few drinks, and Wise listened to them tell their tales of battle with the Indians on the trail to California. He was impressed with a story of poison arrows, deadly accurate rifle

[16]Ibid., 293.
[17]Ibid., 44-45, 50.

shooting, and the taking of an Indian scalp.[18] He also added his own contribution to the developing legend of the indomitable, steely-eyed mountain men. These were American volunteers and irregulars, and he contrasted them favorably with some French troops he met later on his voyage to Tahiti. The French had just succeeded in wresting the island from the natives after a difficult struggle. The Tahitian warriors, Wise thought, could not compare to the American Indian in "courage, hardihood, or sagacity [this was, incidentally, about the only place where Wise had anything complimentary to say about Indians] ; and without any disparagement of French valor or gallantry, in our innocence we sincerely believed that two hundred of our back-woodsmen would have hunted every copper-colored warrior into the ocean."[19] The men of Fremont's California Battalion were just such "good men and true among their own birth and kindred," but Wise was nevertheless going to blame them for stirring up the Californians: "their mistaken idea of what constituted civilized warfare made them the most unscrupulous of freebooters...."[20]

Wise was ever the gentleman. The backwoodsmen may have been useful and skilled fighters, especially against "savages," but they carried with them some liabilites when it came to "civilized" warfare, and Wise's attitude towards them was ambivalent. He was an early exponent of the Josiah Royce/H. H. Bancroft thesis that the Californians were unnecessarily goaded into war by the ham-handed actions of the Americans, but he tried to exonerate the regular, "civilized" forces from this responsibility.[21]

Wise could see that the Californians were gradually accepting their Yankee conquerors. He and his fellow naval officers were being invited to fandangos, welcomed, and given the privilege "of making as much

---

[118]Ibid., 50.

[19]Ibid., 417.

[20]Ibid., 104.

[21]See Josiah Royce, *California, From the Conquest In 1846 to the Second Vigilance Committee in San Francisco: A Study of American Character*, (New York, Alfred A Knopf, 1948); Hubert Howe Bancroft, *Works*, vol. XXII. There were scholars who considered Bancroft biased against his own countrymen; see, for example, Hiram Martin Chittenden, *The American Fur Trade of the Far West*, vol. I, 243, where he states: "whenever it is a question of an American view as against a Spanish, British, or Indian view, Mr. Bancroft, if circumstances will possibly admit it, ranges himself against his own countrymen."

love, and devouring as many frijoles as may have been polite or palat-
able." The people of Monterey, hospitable but not in Wise's judgement
overly clean, were returning to their homes and resuming their lives.
Even those who had been most hostile and seemingly irreconcilable
were coming around. Wise offered the case of "Dona Augustia
Ximenes" who had sworn an oath never to dance again until she could
wear a necklace of Yankee ears. This woman had so much relented as to
have taken a sick American naval officer into her home and helped to
nurse him back to health.[22]

But the prime example for Wise of the intelligent Californian, a man
who could see the benefits to be conferred on the country through its
new connection to the United States, was General Mariano Vallejo. In
spite of his imprisonment by American settlers during the Bear Flag
Revolt, when Wise visited Vallejo at his home in Sonoma, the General,
"being blessed with a clear head and much discernment," could see that
placing California in the possession of the United States was much to be
preferred to "letting the territory languish under the mis-rule of Mexico,
or , perhaps, at some future period, to maintain the needy soldiery of a
foreign monarchy," or so Wise believed.[23]

Mariano Vallejo was an exemplary aristocratic California gentleman,
and as such he piqued the interest of an officer and gentleman like
Henry Wise. Wise observed that Vallejo owned about one hundred
square leagues of some of the finest agricultural lands in the area. His
adobe house was one of the largest Wise had seen in California, two stories high and two hundred feet long, and Wise was surprised at the
refinements inside the home: It was well furnished, the walls were taste-
fully papered, there were plenty of books in their cases and prints and
mirrors on the walls. Wise and his fellow officers were fed an excellent
supper and entertained by some visiting Russians and Germans who
were enjoying the General's hospitality. But the most pleasant surprise
of all for Wise were the General's two charming daughters who played
the piano. Wise paid the young ladies a typical compliment. "They had
been properly instructed," he said, "and performed remarkably well;
besides, they were pretty, becomingly attired, and, what is still more

---

[22]Wise, *Los Gringos*, 53-54.
[23]Ibid., 124.

commendable, exceedingly well bred." Were this Wise's last word on the Vallejo family, we might be led to believe that he thought at least some elements of California society were on a par with the best to be found in the United States. But no, the elegance of the Vallejo hacienda and the charm and grace of the ladies were not to be Wise's final remarks on his visit to the famous General. He ended his observations with a complaint about the ever-present fleas in his accomodations, which made sleeping difficult.[24]

Wise had something to say about all levels of California society. As was usual with him, he found most of the women of interest, though his tone toward those of the lower classes was one of condescension. Once while hunting he got lost and finally ended up at the Mission of Carmel where he was fed and given a bed. When he woke up, a party was in progress. Leaping out of bed, he said he "made a dash at the Patrona, drank all the licores on the tray, and seizing her around the waist, away we spun through the fandango." Next he bought a pack of cards and proved himself adept enough to win a few centavos and some cigarettes from the Indians who were there, thus showing them that he was not quite the greenhorn they believed him to be. Finally, sounding some-what like William Henry Thomes, he said, "I busied myself swearing love, and sipping dulces with the brunettas; vowing friendship to the men; drinking strong waters; promising to redress all grievances, to pay all claims out of my own pocket for the government; and ended up by repudiating the Yankees, and swearing myself a full-blooded Californ-ian."[25]

Later, in Lower California, he met another young woman named Eugenia, "a charming little brunette, who shared my dinner, and, by way of frolic, cunningly squeezed lime juice in my mouth when asleep." Eugenia also apparently did duty as his laundress. She washed his pants and shirt while he napped, and he rewarded her with his handkerchief.[26]

These episodes perhaps have the ring of what a typical young naval officer would do to amuse himself on shore in any age. Yet Wise could become romantically sentimental when he met a woman whom he con-

---

[24]Ibid., 125.
[25]Ibid., 63-64.
[26]Ibid., 141.

sidered a peer. While at Mazatlan, he met Dolores, a young Mexican woman who he maintained was far more intelligent and better educated than the generality of her countrywomen. Wise became acquainted with Dolores while she was waiting faithfully and lovingly (as he put it) for news of her husband, a Mexican officer with the troops outside occupied Mazatlan. One evening this "villainous" character slipped into town and pistol whipped Dolores, either as Wise speculated, "from idle jealousy, or natural brutality of disposition...." Dolores died several days later. Wise was incensed at this cruel treatment and wished that he could get the husband in the sights of his rifle. But he never seemed to consider the idea that his own friendship for the lady—as an enemy officer in an occupied town—could have provoked the tragedy. He attended the woman at her death bed and accompanied her coffin to the cemetery. His closing sentences capture the effusive tone of his style, and could have been used by Mark Twain himself as a model for some of his satire on American sentimentality: "Alas! poor Dolores! I have preserved your tress and ring, and time has not erased the remembrance of your love and sufferings from a stranger's breast."[27]

If Wise occasionally waxed sentimental, he could also be revealingly facetious. A career naval man, he proclaimed his hatred for boats, ships, and anything that floated. He said that he hated these things "even more than I detest poor people; but at times they are all endurable, and marine misanthropic as I am, once in a great while I become reconciled...." This was not meant to be taken seriously, yet his narrative is punctuated with caricatures of the "lower orders." At Mazatlan there is a comic-opera black cook who claimed to have escaped from the Mexicans. He came aboard Wise's ship telling the crew that he had contracted a debt of nine dollars which he was unable to pay. Then there was the Irishman in the ship's crew—of course called Paddy—who was hit in the nose by a fish and became the butt of much laughter when he screamed "Take him off, be Jasus!" While in California, Wise had only one unfriendly encounter with a vaquero who could perhaps have been from the lower classes. But in Mexico and Lower California, he was plagued by the "leperos," who in their extreme poverty resorted to pickpocketing and thefts. While attending a dance in Mazatlan, a thief took his sword right out of his

[27]Ibid., 185.

scabbard. His pistol was also stolen from under the nose of one of his men whom he had set to guard his horse and effects. His response was to be philosophical about it, but when he actually caught a young man stealing, he turned the fellow over to his sailors for punishment. The sailors made "what they call a 'spread eagle' of him, over the long gun." Wise claimed to believe that this would cure the young man of any future tendencies toward thievery.[28]

In California, Wise himself administered the punishment. On his way back to Monterey from the Pueblo of San Jose—he called it "a detestable spot"—he was accosted by a young vaquero who tried to intimidate Wise into handing over his tobacco, and then made a grab for Wise's money bag. Wise smacked him in the nose with the barrel of his rifle, and when the vaquero made a feint at him with the lasso, Wise then leveled his gun at him. He noted that this was enough to prevent any further unpleasantness.[29]

While in California, Wise had no more trouble of this nature, in spite of his frequent attendance at fandangos where he gambled and romanced the ladies. On duty in Mexico, however, he did run into some bandits and narrowly escaped with his life. After the armistice, Wise was entrusted with dispatches and had to ride overland from San Blas to Mexico City. It was an arduous and dangerous journey. He and his Mexican guide were armed when they were held up, but could make no resistance against the much more numerous bandits. Fortunately, they were rescued by some Mexican dragoons.[30] And the courage of the Mexican guide who accompanied him won Wise's respect. The guide never thought of deserting Wise in the face of danger. The men who acted as guides, and the *arrieros* or muleteers, impressed Wise with their fortitude and fidelity. He said of them: "In no other part of the world do I believe there can be found such a worthy, brave, hardworking, and industrious class of persons...."[31]

He was thus not entirely blind to the virtues to be displayed by at least some members of the lower classes. In fact, in California his closest

---

[28]Ibid., 315, 90-91, 96, 193.
[29]Ibid., 118.
[30]Ibid., 246-249.
[31]Ibid., 246-249, 282, 290

friendship was with a boy of ten or eleven. Like all of the Californians, the boy was a superb horseman; he was also a good shot and a skilled woodsman. He quickly became indispensable to Wise on his hunting trips into the hills in back of Monterey and Carmel. For the boy, Juaquinito, it was an excellent opportunity—to earn some money and to escape from his own house where his drunken mother lived with her equally inebriated lover. To Wise, the boy was a marvelous companion. They roamed the lovely hills together, the boy showing Wise where to find game. Wise described their relationship: "At night we made a fire, ate broiled partridges without stint, and slept under the same blanket."[32]

Wise's amused, condescending tolerance and willingness to befriend certain of the Mexicans and Californians he met seemed to disappear when it came to the Indians. He was a witness to the disruption and death of their culture, yet he displayed little understanding of the price exacted from them by diseases and the requirements of civilization. This is strange in the light of what he would later say about the natives of the Hawaiian Islands and the South Pacific. He seemed to have a much clearer grasp of what the intrusion of western civilization meant to these peoples. The same process was taking its toll on Indians everywhere. In another book Wise most starkly revealed his opinion of Indians. In 1834 at Buenos Aires he was a witness to the mass execution of some sixty-three Indians. He said of them:

> a more hideous set of human beings I never beheld. Their long, matted black locks...fell in disordered masses around their gleaming bloodshot eyes, pinched, yellow, parchment-looking faces, and over their shoulders. [When given a last cigarette] I never saw such intense satisfaction as spread over the ugly faces of those swarthy, filthy Indios....Many of them smiled, too, showing their teeth like the sharp fangs of a bloodhound.[33]

In California Wise did not change his assessment. He saw the Indians gathered in the town square at Monterey where they customarily went, after working all week, to gamble and drink aguardiente until they finally passed out in the street. He called them "crowds of degraded Indians, of both sexes," whose diets he believed were made up of locusts and

---

[32]Ibid., 65.

[33]Harry Gringo [Henry Wise] *Tales for the Marines*, (Boston, Phillips, Sampson & Co., 1855), 371-372.

grasshoppers.[34] One morning after Mass he was a witness to an incident between two Indians who had been drinking. They went after a runaway horse belonging to one of Wise's acquaintances. On their way they quarreled and one of them stabbed the other in the thigh with his knife. To Wise, the loss of the horse and saddle, which he said "was worth half-a-dozen Indian lives," was of more significance than the fate of the injured Indian. He also saw a public hanging. This was punishment meted out for murder by the American military governor of California, Colonel Mason. Wise claimed that such a punishment was unknown at that time in California, and the first two men to be hanged were Indians. At the first attempt the rope broke; because of this, the padres of Monterey urged Mason to pardon the men. But he would not do it, and they were hanged again, this time to death. Wise said that this execution caused bad feelings on the part of the clergy toward the American regime, though he went on to point out that the local population supported the measures taken. Indians, at the very bottom of Wise's social hierarchy, seemed always to be regarded as dirty, thieving and squalid, like those he saw fishing for pearls at La Paz. They knew no more about civilized values than to exchange these pearls for jerked beef and paper cigars.[35]

California was now the United States' window on the Pacific, and Lieutenant Henry Wise of the United States Navy would be one of the first to reflect on the potential benefits of a Pacific empire. He could take what he had seen in California—the beginnings of an industrious Yankee commercial society on Pacific shores—as a harbinger of the future for the entire Pacific region. He could already see that the United States had interests in the Pacific which would call for the protection of the United States government. The American whaling industry was beginning to dominate the entire South Pacific area, with an important port of call at Lahaina on the island of Maui. In Wise's opinion, the United States should begin at once to deploy a few Navy corvettes to protect the whale ships from any possible attacks by natives. After observing some of the deserters from the whaling vessels who were leading what he called licentious lives among the natives, Wise also felt that the conditions

---

[34]Wise, *Los Gringos*, 133.
[35]Ibid., 115, 132-133, 320-321.

aboard the whalers had to be improved to prevent excessive desertions. He looked forward to a United States that was on the way to becoming a Pacific power.[36]

Wise was aware of the costs to the native peoples in the region exacted by the acquisitive U.S. and European societies. At Hawaii he could see the devastating impact of European diseases on the aboriginal population. He considered the missionary efforts to have been essentially a failure, placing only a veneer over the basic savagery of the natives, though he did commend the missionaries for keeping alcohol away from them. He concluded that they were actually happier and better off before the arrival of Captain Cook. He showed a certain understanding for the connection between their work habits and the land and climate where they lived when he said that "their very indolence" was "induced by an equable and delicious climate, where Nature so bountifully scatters her fruits in their path, produced an enervating languour, where neither cares nor sorrows surrounded them!" This paradise, however, was to be replaced by white civilization. According to Wise even the natives understood that "they cannot cope with the skill and energy of the foreigner, and hopelessly and inevitably they must look forward to the rapid future, when their lands will be in strange hands, and the few remnants of their race the slaves or puppets of their white masters." Wise would thus close his narrative as he had begun it, with a prophetic vision of the fate of "backward" people unable to compete with enterprising foreigners from Europe and the United States. He admitted that this was a sad vision; yet for him the destruction of native cultures (with even a hint of genocide) weighed very little in the balance when compared to the benefits to be derived for civilization by getting a foothold in the Pacific islands. As with his assessment of commercial potential in Chile, confirmed by events in California, so too in the Pacific he saw that foreigners would end up dominating.[37]

Already a certain Mr. Judd, an American, had worked his way into the high councils of the Hawaiian King, Kamehameha, where as Minister of Finance he was making his own personal fortune. Ironically, when confronted with an actual working representative of that commercial

---

[36]Ibid., 350-353, 387-392.
[37]Ibid., 357-358, 375.

society Wise considered so superior and inevitable, he turned up his nose! He had some sarcastic things to say about how a "staunch democrat" (Judd) could possibly bear "the tainted air of a monarchical court in his republican nostrils." In Wise's estimation, Judd had learned to calculate his patriotism at so much money per year and would kneel before a throne if there were dollars under it. Wise, who favored progress in the abstract, failed to see that it was to be precisely such people as Judd who would open up and "develop" the islands and carry American commerce to the four corners of the globe.[38]

Yet perhaps this is asking a great deal of a young navy lieutenant of the late eighteen forties. He was a man of his times, essentially optimistic and forward looking, an American with many of the more positive traits produced by his culture. He may have had his blind spots, as with the Indians, but he was more open minded than many Americans who went west, and he could be kind and capable of generosity. He tried to be fair to all he encountered and gave credit where he felt it was due. He enjoyed his fun, but would risk his life for what he thought were the best interests of his country, which he served throughout his lifetime. He worked with what he had to work with and spoke for what he considered to be progress. He was privileged to visit an early, unspoiled, fascinating and romantic California, where he enjoyed himself immensely. Like all of the Americans, merchants, mountain men and adventurers, who wrote about their experiences in California, he was a witness to the expansion of American power to the Pacific shores and beyond, a process about which he could at that time still be unreservedly positive. It was merely a

> sickly sympathy...to talk of the wrongs and aggressions, or the rights and laws of European nations as having a bearing upon a handful of barbarians, subjected to the savage sway of tyrannical native masters, when contrasted with the benefits conferred upon the world at large, by their being under the enlightened rule of a civilized government.[39]

[38]Ibid., 396.
[39]Ibid., 396.

Conclusion

The Americans who wrote about their experiences in California during the Mexican period were working in a generic tradition that went back to the very beginnings of European colonization in the New World. Narratives of travel, exploration, adventure and conflict with the Indians were among the first literary means by which Americans began to define themselves as such. Their journeys were often presented as tests of character, manhood and mettle. Their identities as Americans were frequently forged in opposition to the peoples whom they found already in possession of the land, or in struggle with an environment that could be death-dealing, but which also contained elements of the sublime and the pastoral, the promise of riches and renewal.[1]

All of the people who chronicled their California adventures and impressions expressed these common themes. They were optimistic about the tremendous potential for prosperity that California represented, a prosperity which would be realized, they believed, once the blessings of a more effective and efficient civilization replaced the backwardness of Mexican rule. They expressed this clearly, even when they were not militant proponents of Manifest Destiny, and they had a concomitant sense of their own superiority, or the superiority of United States institutions and American work-habits.[2] The Spanish-Mexican and Indian population of California was not infrequently judged harshly. But those who had lived for a longer period of time among the Californians expressed more ambivalence in their attitudes toward these people. They knew the Californians and participated with them in their social and political lives. They were more willing to recognize the virtues in the life-style of the Californians, and more capable of understanding their vices. Some—like Alfred Robinson, William Heath Davis, and Benjamin Davis Wilson—

---

[1]See Richard Slotkin, *Regeneration Through Violence: The Mythology of the American Frontier, 1600-1860,* (Middletown, Connecticut, Wesleyan University Press, 1973), 230-250.

[2]See ibid., 205-206, where Slotkin points out the need for a "moral rationale" for displacing the Indians; clearly such a rationale was at work in this American sense of superiority over the Californians.

had married into the leading ranchero families. Mountain man George Nidever also married a Californian, though she was not from a family of such social prominence as the wives of Robinson, Davis or Wilson. Nevertheless, time and intimacy served to soften and qualify the assessments these Americans made of their Californian neighbors. They never ceased to be Americans in their patriotism, but they regarded the Californians whom they had come to know and respect with a less jaundiced eye.

A substantial number of our autobiographers were visitors to California. When they returned to the United States, these people were sufficiently moved by the country to write down their impressions of the land and its people. They almost always emphasized the fertility and desireability of the former, and the indolence or degeneracy of the latter. Thus Zenas Leonard and James Pattie, after enduring the test of tremendous hardships in their overland treks to California, marveled at the country; but when they generalized about the people of California, it was usually in the most unflattering of terms. Richard Henry Dana too endured his trials on board the *Pilgrim* and in California. He was on the coast for just over a year and found little to admire in the Californians. As a hardworking sailor he had not been given much opportunity to understand them in spite of his efforts to learn Spanish. Thomas Jefferson Farnham's stay in California was shorter and his portrayal of the Californians the harshest of any of the visitors. He arrived just when the California authorities had arrested a large number of American citizens for allegedly plotting against the government. Lieutenant Henry Wise's time in California was also brief. He affected a tolerant manner, but he too was generally true to this pattern in his characterization of the Californians he met. He had proven himself a courageous man in his trek across Mexico, so he had acquired the necessary moral stature to judge the Californians. All of these visitors helped to create an image of California as a land of opportunity, an image that contributed strongly to the westward movement which was just beginning to draw more and more Americans to the west coast. And they reinforced an already powerful sense of national pride Americans felt in their particular fitness to possess a country whose potential for riches only they could develop. American "civilization" was clearly the preferable alternative to what was encountered in Mexican

California, from the "savagery" of Indians to the less efficient, more indolent culture of the Spanish-Mexican Californians.[3]

Those who were literary or articulate enough to have set down their observations and experiences at the time, seem to have foreshadowed at least the outline of California's future greatness. The autobiographers who reflected on what they had seen and done from the vantage point of thirty or forty years' hindsight also wished to display their prophetic gifts, but they were even more interested in showing themselves as actors in the drama of California's history. William Heath Davis commented on and connected himself with almost all of the events and people of the Mexican period, and William Dane Phelps emphasized his value as an eyewitness to—and at times a participant in— the events of the Mexican War in California. William H. Thomes too, who like Dana had only been a visitor to California, placed himself at the center of the action. In his first book he was content to give a modest account of his experiences there, but in his partially fictionalized sequel he succumbed to a desire to assume a more historical persona. These people had seen California transformed from a sparsely populated wilderness outpost of the infant Mexican Republic, to a new American empire on the Pacific in some forty years, and they took justifiable pride in their part in such a process.

The autobiographers who dictated their reminiscences—mountain men Kit Carson and George Nidever—were primarily men of action. Their experiences were conveyed with a vivid sense for the daily life of hunters, scouts and adventurers, despite a matter-of-fact tone. Indeed, such a tone may have heightened the impact on readers of the dangers and hardships they described. The hardships and trials undergone by these men made them truly valiant figures, in the tradition of the particularly American heroics established by Daniel Boone.[4] As one would expect, these men too displayed some of the same characteristic thought patterns that the other Americans in California revealed. Nidever chose

---

[3]See Roy Harvey Pearce, *Savagism and Civilization*. Pearce focuses primarily upon the white view of Indians as savages antithetical to civilization, but the autobiographers in Mexican California did not confine their invidious comparison of American civilization to just the Indians.

[4]See Slotkin, *Regeneration Through Violence*, chapters 9 and 10.

to live in California, but remained a citizen of the United States. During the Mexican War, he had his little conflicts with some Californians, his neighbors, but neither Nidever nor the Californians allowed these incidents to escalate into violence. Kit Carson's name and fame became intimately connected with this period of California history, though he continued to reside in New Mexico. Kit may have underestimated the Californians' courage at the Battle of San Pascual, but he was not the only one to do so, and in his autobiography he almost always made a fair assessment of anyone with whom he had had any very extensive personal dealings. Both of these men had steeled themselves all of their lives in an almost constant struggle to survive in a hostile wilderness where death was ever-present. California would prove to be more than sufficient recompense for such struggles.

All of the autobiographers, finally, even the most hardened and unreflective of the mountain men, expressed a certain feel for the beauties of the landscape. From Alfred Robinson's moonlight ride near Ventura, to Zenas Leonard's awareness of the sublimity of the Yosemite valley in the midst of an arduous crossing of the Sierra, they marveled at the magnificence of the country. California had come to embody the enduring American dream of riches and fulfillment for the fortunate and the deserving, those who could pass the testing of their courage and prove the superiority of their way of life. But the greatest sense of happiness and contentment in these autobiographical works comes through not in the struggles, or even in the promise of prosperity, but rather in the loveliness of the land.

Bibliography and Index

Bibliography

Unpublished Sources:

Brown, Charles. "Statement of Recollections of Early Events in California." Bancroft Library, Univ. of Calif., Berkeley, CA.

Cahill, Luke. "Recollections of Kit Carson." Bancroft Library, Univ. of Calif., Berkeley, CA.

Dallas, Sherman Forbes. "The Hide and Tallow Trade in Alta California, 1822-1846." Unpublished Ph. D. Dissertation, Indiana Univ., 1955.

Davis, William Heath, Jr. "Sixty Years in California; The 'Volunteer', 'Ayacucho' and other Vessels," three variants. Huntington Library, San Marino, CA.

Dittman, Carl. "Narrative of a Seafaring Life on the Coast of California." Bancroft Library, Univ. of Calif., Berkeley, CA.

Dye, Job Francis. "Recollections of California," Bancroft Library, Univ. of Calif., Berkeley, CA.

Farnham, Thomas Jefferson. Letter to W. E. P. Hartnell. In *Documentos para la Historia de California, 1827-1858*. Bancroft Library, Univ. of Calif., Berkeley, CA.

_____. Letter to John Marsh. Bancroft Library, Univ. of Calif., Berkeley, CA. (Photocopy of original in California State Library).

Hart, James D. "Richard Henry Dana, Jr." Unpublished Ph. D. Dissertation, Harvard Univ., 1936.

Hertzog, Dorothy Allen. "Isaac Graham, California Pioneer." Unpublished Master's Thesis, Univ. of Calif., 1942.

Phelps, William Dane. "Journal, 1841-1843." Bancroft Library, Univ. of Calif., Berkeley, CA. (Microfilm of original in Widener Library, Harvard Univ.).

Robinson, Alfred. "Diary, September 11, 1839 - February 29, 1840." Bancroft Library, Univ. of Calif., Berkeley, CA.

_____. "Statement of Recollections of early years of California." Bancroft Library, Univ. of Calif., Berkeley, CA.

_____. "Letters to Abel Stearns." Huntington Library, San Marino, CA.

Tays, George. "The Political History of California during the Mexican period, 1822-1846." Unpublished Ph. D. Dissertation, Univ. of Calif., 1932.

Thomson, Virginia W. "George Nidever: A Pioneer of California." Unpublished Master's Thesis, Univ. of Calif., 1952.

Wilson, Benjamin Davis. "Observations on Early Days in California and New Mexico." Bancroft Library, Univ. of Calif., Berkeley, CA.

———. "Some Facts about Isaac Graham and John A. Sutter, by a Pioneer of 1841." Bancroft Library, Univ. of Calif., Berkeley, CA.

Wise, Henry A. "California and Mexico, 1846-8." Bancroft Library, Univ. of Calif., Berkeley, CA.

Published Sources:

Anderson, Charles Roberts, (ed.). *Journal of a Cruise to the Pacific Ocean, 1842-1844.* Durham: Duke Univ. Press, 1937.

Arnaz, Jose. "Memoirs of a Merchant: being the recollections of life and customs in California," [Trans. and ed. by Nellie van de Grift Sanchez] *Touring Topics,* XX, No. 9 (Sept. 1928), 14-47, and No. 10 (Oct. 1928), 36-47.

Bandini, Jose. *A Description of California in 1828.* [Trans. by Doris Marion Wright] Berkeley: Friends of the Bancroft Library, 1951.

Brewerton, George D. *A Ride with Kit Carson....* Palo Alto: Lewis Osborne, 1969.

Carter, Harvey Lewis. *'Dear Old Kit', the Historical Kit Carson.* [Kit Carson's Memoirs, 1809-1856] Norman: Univ. of Oklahoma Press, 1968.

Colton, Walter. *Three Years in California.* Stanford Univ. Press, 1949.

Cooke, Philip St. George. *The Conquest of New Mexico and California: An Historical and Personal Narrative.* Oakland: Biobooks, 1952.

Dana, Richard Henry Jr. *An Autobiographical Sketch.* Hamden, Conn.: The Shoestring Press, 1953.

———. "Cruelty to Seamen: Being the Case of Nichol & Couch [original appeared in 1839 issue of *American Jurist*] Berkeley, Privately Printed, 1937.

———. *The Journal of Richard Henry Dana, Jr.* [Robert F. Lucid, ed.] Vol. III. Cambridge: Harvard Univ. Press, 1968.

———. *Two Years Before the Mast.* 2 vols. [John Haskell Kemble, ed.] Los Angeles: Ward Ritchie Press, 1964.

Davis, William Heath. *Sixty Years in California.* San Francisco: A.J. Leary, 1889.

———. *Seventy Five Years in California.* [Third ed. , Harold A. Small, ed.] San Francisco: John Howell - Books, 1967.

Farnham, Thomas Jefferson. *Travels in the Californias, and Scenes in the Pacific Ocean:* N.Y: Saxton & Miles, 1844.

———. *Travels in the Great Western Prairies, the Anahuac and Rocky Mountains, and in the Oregon Territory.* Poughkeepsie: Killey and Lossing, Printers, 1841.

Hafen, Leroy and Ann W., (eds). *To the Rockies and Oregon, 1839-1842,* [with diaries and accounts by Sidney Smith, Amos Cook, Joseph Holman, E. Willard Smith, Francis Fletcher, Joseph Williams, Obadiah Oakley, Robert

Shortess, T. J. Farnham] Vol. III in *The Far West and the Rockies Historical Series, 1820-1875*, Glendale: The Arthur H. Clark Co., 1955.

Hammond, George P., (ed). *The Larkin Papers: Personal, Business, and Official Correspondence of Thomas Oliver Larkin, Merchant and United States Consul in California.* 10 Vols. Berkeley and Los Angeles: Univ. of Calif. Press, 1951-1964.

Jackson, Donald L., and Spence, Mary Lee, (eds.). *The Expeditions of John Charles Fremont.* 3 Vols. Urbana, Chicago and London: Univ. of Illinois Press, 1970-1984.

Leonard, Zenas. *The Adventures of Zenas Leonard.* [Milo Milton Quaife, ed.] Chicago: The Lakeside Press, 1934.

_____. *The Adventures of Zenas Leonard.* [John C. Ewers, ed] Norman: Univ. of Oklahoma Press, 1959.

Lugo, Jose del Carmen. "Life of a Rancher," *The Hist. Soc. of So. Calif. Qtly.*, XXXII, No. 3 (Sept. 1950), 185-236.

Machado, Juana. "Times Gone By in Alta California," [translated and annotated by Raymond S. Brandes] *The Hist. Soc. of So. Calif. Qtly.*, XLI, No. 3 (Sept. 1959), 198-217.

Martin, Thomas S. *With Fremont to California and the Southwest, 1845-1849.* [Ferol Egan, ed.] Ashland, Oregon: Lewis Osborne, 1975.

Nidever, George. *The Life and Adventures of George Nidever, 1802-1883.* [William Henry Ellison, ed.] Santa Barbara: McNally & Loftin, Publishers, 1984.

Pattie, James O. *The Personal Narrative of James O. Pattie of Kentucky.* [Timothy Flint, ed.] Cincinnati: J.H. Wood, 1831.

_____. *The Personal Narrative of James O. Pattie.* Lincoln/London: Univ. of Nebraska Press, 1984.

Pryor, Nathaniel M. "A Sketch of Some of the Earliest Kentucky Pioneers of Los Angeles," [N. M. Pryor's story of the Pattie expedition as told to Stephen C. Foster] *The Hist. Soc. of So. Calif. Publications*, I, 1884-91 (1887. pt. 3), 30-35.

Phelps, William Dane. *Alta California 1840-1842: The Journal and Observations of William Dane Phelps, Master of the Ship "Alert".* [Briton Cooper Busch, ed.] Glendale: The Arthur H. Clark Co., 1983.

Phelps, William Dane ["Webfoot"]. *Fore and Aft; or Leaves from the Life of An Old Sailor.* Boston: Nichols & Hale, 1871.

_____. *Fremont's Private Navy: The 1846 Journal of Captain William Dane Phelps.* [Briton Cooper Busch, ed.] Glendale: The Arthur H. Clark Co., 1987.

Pico, Pío. *Don Pio Pico's Historical Narrative.* [translated by Arthur P. Botello] Glendale: The Arthur H. Clark Co., 1973.

Revere, Joseph Warren. *Naval Duty in California.* Oakland: Biobooks, 1947.

Reviews of *Sixty Years in California* by William Heath Davis. [Huntington Library, San Marino, CA, Rare Book] San Francisco? 1890?

Robinson, Alfred. "Business Letters," *Calif. Hist. Soc. Qtly.*, XXIII, No. 4 (December, 1944), 301-334.

_____. "José de la Guerra," *Representative and Leading Men of the Pacific.* [Oscar T. Shuck, ed.] San Francisco: Bacon and Co., 1870.

_____. *The Letters of Alfred Robinson to the De la Guerra family of Santa Barbara, 1834-1873.* [Trans. and annotated by Maynard Geiger] Los Angeles: The Zamorano Club, 1972.

_____. *Life in California....* 1846; Santa Barbara and Salt Lake City: Peregrine Pubs., Inc., 1970.

_____. "Sketch of California," *Fisher's National Magazine and Industrial Record*, III, No. 1 (June, 1846), 36-42.

Simpson, Sir George. *Narrative of a Voyage to California Parts in 1841-42.* San Francisco: Thomas C. Russell, 1930.

Streeter, William A. "Recollections of Historical Events in California, 1843-1878," *Calif. Hist. Soc. Qtly.*, XVIII, (1939), 64-71; 157-179; 254-278.

Thomes, William H. *Lewey and I; or Sailor Boys' Wanderings....* Boston: DeWolfe, Fiske & Co., 1885.

_____. *On Land and Sea, or California in the Years 1843, '44, and '45.* Boston: DeWolfe, Fiske & Co., 1884.

_____. *Recollections of Old Times in California or, California Life in 1843.* [George R. Stewart, ed.] Berkeley: The Friends of the Bancroft Library, 1974.

Wilson, Benjamin Davis. *The Indians of Southern California in 1852.* [John Walton Caughey, ed.] San Marino: The Huntington Library, 1952.

_____. *Benjamin Davis Wilson, 1811-1878.* [Original in Bancroft Library, Univ. of Calif., Berkeley CA] Pasadena: A.C. Vroman, Inc., n.d.

Wise, Henry Augustus. *Los Gringos or, An Inside View of Mexico and Calfornia, with Wanderings in Peru, Chili, and Polynesia.* N.Y: Baker and Scribner, 1849.

_____. *Los Gringos....* N.Y: C. Scribner, 1857.

_____. *Tales for the Marines.* Boston: Phillips, Sampson & Co., 1855.

Yount, George C. *George C. Yount and his Chronicles of the West, Comprising Extracts from His "Memoirs" and from the Orange Clark "Narrative".* [Charles L. Camp, ed] Denver: Old West Publishing Co., 1966

Secondary Sources:

Axtell, James. *The Invasion Within: The Contest of Cultures in Colonial North America.* N.Y. and Oxford: Oxford Univ. Press, 1985.

Bancroft, Hubert Howe. *Works.* Vols. XIX - XXII (*History of California*, Vols. II - V). San Francisco: The History Co., Pubs., 1886.

Barrows, Henry D. "Alfred Robinson," *Annual Publication of the Hist. Soc. of So. Calif. and Pioneer Register*, IV (1897) 234-236.

_____. "Juan Bandini," *The Hist. Soc. of So. Calif. Publications*, IV (1900), 243-246.

Batman, Richard. *American Ecclesiastes: The Story of James Pattie*. N.Y: Harcourt Brace Jovanovich, 1984.

_____. *The Outer Coast*. N.Y: Harcourt Brace Jovanovich, 1985.

Bean, Walton E. *California: An Interpretive History*. 2d. ed. N.Y: McGraw-Hill Book Co., 1973.

"Benjamin Davis Wilson," *American Biography A New Cyclopedia*, XL. N.Y: The American Historical Society, Inc., 1932.

Camp, Charles L. "Kit Carson in California," *Calif. Hist. Soc. Qtly.*, I (1922-23), 111-151.

Caughey, John W. *California: A Remarkable State's Life History*. 3rd ed. Englewood Cliffs, N.J: Prentice-Hall, Inc., 1970.

Chittenden, Hiram Martin. *The American Fur Trade of the Far West*. 2 vols. Lincoln/London: Univ. of Nebraska Press, 1986.

Clarke, S. A. *Pioneer Days of Oregon History*. Portland: J.K. Gill Co., 1905.

Cook, Sherburne F. *The Conflict between the California Indians and White Civilization.* Berkeley: Univ. of Calif. Press, 1976.

Cott, Nancy F., (ed.). *Root of Bitterness: Documents of the Social History of American Women*. N.Y: E.P. Dutton & Co., 1972.

Dakin, Susanna Bryant. *The Lives of William Hartnell*. Stanford: Stanford Univ. Press, 1949.

_____. *A Scotch Paisano in Old Los Angeles*. Berkeley: Univ. of Calif. Press, 1939.

DeVoto, Bernard. *Across the Wide Missouri*. Boston: Houghton Mifflin Co., 1947.

Dillon, Richard. *Captain John Sutter: Sacramento Valley's Sainted Sinner*. Santa Cruz, CA: Western Tanager, 1981.

Drake, Francis S. "Henry Augustus Wise," *Dictionary of American Biography*. Cambridge: The Riverside Press, 1879.

Eakin, John Paul. *Fictions in Autobiography: Studies in the Art of Self-Invention*. Princeton: Princeton Univ. Press, 1985.

Egan, Ferol. *Fremont: Explorer for a Restless Nation*. Reno: Univ. of Nevada Press, 1985.

Gale, Robert L. *Richard Henry Dana*. N.Y: Twayne Publishers, Inc, 1969.

Geertz, Clifford. *The Interpretation of Cultures*. N.Y: Basic Books Inc., 1973.

Gilbert, Bil. *Westering Man: The Life of Joseph Walker*. Norman: Univ. of Oklahoma Press, 1983.

Goetzmann, William H. *Exploration and Empire: The Explorer and the Scientist in the Winning of the American West*. N.Y: W.W. Norton & Co., 1966.

Gould, Stephen Jay. *The Mismeasure of Man*. N.Y: W.W. Norton, 1981.

Griffen, William B. "The Compas: A Chiracahua Apache Family of the Late 18th and Early 19th Centuries." *American Indian Quarterly* VII:2 (Spring, 1983), 21-48.

Guild, Thelma S. and Carter, Harvey L. *Kit Carson: A Pattern for Heroes*. Lincoln/London: Univ. of Nebraska Press, 1984.

Haley, James L. *Apaches: A History and Culture Portrait*. N.Y: Doubleday and Co., Inc., 1981.

Hall, Thomas D. *Social Change in the Southwest, 1350-1880*. Lawrence: University Press of Kansas, 1989.

Hansen, Woodrow James. *The Search for Authority in California*. Oakland: Biobooks, 1960.

Harlow, Neal. *California Conquered: War and Peace on the Pacific 1846-1850*. Berkeley: Univ. of Calif. Press, 1982.

Hart, James D. *American Images of Spanish California*. Berkeley: The Friends of the Bancroft Library, 1960.

_____. "The Education of Richard Henry Dana, Jr.," *The New England Qtly.*, IX (March 1936), 3-25.

Hill, Joseph J. "Ewing Young in the Fur Trade of the Far Southwest, 1822-1834," *Oregon Hist. Soc. Qtly.*, XXIV, No. 1 (March 1923), 6-32.

Holmes, Kenneth L. *Ewing Young: Master Trapper*. Portland, Oregon: Binford & Mort, Pubs., 1967.

Horsman, Reginald. *Race and Manifest Destiny: The Origins of American Racial Anglo-Saxonism*, Cambridge: Harvard Univ. Press, 1981.

Hutchinson, C. Alan. *Frontier Settlement in Mexican California: The Hijar-Padres Colony, and Its Origins, 1769-1835*. New Haven and London: Yale University Press, 1969.

Johnson, Allen, and Malone, Dumas, (eds.). "Thomas Jefferson Farnham," *Dictionary of American Biography*, Vol. VI, 283-284. N.Y: Charles Scribner's Sons, 1931.

Jordan, Winthrop D. *White Over Black: American Attitudes toward the Negro, 1550-1812*. Baltimore: Penguin Books, 1969.

Langum, David J. "Californios and the Image of Indolence," *The Western Hist. Qtly.*, IX, No. 2 (April 1978), 181-196.

Lockwood, Frank C. *The Apache Indians*. N.Y: The Macmillan Co., 1938.

Lynch, John. *The Spanish American Revolutions, 1808-1826*. 2nd ed. N.Y: W.W. Norton & Co., 1986.

Malone, Michael P., (ed.). *Historians and the American West*. Lincoln and London: Univ. of Nebraska Press, 1983.

McGiffert, Michael, (ed.). *Puritanism and the American Experience.* Reading, Massachusetts: Addison-Wesley Publishing Co., Inc., 1969.

Moore, Arthur K. *The Frontier Mind.* N.Y: McGraw-Hill Book Co., Inc., 1963.

Morgan Dale L. *Jedediah Smith and the Opening of the West.* Lincoln/London: Univ. of Nebraska Press, 1964.

Morison, Samuel Eliot. *The Maritime History of Massachusetts, 1783-1860.* Boston: Houghton Mifflin, 1941.

Nadeau, Remi. *Los Angeles, from Mission to Modern City.* N.Y: Longmans, Green and Co., 1960.

Nash, Gary B. *Race, Class, and Politics: Essays on American Colonial and Revolutionary Society.* Chicago: Univ. of Illinois Press, 1986.

Nunis, Doyce B. Jr. *A Commentary on Alfred Robinson.* Los Angeles: The Zamorano Club, 1970.

————. *The Trials of Isaac Graham.* Los Angeles: Dawson's Book Shop, 1967.

Ogden, Adele. "Alfred Robinson, New England Merchant in Mexican California," *Calif. Hist. Soc. Qtly.*, XXIII, No. 3 (Sept. 1944), 193-218.

————. "Boston Hide Droghers Along California Shores," *Calif. Hist. Soc. Qtly.*, VIII (Dec. 1929), 289-305.

————. *The California Sea Otter Trade, 1784-1848.* Berkeley: Univ. of Calif. Press, 1941.

Olney, James, (ed.). *Autobiography: Essays Theoretical and Critical.* Princeton: Princeton Univ. Press, 1980.

Pearce, Roy Harvey. *Savagism and Civilization: A Study of the Indian and the American Mind.* Berkeley, London, Los Angeles: Univ. of Calif. Press, 1988.

Pitt, Leonard. *The Decline of the Californios: A Social History of the Spanish-Speaking Californians, 1846-1890.* Berkeley, London, Los Angeles: Univ. of Calif. Press, 1971.

Powell, Philip Wayne. *Tree of Hate: Propaganda and Prejudices Affecting United States Relations with the Hispanic World.* N.Y./London: Basic Books Inc., 1971.

Rawls, James J. *Indians of California: The Changing Image.* Norman and London: Univ. of Oklahoma Press, 1984.

Richman, Irving Berdine. *California under Spain and Mexico, 1535-1857.* N.Y: Cooper Square Publishers, Inc., 1965.

Robinson, W.W. *Land in California....* Berkeley: Univ. of Calif. Press, 1979.

Rolle, Andrew F. *An American in California: The Biography of William Heath Davis 1822-1909.* San Marino: Henry E. Huntington Library, 1956.

Royce, Josiah. *California from the Conquest in 1846 to the Second Vigilance Committee in San Francisco: A Study of American Character.* N.Y: Alfred A. Knopf, 1948.

Saum, Lewis P. *The Popular Mood of Pre-Civil War America*. Westport, Conn: Greenwood Press, 1980.

Saxton, Alexander. *The Indispensable Enemy: Labor and the Anti-Chinese Movement in California*. Berkeley: Univ. of Calif. Press, 1975.

Servin, Manuel P. "The Secularization of the California Missions: A Reappraisal," *So. Calif. Qtly.*, XLVII (June 1965), 133-149.

Shapiro, Samuel. *Richard Henry Dana, Jr., 1815-1882*. East Lansing: Michigan State Univ. Press, 1961.

Sherwood, Midge. *Days of Vintage, Years of Vision*. San Marino, CA: Orizaba Publications, 1982.

Slotkin, Richard. *Regeneration Through Violence: The Mythology of the American Frontier, 1600-1860*. Middletown, Conn: Wesleyan Univ. Press, 1973.

_____. *The Fatal Environment: The Myth of the Frontier in the Age of Industrialization, 1800-1890*. Middletown, Conn: Wesleyan Univ. Press, 1985.

Smith, Henry Nash. *Virgin Land: The American West as Symbol and Myth*. N.Y: Vintage Books, 1962.

Stewart, George R. *Take Your Bible in One Hand: The Life of William Henry Thomes*. San Francisco: The Colt Press, 1939.

Strickland, Rex W. "The Birth and Death of a Legend: The Johnson 'Massacre' of 1837." *Arizona and the West* 18:3 (August, 1976), 257-286.

Taylor, William R. *Calvalier & Yankee: The Old South and American National Character*. N.Y: Doubleday & Co., Inc., 1963.

Thwaites, Reuben Gold (ed.). *Early Western Travels, 1748-1846*. vol. XXVIII (Farnham's Travels). Cleveland: Arthur H. Clark Co., 1906.

Vestal, Stanley. *Kit Carson: The Happy Warrior of the Old West*. N.Y: Houghton Mifflin Co., 1928.

Weber, David J. (ed.). *Foreigners in Their Native Land: The Historical Roots of the Mexican Americans*. Albuquerque: Univ. of N.M. Press, 1973.

_____. *The Mexican Frontier, 1821-1846: The American Southwest under Mexico*. Albuquerque: Univ. of New Mexico Press, 1982.

_____. *The Taos Trappers: The Fur Trade in the Far Southwest, 1540-1846*. Norman: Univ. of Oklahoma Press, 1971.

Whitehead, Roy Elmer, M.D. *Lugo: A Chronicle of Early California*. Redlands, CA: San Bernardino Co. Museum Assn., 1978.

Woodward, Arthur. "Isaac Sparks—Sea Otter Hunter," *The Hist. Soc. of So. Calif. Qtly.*, XX, No. 2 (June 1938), 43-55.

Index